3 935

D1431377

W/D

PR
4754
.P56

1-43674

JUN. 24. 1992

DATE DUE

MAY 1 5 2006		
APR 0 3 2011		
APR 2 7 2011		

DEMCO 25-380

TEXAS WOMAN'S UNIVERSITY
LIBRARY
DENTON, TEXAS

DEMCO

THOMAS HARDY: ART AND THOUGHT

Thomas Hardy: Art and Thought

F. B. Pinion

ROWMAN AND LITTLEFIELD
Totowa, New Jersey

First published in the United States 1977
by ROWMAN AND LITTLEFIELD, Totowa, N.J.

© F. B. Pinion 1977
All rights reserved. No part of this publication may be
reproduced or transmitted, in any form or by any means,
without permission

First published 1977 by
THE MACMILLAN PRESS LTD
London and Basingstoke

ISBN 0–87471–975–5

Printed in Great Britain

PR
4754
.P5L

To MARJORIE,
particularly for encouraging a Hardy companionship

1—43674

WOMAN'S UNIVERSITY
LIBRARY

Contents

Preface

The essays which comprise the main part of this volume are closely related to Hardy's art and thought, though no attempt has been made to explore this area as a whole. Such an aim must be rather self-defeating, since all the important influences which combined to generate and mould his works are not yet known. I have, moreover, tried in general to avoid familiar approaches, and to present new points of view or relatively unexplored territory.

Most of the essays have been written recently, developing from notes made since the publication of *A Hardy Companion* in 1968. The only two to be published in any form (4, 9) were read as papers at schools organized by the Thomas Hardy Society in 1972 and 1975. Another (8) was given at Manchester in 1974; and a fourth (3), at Kansas State University in 1975. All these have been revised, principally with the aim of reducing repetition to a minimum consonant with clarity, and of increasing the range and variety of illustrative material. Two others (6, 12) are more complete expositions of subjects which were outlined with fewer references in *A Hardy Companion*, and another (15) enlarges considerably on the final section of my Thomas Hardy Birthday Lecture in 1974.

One question which emerges from these studies is the extent to which Hardy's art was influenced by other writers. *The Mayor of Caster-bridge*, for example, was written to be popular, yet, as other critics have shown, the Old Testament, the *Oedipus Rex* of Sophocles, and *King Lear* all contributed significantly to its imaginative growth. It is now clear that its tragic conclusion owes a great deal to *Les Misérables*. I have discussed several other literary influences at various points, none more important in the aggregate than that of Shelley.

The supplement consists of shorter articles, most of which are related to the main work. All, I believe, throw new light on Hardy's writings, some on particular places, some with wider implications. '*The Return of the Native* in the Making' is included by kind permission of the editor of *The Times Literary Supplement*, where it appeared as part of a slightly longer article on 21 August 1970.

Reference Abbreviations

Life F. E. Hardy, *The Life of Thomas Hardy*, London and New York, 1962.

Orel H. Orel, *Thomas Hardy's Personal Writings*, Lawrence, Kans., 1966 and London, 1967.

ORFW Evelyn Hardy and F. B. Pinion (eds.), *One Rare Fair Woman, Thomas Hardy's Letters to Florence Henniker, 1893–1922*, London and Coral Gables, Fla., 1972.

Purdy R. L. Purdy, *Thomas Hardy, A Bibliographical Study*, Oxford, 1954.

1 An Early Influence

Hardy's indebtedness to Wilkie Collins is readily and rightly assumed but, except in general terms, its range is difficult to assess. How much he was influenced by particular incidents or scenes must remain largely conjectural. To take a minor example: it would be interesting to know whether, at a time when the public might have expected greater realism, Hardy was in any way encouraged to adapt the Lady Macbeth scene (for the dramatization of Angel Clare's deeply suppressed feelings) by the recollection of Admiral Bartram's sleep-walking in *No Name*.

Hardy admired Collins' art in constructing 'novels of complicated pattern';[1] he had read him, particularly with an eye to structural ingenuity and the creation of suspense, during his early apprenticeship, after George Meredith, reader for Chapman and Hall, had recommended him to rewrite *The Poor Man and the Lady*, or put it aside and attempt a different kind of novel, devoid of satire and with a more complicated plot. Adopting the latter course, Hardy wrote *Desperate Remedies*, his first novel to be published.

One of its reviewers unerringly described the cruder elements of the story as ' "desperate remedies" . . . adopted for ennui or an emaciated purse'. Hardy had advanced a large sum for the publication of this novel and, being 'virtually if not distinctly engaged to be married to a girl with no money except in reversion after the death of relatives', was extremely anxious to succeed financially; 'finding himself in a corner', he thought it 'necessary to attract public attention at all hazards'. *Desperate Remedies* is much more than a sensational story, however. Once under way, it is compelling, though it never attains the perspicuous fluency of Collins' style. It is richer and more thoughtful, often poetic in conception, any defects of immaturity being far outweighed by imaginative effects and the creation of character, especially in the heroine Cytherea Graye and the rather crazed Miss Aldclyffe. Only after the tragic climax, when the unravelling of crime takes over and narrative gets the upper hand, is there a marked decline in Hardy's creative energy – just at the point where Collins' would have gained momentum. Sir George Douglas rightly refers to the poetry in the novel, and describes it as 'the work of a literary architect, built up from foundation-stone to finial with an accuracy and finish which surpass the best of Wilkie Collins's mosaic work'.[2]

Mystification and a tight time-schedule which demands notation in hours and minutes as the story reaches a sensational climax are features which *Desperate Remedies* (1871) obviously shares with some of Collins' fiction. More particularly, *The Woman in White* (1860) has a villain of illegitimate descent (like Manston in this respect), a mystery surrounding the identity and past of one woman (as with Miss Aldclyffe of Knapwater House), and a woman masquerading as another (as Anne Seaway impersonates Manston's dead wife).

Yet, in *Desperate Remedies* and elsewhere, none of Wilkie Collins' novels seems to have influenced Hardy more than *Basil* (1852). It is a highly-geared melodrama in autobiographical or confessional form, beginning with a compulsive story of love at first sight, followed by the base deception of a hero activated by noble sentiments, revelations of the villain's monomaniacal pursuit of revenge, a delirious death-bed scene for the unfaithful 'heroine', and a happy ending without wedding-bells. The style is as effective as the plot; it has a facility which carries the reader forward without impediment, leaving little to admire but its functional lucidity, and nothing to ponder on. When the end is reached, the story is already evanescent; not one of its characters seems real.

Though obviously moral in substance and aim, and a 'warning' for the inexperienced, *Basil* provoked sufficient Grundyan disapproval as well as admiration to warrant the assumption that Hardy's interest in Collins' novels would soon draw him to it. It contains several features which collectively constitute more than a likelihood that its influence on Hardy in his early years as a writer of prose fiction is of special interest; and a strong case can be made for claiming that it gave Hardy the title of his first published novel. When Ralph, the hero's brother, becomes involved in 'an awkward love adventure' with one of the tenant's daughters, his father applies a 'desperate remedy' and secures a place for him in a foreign embassy (I. iv). When he finally returns with a 'morganatic' wife to London, and comes to Basil's rescue, he counters the threat of family exposure with court proceedings: 'we shall have no exposure to dread after you have exposed us', he tells Mr Sherwin; 'we shall have no remedy left, but a desperate remedy, and we'll go to law – boldly, openly go to law, and get a divorce' (III. vi).

Perhaps *Basil* gave Hardy the spur he needed to dare to present a social impropriety, 'the violation of a lady' and the 'subsequent birth of a child' as 'a central incident' from which the action of *Desperate Remedies* moved. John Morley, Macmillan's reader, was shocked; the novel was rejected on his advice; and Hardy no doubt took pains to make the 'abominable' affair less obtrusive and offensive.[3]

The satirist of *The Poor Man and the Lady* would relish the irony latent in the highly dramatic scene in which the hero's aristocratic father is more revolted by Basil's marrying a linen-draper's daughter than by his previous surmise that their association had been licentious.

(Charlotte Brontë discovered soon after the publication of *Jane Eyre* that hardly anything was more 'disgusting' to contemporary reviewers than the breaking of class barriers in fictional marriages.) The prevalent attitude is underlined by Ralph:

> I've spent time very pleasantly among the ladies of the counter myself. But ... I'm told that you actually married the girl! I don't wish to be hard upon you, my good fellow, but there was an unparalleled insanity about that act, worthier of a patient in Bedlam than of my brother. I am not sure whether I understand what exactly virtuous behaviour is; but if *that* was virtuous behaviour – there, there! don't look shocked. Let's have done with the marriage, and get on.[4]

Basil had fallen in love with Margaret, Mr. Sherwin's beautiful daughter; but as she is only seventeen the mercenary father persuades him to marry her, and keep the marriage secret and purely nominal for one year. Margaret hopes to be a rich lady, but Mr Mannion, her tutor and Mr Sherwin's confidential clerk (now abroad), intends to marry her. When he returns and discovers that Basil is the son of one who was responsible for his father's death, Mannion's campaign for revenge begins. He knows that Margaret has 'neither heart nor mind', that she has 'simply instincts' ('most of the bad instincts of the animal; none of the good'); and he has no difficulty in seducing her and wrecking Basil's unconsummated marriage, as the latter discovers on the eve of his expected honeymoon. His rage leads to Mannion's permanent disfigurement, and the determination of the anti-hero to pursue his vendetta to the death.

'Manston', the name of the villain in *Desperate Remedies*, is very similar to 'Mannion', and the two men have pronounced similarities in appearance. Both are extremely handsome. The forehead of the former is square and broad; that of the other is high. It is also 'smooth and massive as marble'; not a wrinkle or line is to be found on Mannion's face. The most striking point about Manston's is the wonderful 'clearness of his complexion. There was not a blemish or speck of any kind to mar the smoothness of its surface or the beauty of its hue.' He had clear, penetrating eyes; those of Mannion never varied from a 'steady, straightforward look'. Only the lips were different: Manston's were full and red, proclaiming the sensualist; those of Mannion were delicately formed and tight, indicative, like his cold eyes and mask-like complexion, of cunning and deceit. In this respect, Hardy has reversed the roles: just as he finds himself more in sympathy with the poor-man-and-the-lady theme rather than with the gentleman-and-the-tradesman's-daughter in Collins, so the full lips and sensuality of Margaret Sherwin, the woman in league with the villain, are transferred to Manston in *Desperate Remedies*.

Both villains have Satanic associations. '*That man* had the power of Satan over me!' Mrs Sherwin told Basil not long before her death. It is significant that the 'thunder, lightning, and rain' which increases to 'a terrific force' when Cytherea first meets Manston (and which evoke the spirits of evil in *Macbeth*) are repeatedly associated with Mannion. Basil takes refuge in his house to their accompaniment just as Cytherea accepts shelter in Manston's to avoid the storm. Here during its peak he plays upon her emotions by drawing from the organ music 'of full orchestral power', just as the Devil in the penny chapbook cheered Faustus and his friend with music such as they had never heard before, after it had thundered and lightened as if the world had come to an end.[5] When Basil leaves Mannion's house,

> The lightning was still in the sky, though it only appeared at long intervals. Strangely enough, at the moment when I addressed him, a flash came, and seemed to pass right over his face. It gave such a hideously livid hue, such a spectral look of ghastliness and distortion to his features, that he absolutely seemed to be glaring and grinning on me like a fiend, in the one instant of its duration (ii. iii).

From this it is but a short step to the harmonization of setting and human situation at critical stages in the novel. It is not suggested that Collins was the only influence on Hardy in this direction; George Eliot could have been another. Nevertheless, the co-existence in *Basil* of several features which are important in Hardy's novels does suggest that he paid it particular interest from a technical angle. The outbreaks of thunder and lightning which punctuate the Mannion scenes make a tremendous impact on the reader, but other scenic parallels are common. For example, Basil's wedding-day is marked with unrelieved black cloud, heavy rain, and mist, after ten days of sunshine; the fog thickens at the time of the marriage ceremony. Comment on Basil's gratitude for Mannion's apparently kind offers of assistance comes in the moaning of the wind. 'It seemed at that moment, to be wailing over *me*, to be wailing over *him*; to be wailing over all mortal things!' Basil's repeated assurance of trust in him is answered by a fiercer blast of wind which shakes the window shutter violently and dies away 'in a low, melancholy, dirging swell, like a spirit-cry of lamentation and despair'. When Basil visits his estranged father in the country, the scene is similarly depressing: evening with drizzling rain, rising fog, and a raw wind which causes 'the ancient leafless elms in the park avenue' to groan and creak drearily. He goes to see Margaret at her home on the eve of the honeymoon he had planned; she is out with Mannion at her aunt's party. As he leaves North Villa to join her (only to discover her shame),

> The moonlight which was just beginning to shine brilliantly on my arrival there, now appeared but at rare intervals; for the clouds were

spreading thicker and thicker over the whole surface of the sky, as the night advanced.

When he leaves the hotel where he has discovered that Margaret and Mannion are lovers,

> It was growing dark. The ragged black clouds, fantastically parted from each other in island shapes over the whole surface of the heavens, were fast drawing together into one huge, formless, lowering mass, and had already hidden the moon for good.

Basil stations himself in 'the pitch darkness' of a passage opposite the hotel, intent on killing Mannion when he emerges.

Hardy's parallels are often more elaborate and subtle, but nobody can dispute that Collins' effects are telling. Like Hardy he can use them ironically. When Basil shocks his father by confessing his marriage to a tradesman's daughter,

> The pleasant rustling of the trees mingled with the softened, monotonous rolling of carriages in the distant street, while the organ-tune, now changed to the lively measure of a song, rang out clear and cheerful above both, and poured into the room as lightly and happily as the very sunshine itself.

The first draft of *Desperate Remedies* had been almost completed when Hardy made his first visit to Cornwall. There seems to be little doubt that he associated one scene in *Basil* with the cliffs with which he became familiar in the company of Emma Lavinia Gifford. When he hears that his sister's visits to him have given his father offence, Basil feels compelled to leave London, and retires to Cornwall, only to be followed by the avenger Mannion. There, on a promontory above 'a black, yawning hole that slanted nearly straight downwards, like a tunnel, to unknown and unfathomable depths . . . into which the waves found entrance through some subterraneous channel', he finds himself face to face with his adversary. He resists the temptation to hurl him over the precipice, and runs the way he had come, to climb to a higher range of rocks. Half-way up he looks back and catches sight of Mannion,

> moving shadow-like below and beyond me, skirting the farther edge of the slippery plane of granite that shelved into the gaping mouth of the hole. The brightening atmosphere showed him that he had risked himself, in the mist, too near to a dangerous place. He stopped – looked up and saw me watching him – raised his hand – and shook it threateningly in the air. The ill-calculated violence of his action, in making that menacing gesture, destroyed his equilibrium – he staggered – tried to recover himself – swayed half round where he stood – then fell heavily backward, right on to the steep shelving rock.

The wet sea-weed slipped through his fingers, as they madly clutched at it. He struggled frantically to throw himself towards the side of the declivity; slipping further and further down it at every effort. Close to the mouth of the abyss, he sprang up as if he had been shot. A tremendous jet of spray hissed out upon him at the same moment. I heard a scream so shrill, so horribly unlike any human cry, that it seemed to silence the very thundering of the water. The spray fell. For one instant, I saw two livid and bloody hands tossed up against the black walls of the hole, as he dropped into it. Then the waves roared again fiercely in their hidden depths; the spray flew out once more; and when it cleared off, nothing was to be seen at the yawning mouth of the chasm – nothing moved over the shelving granite, but some torn particles of sea-weed sliding slowly downwards in the running ooze.

But for this sensational climax to the revenge story in *Basil* Hardy might not have thought of the scene in which Knight hangs perilously on a slope above the Cliff without a Name, clinging to 'the last outlying knot of starved herbage ere the rock appeared in all its bareness', while Elfride employs her wits to save him. With Hardy, the scene is more than a sensational climax.[6] It is the occasion for philosophical reflections on 'pitiless nature' and her 'lawless caprice'. Collins' main preoccupation is with the best narrative means to stimulate excitement and suspense, and in this he is Hardy's superior. His comments on chance would secure Hardy's immediate approval, but such comments are rare. It is a mere accident, a chance encounter, which changes the course of Basil's life. From the moment when Margaret entered, she was all he saw in the omnibus, and he therefore thinks it strange that 'the action of our faculties' should be swayed by 'the capricious rule of chance'. This is how the rule of Chance appeared to Hardy: blind, whimsical, doling out pain as readily as happiness.[7] It was but 'the chance of things' that Elfride should fall in love with a man of such 'keen scrutiny and logical power' as Knight when his suspicions were awakened, and that she should have been inspired with the 'docile devotion' which made her his 'bond-servant'. After meeting and falling in love with Emma Gifford, Hardy mused, 'What bond-servants of Chance/We are all'; later he thought it 'a stupid blunder of God Almighty'.[8]

Basil's temptation to hurl Mannion over the precipice probably influenced Hardy when he wrote 'The Honourable Laura', first published in 1881, and included in *A Group of Noble Dames* ten years later.

Margaret Sherwin seems to have given Hardy hints for Eustacia Vye. They are, of course, far different, Eustacia having a richer and more romantic personality, and being capable of dignity in times of tragic crisis. Even so, the memory of Margaret seems responsible for some of Eustacia's main characteristics. Both dream of society and splendour.

They have strong similarities in appearance. Here is Collins' description of the girl with whom Basil falls in love at first sight (I. vii):

> She was dark. Her hair, eyes, and complexion were darker than usual in English women. The form, the look altogether, of her face, coupled with what I could see of her figure, made me guess her age to be about twenty. There was the appearance of maturity already in the shape of her features; but that expression still remained girlish, unformed, unsettled. The fire in her large dark eyes, when she spoke, was latent. Their languor, when she was silent – that voluptuous languor of black eyes – was still fugitive and unsteady. The smile about her full lips (to other eyes they might have looked *too* full) struggled to be eloquent, yet dared not.

Darkness, languor, voluptuousness, fire, are here merely physical. Hardy's poetical imagination makes much more of these elements in the larger thematic dimensions of Egdon scenes as well as in the physical attributes of Eustacia (I. vii):

> She was in person full-limbed and somewhat heavy; without ruddiness, as without pallor; and soft to the touch as a cloud. To see her hair was to fancy that a whole winter did not contain darkness enough to form its shadow; it closed over her forehead like nightfall extinguishing the western glow.

In enlarging on Eustacia's pagan and Hellenic qualities, Hardy used his story to promote a theme. Yet, before she reached her final status, he had temporized over her, and his indecision over her morality was not easily resolved. At first she had been more on Margaret Sherwin's level. Relations between her and Wildeve had been such that Leslie Stephen refused to serialize *The Return of the Native* until he had seen the whole work. Not until Hardy prepared the novel for the 1895 edition did he dare to state uncompromisingly that Eustacia and Wildeve had been lovers 'body and soul'. He probably came to the conclusion that this debased his tragic heroine in readers' eyes, for he finally changed 'body and soul' to 'life and soul'.

However much Hardy may have been impressed by features of *Basil* and the manner of telling it, nothing influenced him more consistently than two of the tenets in the artistic credo which Collins included in the introduction to his novel. The first of these runs as follows:

> My idea was that the more of the Actual I could garner up as a text to speak from, the more certain I might feel of the genuineness and value of the Ideal which was sure to spring out of it. Fancy and Imagination, Grace and Beauty, all those qualities which are to the work of Art what scent and colour are to the flower, can only grow towards heaven by taking root in the earth. Is not the noblest poetry of prose fiction the poetry of every-day truth?

To illustrate this 'poetry of every-day truth', Collins instances the first love-meeting of Basil and Margaret in an omnibus, 'the very last place and under the very last circumstances which the artifices of sentimental writing would sanction'. Another example is the sound of the street-organ during the fatal interview between Basil and his proud patrician father. 'There is enough poetry in what is left in life, after all the false romance has been abstracted, to make a sweet pattern', Hardy believed.[9] The transformation of a railway-cutting by the alchemy of love is the subject of one of Hardy's poems, and his 'love-meeting' with Emma Gifford at a railway-station creates one of the most moving of his recollections in another.[10]

The second principle which Collins' precept and example encouraged Hardy to adopt explains why he opened *The Mayor of Casterbridge* with a wife-sale, and why readers frequently accuse him of melodrama in *Tess of the d'Urbervilles*, forgetting that the Greek writers of tragedy, and Shakespeare (in *King Lear*, for example), used even more sensational stories to stir their audiences to pity and sober reflections on life. In the belief that drama and the novel were 'twin-sisters in the family of Fiction', Wilkie Collins did not think it 'either politic or necessary' to confine his narrative to quotidian events:

> Those extraordinary accidents and events which happen to few men, seemed to me to be as legitimate materials for fiction to work with – when there was a good object in using them – as the ordinary accidents and events which may, and do, happen to us all. By appealing to genuine sources of interest *within* the reader's own experience, I could certainly gain his attention to begin with; but it would be only by appealing to other sources (as genuine in their way) *beyond* his own experience, that I could hope to fix his interest and excite his suspense, to occupy his deeper feelings, or to stir his nobler thoughts.

As a narrative writer Hardy never lost faith in this view; and he found welcome support for it in Anthony Trollope's *Autobiography* (1883). In 1891 he wrote a comment on the American novelist William Dean Howells: 'Howells and those of his school forget that a story *must* be striking enough to be worth telling. Therein lies the problem – to reconcile the average with that uncommonness which alone makes it natural that a tale or experience would dwell in the memory and induce repetition.' More memorably he wrote in 1893: 'A story must be exceptional enough to justify its telling. We tale-tellers are all Ancient Mariners, and none of us is warranted in stopping Wedding Guests (in other words, the hurrying public) unless he has something more unusual to relate than the ordinary experience of every average man and woman.' 'The uncommonness must be in the events, not in the characters', however. Hardy feared he had spoilt *The Mayor of Casterbridge* by providing sensational turns for the weekly serial reader, but consoled himself with the thought that, 'after all, it is not improbabilities of incident but improbabilities of character that matter'.[11] In the creation of character he is far superior to Collins.

Hardy gives us more to think about in the first twenty or thirty pages of *Desperate Remedies* than one finds in the whole of a Wilkie Collins novel. He never attains the latter's facility of style. For readers in search of a 'good' story, *Basil* is excellent. Hardy, in providing more, demands a diversified set of responses, and runs a greater risk of unevenness. The danger for the novelist of thinking too much (and of attributing too much intelligence to the reader from an overdue sense of self-inferiority) is manifest on the opening page: 'Graye was handsome, frank, and gentle. He had a quality of thought which, exercised on homeliness, was humour; on nature, picturesqueness; on abstractions, poetry. Being, as a rule, broadcast, it was all three.' Elsewhere in the early chapters of the novel one can find much that is smart and sententious, but nothing quite as terse as this; it threatens to out-Bacon Bacon. How habitual this aphoristic, notebook style became with the young Thomas Hardy during an intensive period of reading and writing poetry from 1865 to 1867 can be seen in some of the notes which are preserved in his *Life*.[12] In his fiction Hardy never entirely outgrew an excessive regard for economy of expression; the heavy Latinizations which clog his style (though they are the exception rather than the rule, and not nearly as common as some critics suggest) are another consequence of the same rather laudable but misplaced intention.

2 Poetical Extravagance in Fiction

In his eagerness for success, a writer of great resources who is lacking in self-assurance tends to overload his first published work in both style and substance. Hardy did so in much of *Desperate Remedies*. Only after its tragic climax with the wedding of Cytherea and Manston, when a rather amateurish detective narrative is given its unimpeded course, does it lack for long periods those qualities which are more typical of Hardy, ranging from humour to the creation of tragic scenes through the imaginative perception of setting, character, and chance in unison. Much as one admires these effects, one feels that some at least are an extravagance in such a melodramatic story. A writer with the expertise of Somerset Maugham could have developed such a plot with half the effort and with admirable lucidity, yet without giving us as much to reflect on or as much to appeal to the imagination in scene and character.

Hardy did not spare himself. He was not only a keen observer of human nature, and especially of the female temperament; he was highly intelligent and advanced in modern philosophy; and, after having absorbed much of the best of English poetry, had begun to find imaginative correlatives for his thoughts on life. Probably no other novel by Hardy is strewn with as many quotations from so many poets; they include Virgil, Terence, and Horace; Dante; Shakespeare and Thomas Watson; Carew, Crashaw, and Milton; Collins and Gray; Burns, Thomas Moore, Wordsworth, Keats, and Shelley; Browning, Tennyson, Rossetti, and Whitman. Much more interesting, however, are the ways in which *Desperate Remedies* anticipates descriptions, motifs, situations, and their attendant imagery in the later Wessex novels.

With this in mind, I was surprised to find in a relatively recent 'anthology' of Hardy criticism an editorial statement that *Desperate Remedies* has 'very little of the later Hardy in it', and that 'nothing in the book either anticipates the later novels, or suggests a writer of genius'. All this is untrue of a number of passages, and particularly of one brief scene which, with the omission of ten narrative lines, occupies less than a page. Nowhere else in Hardy is such a concentration of poetic thought to be found, and it is fortunate that its several features are repeated or developed in his more important tragedies.

The scene (xii. 6) expresses the tragic crisis of the story. Marriage between the true lovers Cytherea Graye and Edward Springrove has been made to appear out of the question through misrepresentation. The more sensual and passionate Manston wishes to marry her, and circumstances – her brother's impecuniosity and need of prolonged medical treatment – and pressures from him, Miss Aldclyffe, and Manston, argue in favour of a union which will solve all material problems. The conflict of heart and reason remains unresolved, but circumstances prevail, and Cytherea marries Manston. The story is repeated in *Tess of the d'Urbervilles*. When Tess is deserted by Angel Clare, and her family is destitute after her father's death, she is compelled to accept for their sake her persistent suitor, the wealthy sensualist Alec d'Urberville. Self-sacrifice and selfish loyalty with hardly a glimmer of hope are the alternatives for each heroine, and self-sacrifice is made to self-seeking sensuality. Cytherea shrinks from Manston's 'hot voluptuous nature', knowing how 'animal' is the love which bargains for her. Yet the possibility of her brother's death as a result of her 'self-enforced poverty' makes the proposed marriage seem reasonable, and reason is reinforced by loving-kindness or altruism and by gratitude for Manston's gifts to her brother.

It is the resultant wavering in Cytherea's mind which is reflected in the scene. She and Manston are standing by 'the ruinous foundations of an old mill in the midst of a meadow'; 'the water gurgled down from the old mill-pond to a lower level, under the cloak of rank broad leaves – the sensuous natures of the vegetable world'. The image of the ruinous mill and the stream suggests mortality and the lapse of time ('Time like an ever-rolling stream/Bears all its sons away'). As far as she can see, Cytherea's prospects for a happy life, her 'single opportunity of existence' (xiii. 4) are ruined; the ranker plants fringing the stream represent the 'animal' nature of Manston's love (xii. 4). Cytherea's indecision is reflected in what follows. First she is optimistic, and indulges in the hope of a happy marriage:

> On the right hand the sun, resting on the horizon-line, streamed across the ground from below copper-coloured and lilac clouds, stretched out in flats beneath a sky of pale soft green. All dark objects on the earth that lay towards the sun were overspread by a purple haze, against which a swarm of wailing gnats shone forth luminously, rising upward and floating like sparks of fire.

In this imagery there are three features which call for comment. All 'dark objects' are overspread by a 'purple haze': Cytherea's deep-seated anxieties are momentarily obscured by her emotional euphoria. When she and Edward Springrove fall in love and kiss (iii. 2), 'It was the supremely happy moment of their experience. The "bloom" and the "purple light" were strong on the lineaments of both.' Hardy refers to 'The bloom of young desire, and purple light of love' in 'The Progress of Poesy' by Thomas Gray. Secondly, in the wailing gnats (from Keats's 'To Autumn' – the date for Hardy's scene is 'The Twenty-Seventh of August') which shine forth luminously and float away like sparks of fire, there is, as is more poetically revealed in *Tess of the d'Urbervilles* (see p. 29), an allusion to the ephemerality of human love in the universe of space and time. For Tess it is a passing dream; for Cytherea it is no more than an evanescent hope. Lastly, the pale green of the sky suggests a moderate affection (cf. p. 26), and the lilac clouds passion, but the copper hues are more ominous, and the sunset is inevitably close.

Cytherea's depression soon returns:

> The stillness oppressed and reduced her to mere passivity. The only wish the humidity of the place left in her was to stand motionless. The helpless flatness of the landscape gave her, as it gives all such temperaments, a sense of bare equality with, and no superiority to, a single entity under the sky.

The situation is both physically and morally exhausting; she is reduced to 'mere passivity', and is unequal to the demands which encompass her. Both the passages quoted above are repeated with very slight modifications to express Clym Yeobright's change from romantic feelings when he has fallen in love with Eustacia to a more realistic awareness of the problems they will have to face when they are married.

As Manston takes Cytherea's hand and pleads, 'Do try to love me!', she remembers 'his kindness to her brother, his love for herself, and Edward's fickleness'. The hesitation returns, and

> she looked as far as the autumnal haze on the marshy ground would allow her to see distinctly. There was the fragment of a hedge – all that remained of a 'wet old garden' – standing in the middle of a mead, without a definite beginning or ending, purposeless and value-less. It was overgrown, and choked with mandrakes, and she could almost fancy she could hear their shrieks. . . . Should she withdraw her hand? No, she could not withdraw it now; it was too late, the act would not imply refusal. She felt as one in a boat without oars, drifting with closed eyes down a river – she knew not whither.

Here we have the 'Too late, beloved' theme of *Tess of the d'Urbervilles*. When Tess, against her nature and for altruistic reasons, accepts a *de facto* marriage with Alec d'Urberville, she loses the will to live. On his return, Angel is conscious of 'one thing, though it was not clear to him till later; that his original Tess had spiritually ceased to recognize the body before him as hers – allowing it to drift, like a corpse upon the current, in a direction dissociated from its living will'.

Hardy's first use of the image, to express the resignation of Cytherea Graye, seems to be the encapsulated legacy from a whole scene in George Eliot's *Romola* (lxi).

There is a touch of Gothicism in the shrieking mandrakes (and other scenes in *Desperate Remedies*) which may indicate a Harrison Ainsworth influence, but the 'wet old garden' derives chiefly from Shelley and Swinburne. 'The Sensitive Plant' presents a beautiful garden through which glides a 'soft stream' with 'sweet sound and radiance'. It is an 'Eden' tended by 'the spirit of Love'. With the oncoming of winter, decay and loathsome rot set in. When winter is over,

> The Sensitive Plant was a leafless wreck,
> But the mandrakes, and toadstools, and docks, and darnels,
> Rose like the dead from their ruined charnels.

Fungi and such repellent features of late autumn and winter will be found in scenes at tragic points in *Far from the Madding Crowd, The Return of the Native,* and *The Woodlanders.*[1] They correspond to the 'things rank and gross in nature' of Hamlet's world. Implicit for Hardy in this imagery is his 'Unfulfilled Intention, which makes life what it is'. The best elucidation of this is found in his *Life* (p. 149) and 'The Mother Mourns', a poem which contains the line 'Let me grow, then, but mildews and mandrakes'.

The phrase 'wet old garden' seems to be a recollection or adaptation of the idea and imagery of a poem in the first volume of Swinburne's *Poems and Ballads* (1866), which made a stirring impression on Hardy in London, as he recalls in 'A Singer Asleep':

> O that far morning of a summer day
> When, down a terraced street whose pavement lay
> Glassing the sunshine into my bent eyes,
> I walked and read with a quick glad surprise
> New words, in classic guise –.

Arnold's plea for more Hellenism and less Hebraism was gentlemanly and urbane compared with Swinburne's revolt. Whereas Arnold was primarily concerned with English provincialism, self-satisfaction, and aloofness towards new ideas, Swinburne's passionate and sustained protest was an indictment of Victorian Puritanism in favour of the more sensuous or pagan philosophy of the Greeks:

> Wilt thou yet take all, Galilean? but these thou shalt not take,
> The laurel, the palms and the paean, the breasts of the nymphs in
> the brake;
> Breasts more soft than a dove's, that tremble with tenderer breath;
> And all the wings of the Loves, and all the joy before death . . .
> Nay, for a little we live, and life hath mutable wings.

A little while and we die; shall life not thrive as it may?
For no man under the sky lives twice, outliving his day.
And grief is a grievous thing, and a man hath enough of his tears:
Why should he labour, and bring fresh grief to blacken his years?
Thou hast conquered, O pale Galilean; the world has grown grey
    from thy breath;
We have drunken of things Lethean, and fed on the fulness of death.

In principle Hardy was on Swinburne's side in this debate; paganism
against asceticism is a major theme of *The Return of the Native*, and
Greek joyousness in conflict with Church morality a minor, but more
dramatically and fearlessly presented, motif in *Jude the Obscure*.
Hardy, however, seems to have rejoiced more in Swinburne's impugn-
ment of a God who is judged by his creation; it is eloquently expressed
in one of the choruses in *Atalanta in Calydon* (1865):

Because thou art over all who are over us;
    Because thy name is life and our name death;
Because thou art cruel and men are piteous,
    And our hands labour and thine hand scattereth;
Lo, with hearts rent and knees made tremulous,
    Lo, with ephemeral lips and casual breath,
        At least we witness of thee ere we die
That these things are not otherwise, but thus;
        That each man in his heart sigheth, and saith,
            That all men even as I,
All we are against thee, against thee, O God most high.

Hardy's view was modified by contemporary scientific philosophy. To
him 'the Cause of Things' was 'neither moral nor immoral but
*un*moral'. Unfortunately the figurative use of an Aeschylean phrase
(consonant with Swinburne's indictment of the gods) at the end of *Tess
of the d'Urbervilles* has realized his fear that 'no doubt people will go
on thinking that I really believe the Prime Mover to be a malignant
old gentleman, a sort of King of Dahomey – an idea which, so far from
my holding it, is to me irresistibly comic' (*Life*, 409; cf. *Life*, 243–4).

Many details could be adduced from the first volume of *Poems and
Ballads* to show its influence on Hardy and his sympathy with Swinburne's thought. The 'wet old garden' recalls 'Ilicet':

A little sorrow, a little pleasure,
Fate metes us from the dusty measure
    That holds the date of all of us;
We are born with travail and strong crying,
And from the birth-day to the dying
    The likeness of our life is thus.

One girds himself to serve another,
Whose father was the dust, whose mother
The little dead red worm therein;
They find no fruit of things they cherish;
The goodness of a man shall perish,
It shall be one thing with his sin.

In deep wet ways by grey old gardens
Fed with sharp spring the sweet fruit hardens;
They know not what fruits wane or grow;
Red summer burns to the utmost ember;
They know not, neither can remember,
The old years and flowers they used to know, . . .

The symbolism of 'deep wet ways by grey old gardens' invests a particular rural scene in *Desperate Remedies*. The 'wet old garden' near the ruinous mill is in the middle of a meadow. It is 'overgrown, and choked with mandrakes'; in the words of *Hamlet*, 'things rank and gross in nature/Possess it merely'. Cytherea's marriage to Manston spells spiritual death; in it she can see 'no fruit of things' she cherishes. Like the wet old garden which is in the middle of a fertile meadow for no obvious reason, it makes no sense; it seems as if, measured by the heart's affections, her one life, instead of being happy and fruitful, is condemned to be purposeless and wasted.

The significance of the imagery becomes clearer if we think of Bathsheba's waking up, after discovering the perfidy of her husband Troy, by a malignant swamp, ' a nursery of pestilence small and great, in the immediate neighbourhood of comfort and health'; or of Tess, when her future is blighted by early misfortune, lured by Angel's music through a 'damp and rank' weed-infested garden in the lush meadows of the Froom valley. The contrast between all three settings and their immediate neighbourhoods accentuates what might have been, the love and happiness that all three heroines might have enjoyed but for betrayal of one kind or another.

Leslie Stephen recalled the poetry 'diffused through the prose' of *Far from the Madding Crowd* when Hardy's first volume of poetry, *Wessex Poems*, was published. The congestion of poetic imagery in the scene which reflects Cytherea's crisis carries too much significance for any novel. Whether Hardy had used any of these imaginative crystallizations previously in poetry or fiction will never be known; collectively they comprise the most intensive and most precious writing of his early period. With greater experience, he concluded that their value was lost in a thriller which he had half-dreaded publishing,[2] and which he assumed had no future. Not surprisingly, he decided to retrieve them and use them singly, and to greater advantage, in some of his later tragedies.

3 Pictorial Art

Hardy's interest in painting began during his adolescence, when he and his sister Mary took up water-colouring as a hobby. It reached another stage during his architectural apprenticeship in London, when it 'led him to devote for many months, on every day that the National Gallery was open, twenty minutes after lunch . . . to a single master on each visit'. This interest was not a passing cultural phase, nor was it limited to a study of 'schools and styles'. The evidence indicates not only that pictures helped to quicken and enrich Hardy's own visual impressions, but that his growing experience as a creative writer intensified his interest in the technical aspects of visual presentation. In 1886 he had his first view of the Impressionists, and concluded that they were 'more suggestive in the direction of literature than in that of art'. At the Royal Academy in January 1889 he was especially impressed by Turner's water-colours, and wrote:

> each is a landscape *plus* a man's soul. . . . What he paints chiefly is *light as modified by objects*. He first recognizes the impossibility of really producing on canvas all that is in a landscape; then gives for that which cannot be reproduced a something else which shall have upon the spectator an approximative effect to that of the real.[1]

The effect of paintings on Hardy's observation and imagining may be seen in references to works of old and new masters in the novels. These have led to exaggerated charges of pedantry. A writer unsure of his own powers may overestimate his readers' cultural expectations. Such diffidence can lead to obscurity as in Browning's early work, or to literary ostentatiousness as in D. H. Lawrence's first novel. In defence of Hardy, it should be said that (as with quotations) he was following in the footsteps of Sir Walter Scott, and took pains to ensure that the significance of his pictorial references was not lost on his readers. Three examples follow from his first three published novels:

> And she had in turning looked over her shoulder at the other lady with a faint accent of reproach in her face. Those who remember Greuze's 'Head of a Girl' have an idea of Cytherea's look askance at the turning. (*Desperate Remedies*, iv. 2)

> [Through the open shop-window, Mr Penny could be] invariably seen working inside, like a framed portrait of a shoemaker by some modern Moroni. (*Under the Greenwood Tree*, ii. ii)

A woman with a double chin and thick neck, like the Queen Anne
portrait by Dahl, threw open the lodge gate . . .

(*A Pair of Blue Eyes*, v)

Alistair Smart assures us that 'a reader who knows anything of
Greuze's work will at once receive a most precise impression' of
Cytherea 'at the turning', that the Moroni suggestion is very appropriate, as can be seen from his 'Portrait of a Tailor' in the National
Gallery, and that there is point in the choice of Dahl, 'who seems to
have had no qualms about stressing the plainness and stodginess of his
sitters'.[2]

Authors cull apt similes from various fields of specialized knowledge,
often leaving readers at a greater loss than Hardy does by this method
of enhancing visual effects. No reader is handicapped by the references, which must be a source of pleasure to those who recall the
pictures and recognise the aptness of the comparisons.

Some of Hardy's later pictorial references are more open to criticism.
When the complexion of the youthful astronomer hero of *Two on a
Tower* is described as 'that with which Raffaelle enriches the countenance of the youthful son of Zacharias, – a complexion which,
though clear, is far enough removed from virgin delicacy, and suggests
plenty of sun and wind as its accompaniment', the reference to a picture in the National Gallery is hardly worth while, as few readers know
that the youthful son of Zacharias is John the Baptist in his childhood.
When we are told in *The Mayor of Casterbridge* that Miss Templeman
(Lucetta) 'deposited herself on the sofa in her former flexuous position,
and throwing her arm above her brow – somewhat in the pose of a
well-known conception of Titian's – talked up at Elizabeth-Jane
invertedly across her forehead and arm', we are balked not by the
visual image but by the verbal opacity of 'deposited herself', 'pose' of
a 'conception', and 'talked up . . . invertedly'. The only reference
where almost everything is left to the reader's pictorial imagination is in
Jude the Obscure, the last novel written by Hardy. Jude and Sue are
visiting their great-aunt, and find her wrapped in blankets, 'turning
upon them a countenance like that of Sebastiano's Lazarus'. No more
description is given. It is a first sketch; Hardy, we know, was never
able to revise this novel as he had intended.

His references are often made in such a way that they enhance
impressions even for a reader who lacks the pictorial background.
Bathsheba's face colours with the angry crimson of a Danby sunset,
and who can doubt that the comparison gains from the particulariza-
tion? Similarly with the depiction of 'tender affectionateness', 'such
as is often seen in the women of Correggio when they are painted in
profile'. Such comparisons vary from the humorous, as in *The Hand of
Ethelberta*, where the heroine's dress 'sloped about as high over the

shoulder as would have drawn approval from Reynolds, and expostulation from Lely', to the tragic in *Tess*, where, on returning from Brazil, Angel Clare shows all the effects of severe fever and remorse for his cruel abandonment of Tess:

> You could see the skeleton behind the man, and almost the ghost behind the skeleton. He matched Crivelli's dead *Christus*. His sunken eye-pits were of morbid hue, and the light in his eyes had waned. The angular hollows and lines of his aged ancestors had succeeded to their reign in his face twenty years before their time.

By contrast the ineffectiveness of the attempt at visual presentation through reference to Sebastiano's Lazarus in *Jude* is obvious. The description of Angel illustrates the truth of Hardy's claim: 'My art is to intensify the expression of things, as is done by Crivelli, Bellini, etc., so that the heart and inner meaning is made vividly visible.'[3] It applies to many passages unrelated to painters, particularly (as will be seen) to landscapes and images which parallel or represent the plight or emotion of Hardy's principal characters.

For the subject in hand no 'Laokoon' or 'New Laokoon' differentiations need be drawn between the modes of perceiving different art forms. It is assumed that pictures emerge as we read, and can be stored in the memory; or a few selected features can be so presented that an impression of the whole is flashed upon the 'inward eye'; or, to adapt Hardy's comment on Turner's water-colours, the writer can give 'for that which cannot be reproduced a something else' which has 'an approximative effect to that of the real'. In literature this is best achieved through metaphor or simile; in *Tess*, for example, almost horizontal sunbeams form a 'pollen of radiance over the landscape'; or, in the direction of the afternoon sun, 'a glistening ripple of gossamer webs' in the meadow suggests 'a track of moonlight on the sea'. Art, Hardy concluded his note on Turner's paintings, is 'the secret of how to produce by a false thing the effect of a true'.

If he were merely (in the words of Blake) a writer of single vision, Hardy would not have maintained his hold on readers. His 'pure' description or backcloth settings are usually very economical. The one undoubted lapse in this respect occurs in *A Laodicean*, much of which he dictated in fulfilment of a contract when he was too ill to write. Hardy's artistic genius is complex, and much of it in his novels is conveyed through image and scene. He does not use them to express his own emotions, as T. S. Eliot suggests when, after having read little of him, he accuses him of making landscape the 'vehicle' of decadent emotionalism.[4] In scene and image the poet and the novelist in Hardy combine to express the feelings, moods and situations of characters, particularly in times of stress. An artist will often find a concrete way of expressing experience far more intensely and vividly than the psychological or realistic writer; and here Hardy excels.

*   *   *

This is to anticipate, and I must first make a few observations on pictorial description in Hardy which is basic and direct, with no secondary associations or significant implications. His first novel, *The Poor Man and the Lady*, remained unpublished; it contained a good deal of social satire with West End settings, one of which was utilized in the fourteenth chapter of *A Pair of Blue Eyes*. The scene is Hyde Park at six o'clock on a midsummer afternoon, 'in a melon-frame atmosphere and beneath a violet sky'. One carriage is the centre of interest amid the general throng. Its general colour is 'the rich indigo hue of a midnight sky'; its wheels and margins are 'picked out in delicate lines of ultramarine'; its attendants are dressed in coats of dark blue with silver lace, and breeches of 'neutral Indian red'. Except for the imaginative hint of a midnight sky, this colourful description is that of a copyist.

A hyperaesthetic response to colour may be suspected in Hardy's note of July 1888 (*Life*, 210): 'A letter lies on the red velvet cover of the table; staring up, by reason of the contrast. I cover it over, that it may not hit my eyes so hard.' It appears in *Desperate Remedies* (ii. 4), where the blazing western light adds an orange tint to the vivid purple of the heather, so intensifying the colours 'that they seemed to stand above the surface of the earth and float in mid-air like an exhalation of red'. A striking first impression of Miss Aldclyffe is given in a vivid and dramatic picture, which seems to be the result of careful observation. When Cytherea Graye visits the Belvedere Hotel to be interviewed by her, she is shown into a room on the shady side of the building. Its prevailing colour is blue, rendered pale by light from the north-eastern sky which falls on a wide roof of new slates – all that is visible through the small window. Under the door leading to the next room in the suite gleams 'a very thin line of ruddy light'. When Miss Aldclyffe enters this room, 'the golden line' vanishes in parts 'like the phosphorescent streak caused by the striking of a match'. She taps her foot with impatience and says imperiously, 'There's no one here!' As Cytherea lays her hand on the knob, the door opens, and the direct blaze of the afternoon sun, refracted through crimson curtains and heightened by reflections from the red wallpaper and carpet, shines with a burning glow around the lady holding the door. She stands like a tall black figure in the midst of fire. The framing effect of this ominous climactic presentation is to be found elsewhere in Hardy (but nowhere as dramatically), as in the window pictures of Fancy Day and of Mr Penny (already quoted) in *Under the Greenwood Tree* (I. v, II. ii).

John Morley, Macmillan's reader, thought the 'pictures of Christmas

Eve in the tranter's house' at the opening of *The Poor Man and the Lady* were 'really of good quality. . . . So that we are irresistibly reminded of the paintings of Wilkie and still more perhaps of those of Teniers, etc.' They were transferred to *Under the Greenwood Tree*, which Hardy described as 'a rural painting of the Dutch school'. Of its kind it is almost perfect, but it lacks exciting incident, as Leslie Stephen was quick to point out when he invited Hardy to write a serial for *The Cornhill Magazine*. Yet its pictures are admirably succinct; they reduce the action less than does the dialogue, which is full of mature, thoughtful rustic humour and amusing anecdote. George Eliot's influence weighed with Hardy at least as much as Morley's after the critical reception of the sensationally plotted *Desperate Remedies*. At the opening of the second book of *Adam Bede* she had written:

> It is for this rare, precious quality of truthfulness that I delight in many Dutch paintings, which lofty-minded people despise. I find a source of delicious sympathy in these faithful pictures of a monotonous homely existence . . .
> . . . do not impose on us any aesthetic rules which shall banish from the region of Art those old women scraping carrots with their workworn hands, those heavy clowns taking holiday in a dingy pot-house, those rounded backs and stupid weather-beaten faces that have bent over the spade and done the rough work of the world . . .

This defence of 'low' life, as it was regarded in the pre-Wordsworthian era,[5] encouraged Hardy to write about country life rather than 'society', the satire of which had been the main subject of *The Poor Man and the Lady*. For many years afterwards he was afraid that he would be 'driven to society novels' and 'had kept, at casual times, a record of his experiences in social life' against such a contingency. Some of these impressions entered *The Well-Beloved*, at least twenty years after the writing of *Under the Greenwood Tree*.

To some extent the story of *A Pair of Blue Eyes* is based on Hardy's falling in love with Emma Lavinia Gifford at St Juliot, Cornwall; and the following picture was undoubtedly a most vivid recollection. 'Every woman who makes a permanent impression on a man is usually recalled to his mind's eye as she appeared in one particular scene', he begins:

> Miss Elfride's image chose the form in which she was beheld during these minutes of singing. . . . The profile is seen of a young woman in a pale gray silk dress with trimmings of swan's-down, and opening up from a point in front, like a waistcoat without a shirt; the cool colour contrasting admirably with the warm bloom of her neck and face. The furthermost candle on the piano comes immediately in a line with her head, and half invisible itself, forms the accidentally

frizzled hair into a nebulous haze of light, surrounding her crown like an aureola. Her hands are in their place on the keys, her lips parted, and trilling forth, in a tender diminuendo, the closing words of the sad apostrophe:

> 'O Love, who bewailest
> The frailty of all things here,
> Why choose you the frailest
> For your cradle, your home, and your bier!'

With Shelley's lyric we pass from pictorial realism to the tragic theme. The heroine of *A Laodicean* inherits technological interests and a castle from her father, a prominent railway contractor. Her long indecision between the hero Somerset and Captain de Stancy represents the conflict between the romance of scientific engineering and that of the old aristocratic values. It is appropriate that her love for the architect Somerset quickens near one of her father's scientific triumphs, a railway tunnel. Hardy prefaces his picture of the entrance with these words, 'The popular commonplace that science, steam, and travel must always be unromantic and hideous, was not proven.' The implications of his poem 'After a Romantic Day' are similar, though its railway setting is 'bald' and 'moon-lit':

> The railway bore him through
> An earthen cutting out from a city:
> There was no scope for view,
> Though the frail light shed by a slim young moon
> Fell like a friendly tune.
>
> Fell like a liquid ditty,
> And the blank lack of any charm
> Of landscape did no harm.
> The bald steep cutting, rigid, rough,
> And moon-lit, was enough
> For poetry of place: its weathered face
> Formed a convenient sheet whereon
> The visions of his mind were drawn.

Here, and in a poem to which I refer later, we see that Hardy was not a traditionalist. He was true to human nature, knowing that 'the beauty of association is entirely superior to the beauty of aspect'. With Wilkie Collins he believed in 'the poetry of every-day truth'.

Unlike *Under the Greenwood Tree*, *The Mayor of Casterbridge* was written for weekly serialization, and therefore needed to be sustained by continual incident. After the opening scenes, Hardy had to economize or use another technique when he might have preferred more scenic description. The interior sketch of the Three Mariners, for example, just before Henchard compels the choir to sing a curse on Farfrae, is almost minimal, yet sufficient for imaginative realization. We take a close look at the cups, 'all exactly alike – straight-sided, with two leafless lime-trees done in eel-brown on the sides', before the general scene is presented, as it appears on Sunday afternoons after service in the church opposite. In the large room there would be forty church-goers at least, including the choir,

> forming a ring round the margin of the great sixteen-legged table, like the monolithic circle of Stonehenge in its pristine days. Outside and above the forty cups came a circle of forty smoke-jets from forty clay pipes; outside the pipes the countenances of the forty church-goers, supported at the back by a circle of forty chairs.

Of the skimmington-ride which kills Lucetta there is hardly any direct description, only glimpses conveyed by the comments across the street of two maids at upper windows. The drama of the scene is reinforced by the increasing din and Lucetta's fatal insistence on seeing what she dreaded. Ultimately the tension makes this one of the most imaginative scenes in the book.

The presentation of Marty South at the beginning of *The Woodlanders* is gradual, concluding with an Impressionist picture as seen by the hairdresser whose only interest is the purchase of her beautiful tresses:

> In her present beholder's mind the scene formed by the girlish spar-maker composed itself into an impression-picture of extremest type, wherein the girl's hair alone, as the focus of observation, was depicted with intensity and distinctness, while her face, shoulders, hands, and figure in general, were a blurred mass of unimportant detail, lost in haze and obscurity.

As one of many instances in Hardy's later novels of a '*rapprochement* to the Impressionist vision', Alistair Smart selects the following description of Grace Melbury:

> Just about here the trees were large and wide apart, and there was no undergrowth, so that she could be seen to some distance; a sylph-like greenish-white figure, as toned by the sunlight and the leafage.

*   *   *

We turn now to pictures where more is meant than meets the eye, where, for example, the scene conveys the pathos of the situation or suggests the future in the making. The imagery of such narrative scenes is often poetical in origin and effect. One of the most elaborate is too long to quote, and is derived from Hardy's association of frost with misfortune and adversity. It coincides with the marriage which

Cytherea, the heroine of *Desperate Remedies*, is compelled to make in order to save her brother (see pp. 97–8). A sense of lucklessness is conveyed more swiftly but less surely in *A Pair of Blue Eyes* when the summer-house of the rectory garden at St Juliot is used to present a chiaroscuro picture renewing the note of death which was introduced when Elfride sang 'O Love, who bewailest'. Stephen Smith, returning from India, reaches the garden in time to see her and a man whose voice is familiar enter the Belvedere. Within its trellis-work the 'scratch of a striking light' is heard, and in the 'strongly illuminated picture' which results he sees his friend Henry Knight, his left arm round the waist of Elfride, as they look at her watch. Horizontal bars of woodwork 'crossed their forms like the ribs of a skeleton'.

It is when the love that grew up between Knight and Elfride is threatened that they sit on the altar steps of the partially demolished church. (The tower which had fallen had been her 'strong tower . . . against the enemy'.)

> The heavy arch spanning the junction of the tower and nave formed to-night a black frame to a distant misty view, stretching far westward. Just outside the arch came the heap of fallen stones, then a portion of moonlit churchyard, then the wide and convex sea behind. . . . Rays of crimson, blue, and purple shone upon the twain from the east window behind them, wherein saints and angels vied with each other in primitive surroundings of landscape and sky, and threw upon the pavement at the sitters' feet a softer reproduction of the same translucent hues, amid which the shadows of Knight and Elfride were opaque and prominent blots. Presently the moon became covered by a cloud, and the iridescence died away.

The moonlight returns, irradiating a further portion of the churchyard and revealing, brightest of all, a tomb. The first moonlight scene recalls the casement in Keats's 'The Eve of St Agnes', but the thought is related figuratively to Wordsworth's 'Intimations of Immortality', as Hardy indicates later, when the train of jealous probings started by the tomb has taken its tragic and irreversible course:

> He supported her lightly over the style, and was practically as attentive as a lover can be. But there had passed away a glory, and the dream was not as it had been of yore.

Hardy sometimes presents the moon in a baleful aspect, as in the scene confronting Gabriel Oak, when he is horrified to find that he has lost the two hundred sheep for which he had not wholly paid. Sinister chance and the extinction of all the hopes on which he had built are conveyed in the imagery:

> By the outer margin of the pit was an oval pond, and over it hung the attenuated skeleton of a chrome-yellow moon, which had only

a few days to last – the morning star dogging her on the left hand. The pool glittered like a dead man's eye, and as the world awoke a breeze blew, shaking and elongating the reflection of the moon without breaking it, and turning the image of the star to a phosphoric streak upon the water.

This is one of the most memorable figurative scenes in *Far from the Madding Crowd*. The most brilliant is Troy's sword display around the form of the helplessly dazzled Bathsheba. The greatest *tour de force* is the lightning storm scene, when Troy and his men lie in drunken stupor in the barn, and only Oak, aided by Bathsheba, works against time to save the stacked corn. The climactic flash reflects her final realization of Oak's worth and of her own folly in marrying Troy.

'Outside the Barracks', a late addition to the novel, is a depressing wintry picture, painted in white and varying degrees of darkness by an artist who proceeds step by step with cool deliberation. The first impression is of the unsurpassed dreariness of a snowy evening. Then follow the main features: a public path; to the left, 'a river, beyond which rose a high wall'; to the right, meadow and moorland. The snow gradually makes forms featureless, and the low arching cloud sinks lower until 'the instinctive thought was that the snow lining the heavens and that encrusting the earth would soon unite into one mass without any intervening stratum of air at all'. The psychological effect of this seems to be the elimination of hope, and this impression is reinforced by 'the left-hand characteristics': 'If anything could be darker than the sky, it was the wall, and if anything could be gloomier than the wall it was the river beneath.' The dialogue between Troy within and the fated Fanny Robin beyond the river ends with ironic echoes. What a contrast this scene makes with the colour picture which first reveals Troy to Bathsheba!

Again it is evening, and Bathsheba, after dismissing her bailiff, is compelled to make a late inspection of the farm herself. She carries a dark lantern, which she uses intermittently. On her way from the paddock she passes through a small fir plantation, the interior of which is 'as black as the ninth plague of Egypt at midnight'. She hears the rustle of approaching steps, finds her skirt caught, and is addressed by a man who opens the lantern to set her free:

> The man to whom she was hooked was brilliant in brass and scarlet. He was a soldier. His sudden appearance was to darkness what the sound of a trumpet is to silence. Gloom, the *genius loci* at all times hitherto, was now totally overthrown, less by the lantern-light than by what the lantern lighted.

For the reader, the sound of the trumpet heightens the romance of the colours. The scene is unforgettable, and part of its symbolism is dramatically defined by Boldwood. In his protest, 'Dazzled by brass and scarlet – O, Bathsheba – this is woman's folly indeed!', can be felt the suppressed agony of a tender-hearted man. Jealousy in love is hardly more than a passing twinge in *Under the Greenwood Tree*; in *A Pair of Blue Eyes* it is an obstinate hardening of feeling; in the passionate intensity of Boldwood its crescendo reaches a climax.

In isolation the picture of Sergeant Troy in colourful chiaroscuro might suggest the art of a young man 'unawakened to the tragical mysteries of life'. The scene outside the barracks, however, is in complete accord with the view Hardy expressed in the thematic opening of *The Return of the Native:*

> human souls may find themselves in closer and closer harmony with external things wearing a sombreness distasteful to our race when it was young. The time seems near, if it has not actually arrived, when the chastened sublimity of a moor, a sea, or a mountain will be all of nature that is absolutely in keeping with the moods of the more thinking of mankind.

This outlook in association with the barracks scene helps to explain the fascination for Hardy of N. Mangiarelli's painting 'Near Porta-Salara', which he studied at a private viewing in November 1878. It showed, he wrote, '3 travellers on a dull uninteresting road before a gaunt blank-walled inn – the woman of which comes out to them. In the distance waste and dreariness.'[6] One does not expect the thoughts and feelings of the people in this picture to coincide with the painter's or with Hardy's. Similarly those of Elfride, Knight, Oak, Fanny Robin, and Bathsheba are not identical with the author's. Unlike those in the next category, the pictures in this group illustrate an artistic medium whereby Hardy conveys to the reader his assessment of situations. Whatever the view of the protagonists, his view is detached, and to this extent external.

*   *   *

The third type of scene may be broadly described as 'psychological'. It is a concrete and sometimes poetic way of expressing states of mind, feelings, and moods in the protagonists themselves. One of the finest examples occurs in *The Woodlanders*, a novel in which scenery often has what Hardy described in *Tess* as 'a negative beauty of tone'. Tragic workings of chance are stressed by their collocation with grey and grim impressions of winter, fog, and Darwinian cruelty. There are brighter scenes, the largest canvas among them being that of 'the gorgeous autumn landscape of White-Hart Vale', when Grace, suspecting her husband's infidelity, watches him riding off in the distance on her white horse Darling, an object like 'a Wouvermans eccentricity' of microscopic proportions against the deep violet sky. Nearer she catches sight of a cider machine being drawn up the valley by two horses, a stray sunbeam being reflected now and then like a star on the steely mirrors of the pomace shovels.[7] She recognises Giles Winterborne, and walks down to meet him. Then follows the familiar description:

> He looked and smelt like Autumn's very brother, his face being sun-burnt to wheat-colour, his eyes blue as corn-flowers, his sleeves and leggings dyed with fruit-stains, his hands clammy with the sweet juice of apples, his hat sprinkled with pips, and everywhere about him that atmosphere of cider which at its return each season has such an indescribable fascination for those who have been born and bred among the orchards. Her heart rose from its late sadness like a released bough; her senses revelled in the sudden lapse back to Nature unadorned.

So we proceed from bright colourful landscape detail, alive with narra-tive and visual movement, to this rich, almost Keatsian description of Giles. It is as Grace sees him, and leads inevitably to a release of her true feelings. She had thrown off 'the veneer of artificiality which she had acquired at the fashionable schools', and become her natural, instinctive self: 'Nature was bountiful, she thought. No sooner had she been cast aside by Eldred Fitzpiers than another being, impersonating chivalrous and undiluted manliness, had arisen out of the earth ready to hand.' As they passed round a hill, 'the whole west sky was revealed':

> Between the broken clouds they could see far into the recesses of heaven as they mused and walked, the eye journeying on under a species of golden arcades, and past fiery obstructions, fancied cairns, logan-stones, stalactites and stalagmite of topaz. Deeper than this their gaze passed thin flakes of incandescence, till it plunged into a bottomless medium of soft green fire.

In this skyscape Hardy expresses the true, immeasurable love which stirs in both. Grace, he tells us, is abandoned to the seductive hour, and Giles like a somnambulist forgets himself and caresses the flower she wears in her bosom.

Hardy had used another western sky to express Bathsheba's fears and indecision when she thinks of Boldwood's rage and jealousy should she marry Troy:

> Above the dark margin of the earth appeared foreshores and pro-montories of coppery cloud, bounding a green and pellucid expanse in the western sky. Amaranthine glosses cames over them then, and the unresting world wheeled her round to a contrasting prospect eastward, in the shape of indecisive stars. She gazed upon their silent throes . . . but realized none at all. Her troubled spirit was far away with Troy.

It is not just in the 'silent throes' of the stars that the outer world registers Bathsheba's perturbation.

With the deeper artistic implications of these skyscapes one may compare a cloud scene in Virginia Woolf's *Mrs Dalloway* which has no bearing on the narrative situation, and conveys no more than a writer's own fanciful impressions:

A puff of wind ... blew a thin veil over the sun and over the Strand. The faces faded; the omnibuses suddenly lost their glow. For although the clouds were of mountainous white so that one could fancy hacking hard chips off with a hatchet, with broad golden slopes, lawns of celestial pleasure gardens, on their flanks, and had all the appearance of settled habitations assembled for the conference of the gods above the world ... now a summit dwindled, now a whole block of pyramidal size which had kept its station inalterably advanced into the midst or gravely led the procession to fresh anchorage ... now they struck light to the earth, now darkness.

Calmly and competently, Elizabeth Dalloway mounted the Westminster omnibus.

When Boldwood receives Bathsheba's valentine he is so emotionally unbalanced that he does not know whether he is on his head or his feet. 'His equilibrium disturbed, he was in extremity at once.' Before going to bed, he places the valentine in a corner of the looking-glass, and is conscious of it, even when his back is turned towards it. The moonlight in the room is unusual: 'the pale sheen had that reversed direction which snow gives, coming upward and lighting his ceiling in an unnatural way, casting shadows in strange places, and putting lights where shadows had used to be'. The sunrise is like a sunset, and the snow-covered fields show 'that before-mentioned preternatural inversion of light and shade which attends the prospect when the garish brightness commonly in the sky is found on earth, and the shades of earth are in the sky'. The wasting moon, like tarnished brass, looks unpropitious, but the principal effect of the scenes is to emphasize the mental *bouleversement* which is to result in Boldwood's neglect of his farm and the murder of Troy.

When Clym Yeobright and Eustacia Vye are ardently in love just before they decide to marry,

All dark objects on the earth that lay towards the sun were overspread by a purple haze, against which groups of wailing gnats shone, rising upwards and dancing like sparks of fire.

Keats's ode 'To Autumn' obviously contributes to this picture, but more important is Thomas Gray's 'purple light of love', which is here used to conceal all 'dark objects'. After Eustacia's departure, Clym has time to reflect, and realizes that a less hasty marriage would be more sensible:

> As he watched, the dead flat of the scenery overpowered him. . . . There was something in its oppressive horizontality which too much reminded him of the arena of life; it gave him a sense of bare equality with, and no superiority to, a single living thing under the sun.
> Eustacia was no longer the goddess but the woman to him . . .

Hardy probably had a notebook for such mirror effects, for he had employed the same descriptions, almost word for word, in *Desperate Remedies* as part of a ground and sky setting to reflect the changing emotions of the heroine when she is pressed to marry Manston (see pp. 11–12). Another reflective image in *The Return of the Native* is that of the heron flying towards the sun, as seen by the dying Mrs Yeobright in the torrid heat of Egdon Heath: 'as he flew the edges and linings of his wings, his thighs, and his breast were so caught by the bright sunbeams that he appeared as if formed of burnished silver.' As Hardy indicates, it embodies Mrs Yeobright's wish to be released from earthly pain.

An acoustic picture in *The Mayor of Casterbridge* presents one of Hardy's more subtle psychological scenes. Henchard is certain that Newson will return, expose his appalling deceit, and take away Elizabeth-Jane – all he has to live for. The prospect is reflected in the landscape; it is dark and unendurable. 'If he could have summoned music to his aid,' Hardy writes, 'his existence might even now have been borne; for with Henchard music was of regal power.' Ironically what he hears suggests the most appropriate place for suicide; it draws him like music. Hardy uses the same meadow and moorland scenery he had recreated outside the barracks in *Far from the Madding Crowd*, but with a different emphasis. Its waters are heard like 'singular symphonies' in 'sundry tones, from near and far', but loudest of all at Ten Hatches, Henchard's goal, where their instrumentation becomes 'a very fugue of sounds'.

Three pictures express the state of mind of Tess when she is in love with Angel Clare at the dairy-farm. The first suggests a painting in which the objects appear to be animated with the terror that mars her ecstasy at the thought of marrying him without revealing her past:

> the sun settled down upon the levels, with the aspect of a great forge[8] in the heavens, and presently a monstrous pumpkin-like moon arose on the other hand. The pollard willows, tortured out of their natural shape by incessant choppings, became spiny-haired monsters as they stood up against it.

During their courtship they spent 'wonderful afternoons' roving the meadows. Tess's almost unalloyed happiness is transmuted into a Turneresque scene:

> They were never out of the sound of some purling weir, whose buzz accompanied their own murmuring, while the beams of the sun, almost as horizontal as the mead itself, formed a pollen of radiance over the landscape. They saw tiny blue fogs in the shadows of the trees and hedges, all the time that there was bright sunshine elsewhere.

By the late autumn 'Tess's desire seemed to be for a perpetual betrothal in which everything should remain as it was then'. In the early afternoons she and Angel lingered in the warm meadows. 'Looking over the damp sod in the direction of the sun', they saw

> a glistening ripple of gossamer webs . . . like the track of moonlight on the sea. Gnats, knowing nothing of their brief glorification, wandered across the shimmer of this pathway, irradiated as if they bore fire within them, then passed out of its line, and were quite extinct.

Here we have a marvellously artistic and philosophical picture of love, its radiance and its ephemerality, for Tess far shorter-lived than for most. The significance of the 'wailing gnats . . . like sparks of fire' in Hardy's previous scenes is now explicit; it is the insignificance of the individual in the vast expanse of time and space.

Harmonization of landscape and situation is to be found in several of Hardy's novels, but never more felicitously or abundantly than in *Tess*. A golden harvest scene accords with Tess's resolution to shake off the past, though it is a reminder of Nature's indifference to her lot, and there are menacing signs in the red revolving arms of the reaping-machine, and in the foretold doom of the animals within the shrinking covert of corn. Tess's summer in the lush green meadows of the Vale of Great Dairies coincides with love and relative happiness, and contrasts with the winter on the chalk hills of Flintcomb-Ash Farm after her abandonment by Angel Clare. Her intense misery is expressed in the frost and snow, but most intensively in the eyes of those Arctic birds that come near her and Marian as they toil in the fields:

> gaunt spectral creatures with tragical eyes – eyes which had witnessed scenes of cataclysmal horror in inaccessible polar regions of a magnitude such as no human being had ever conceived . . .; which had beheld the crash of icebergs and the slide of snow-hills by the shooting light of the Aurora; been blinded by the whirl of colossal storms and terraqueous distortions; and retained the expression of feature that such scenes had engendered.

This is more than a picture; it is an outcry against what Hardy calls
'the Frost's decree', the pitilessness of nature and chance, or the indifference of 'the Cause of Things'. There are great and moving scenes
in *Tess* – the christening scene by candlelight which bestows grandeur
on a poor peasant girl in a dingy bedroom ('The business of the poet
and the novelist is to show ... the grandeur underlying the sorriest
things'), and the Stonehenge scene, for example – but nowhere is the
tragedy more intensely conveyed than in this passage, where the endurance of pain is doubly impressed through the superimposition of the
Flintcomb-Ash bird picture on the horrors of the Arctic Circle.

*   *   *

Some of Hardy's most vivid and economical descriptive prose occurs in
his neglected major work *The Dynasts*. It is the distilled result of highly
visualized historical research, and provides panoramic settings for many
scenes and battles. Perhaps the finest is that which begins with an
aerial view of the French army in retreat from Moscow:

> An object like a dun-piled caterpillar
> Shuffling its length in painful heaves along.

It has left Smolensko, and snow begins to fall:

What has floated down from the sky upon the Army is a flake of snow.
Then come another and another, till natural features, hitherto varied
with the tints of autumn, are confounded, and all is phantasmal grey
and white.

The caterpillar shape still creeps laboriously nearer, but instead of
increasing in size by the rules of perpective, it gets more attenuated,
and there are left upon the ground behind it minute parts of itself,
which are speedily flaked over, and remain as white pimples by the
wayside.

Pines rise mournfully on each side of the nearing object; ravens in
flocks advance with it overhead, waiting to pick out the eyes of strays
who fall. The snowstorm increases, descending in tufts which can
hardly be shaken off. The sky seems to join itself to the land. The
marching figures drop rapidly, and almost immediately become white
grave-mounds.

Endowed with larger powers of audition as of vision, we are struck
with the mournful taciturnity which prevails. Nature is mute. Save for
the incessant flogging of the wind-broken and lacerated horses there
are no sounds.

With growing nearness more is revealed. In the glades of the forest,
parallel to the French columns, columns of Russians are seen to be
moving. And when the French presently reach Krasnoye they are
surrounded by packs of cloaked Cossacks, bearing lances like huge
needles a dozen feet long.

So they make their painful way until they reach the Beresina river, when 'the point of vision descends to earth, close to the scene of action'. Hardy's technique is that of the cinematographer.

*　　*　　*

It is difficult to generalize about Hardy's poems. Most of their pictorialism comes in flashes; when it is more extensive, it is usually subordinated to story or theme, as in 'On the Esplanade', where the time 'Midsummer: 10 p.m.' and the cryptic last line suggest a development in accordance with a recurrent Hardy superstition. The scene is one with which he was familiar at Weymouth in 1869, and its description occupies most of the poem. An evocative picture of the moonlit bay is followed by one of the lamp-lit esplanade, and it is interesting to compare this with the same scene in *Desperate Remedies*. In the one the lamps on the sea-wall 'make a long display/As a pearl-strung row,/ Under which in the waves they bore their gimlets of light'; in the other, 'looking small and yellow', they seem to 'send long tap-roots of fire quivering down deep into the sea'.

With half of each stanza devoted to background, 'The Wind's Prophecy' is relatively prodigal in scene and sound effects:

> I travel on by barren farms,
> And gulls glint out like silver flecks
> Against a cloud that speaks of wrecks,
> And bellies down with black alarms.
> . . .
> Yonder the headland, vulturine,
> Snores like old Skrymer in his sleep,
> And every chasm and every steep
> Blackens as wakes each pharos-shine.
> . . .

Among the later poems are many vignettes. One of the best is the frequently anthologized 'Snow in the Suburbs', a picture in which movement is skilfully conveyed through metrical changes. Another is that of 'The Harbour Bridge', leading to snatches of conversation which suffice to tell a common tale of broken marriage. Sometimes they are drab and commonplace, as the poem 'In a Waiting-Room' exemplifies. A radiance is shed on 'fly-blown pictures' by the hope and vitality of children:

> 'Here are the lovely ships that we,
> Mother, are by and by going to see!
> When we get there, it's 'most sure to be fine,
> And the band will play, and the sun will shine.'

It is the poetry of ordinary life. 'To find beauty in ugliness is the province of the poet', Hardy wrote in 1888; 'others find/Poesy ever lurk where pit-pats poor mankind', he wrote in *The Dynasts* (2. III. i). His note of 22 April 1878 shows that this conviction had been reinforced by the work of painters:

> The method of Boldini [and] Hobbema . . . is that of infusing emotion into the baldest external subjects either by the presence of a human figure among them, or by a mark of some human connection with them.

This accords with my feeling about, say, Heidelberg and Baden *versus* Scheveningen – as I wrote at the beginning of *The Return of the Native* – that the beauty of association is entirely superior to the beauty of aspect, and a beloved relative's old battered tankard to the finest Greek vase. Paradoxically put, it is to see the beauty in ugliness.

Almost at the opposite extreme is 'Beeny Cliff', a poem recalling Hardy's happy love. It is colourful, and much in recent years has been made of its Virgilian purples, though the poet was simply reflecting the colours he had seen. It contains a remarkable evocation of sound and scene, height and depth, sea and headland, movement and change:

> The pale mews plained below us, and the waves seemed far away
> In a nether sky engrossed in saying their ceaseless babbling say,
> As we laughed light-heartedly aloft on that clear-sunned March day.
>
> A little cloud then cloaked us, and there flew an irised rain,
> And the Atlantic dyed its levels with a dull misfeatured stain,
> And then the sun burst out again, and purples prinked the main.

'Neutral Tones' is a rare experiment in achromatic visualisation, with the bitterness of love's disillusionment fixed in a wintry scene, featuring a face, a white 'God-curst' sun, a tree, and 'a pond edged with grayish leaves'. The poem is probably an imaginative re-creation, the germ of which is to be found in Shelley (see p. 92).

A frosty scene in 'The Darkling Thrush' presents one of Hardy's most pessimistic moods. It contrasts the poet's outlook with the bird's instinctive and full-hearted joy as the poor light wanes on the last day of the last century. Lifelessness, wintry externalities, suggestions of broken lyre-strings and death, are distinctly imaged and grouped in a scenic expression of unrelieved gloom:

> I leant upon a coppice gate
> When Frost was spectre-gray,
> And Winter's dregs made desolate
> The weakening eye of day.
> The tangled bine-stems scored the sky
> Like strings of broken lyres,

> And all mankind that haunted nigh
> Had sought their household fires.
>
> The land's sharp features seemed to be
> The Century's corpse outleant,
> His crypt the cloudy canopy,
> The wind his death-lament.
> The ancient pulse of germ and birth
> Was shrunken hard and dry,
> And every spirit upon earth
> Seemed fervourless as I.

One of the most powerful and haunting images in Hardy's poetry is that of the old moon as it casts its spell in 'The Pedigree'. A skyscape in motion is admirably created in a few lines:

> and as I bent there, half unrobed,
> The uncurtained panes of my window-square let in the watery light
> Of the moon in its old age:
> And green-rheumed clouds were hurrying past where mute and cold it
> globed
> Like a drifting dolphin's eye seen through a lapping wave.

* * *

Whether this sampling does justice to the subject is highly doubtful, but one cannot fairly end without brief reference to countless miniature pictures in the incidental imagery which helps to keep Hardy's style alive. They may be presented directly, as when, in *A Pair of Blue Eyes*, the ruts of a wet uphill road are transformed by sunset rays into 'shining bars of gold, tapering to nothing in the distance' or, in *Tess of the d'Urbervilles*, 'the wheels of the dairyman's spring cart, as he sped from the market, licked up the pulverized surface of the highway, and were followed by white ribands of dust, as if they had set a thin powder-train on fire'. More often they appear as auxiliars, as in the description of Marty South's shorn tresses on the pale scrubbed deal top of the coffin-stool table, 'like waving and ropy weeds over the washed white bed of a stream'. In the poem 'Overlooking the River Stour', a moor-hen planes up 'shavings of crystal spray', and swallows fly like 'little crossbows . . . in the curves of an eight'. The evening after their wedding, Tess and Angel sit in the glare of flameless embers, and each gem of her necklace turns into 'an Aldebaran or a Sirius – a constellation of white, red, and green flashes' that interchange their hues with every pulsation. Later, in the glow of a fire that is already turning ashen, each diamond on her neck gives 'a sinister wink like a toad's', as she bends forward to tell the story which shatters their marriage before it has begun, reducing her and Angel to mere ashes of their former selves.

Hardy's imagination was animated from many sources, pre-eminently by the sights and sounds of nature. His interest was widespread, ranging, as we see in *Far from the Madding Crowd*, from 'fern-sprouts like bishops' croziers' in June to the colours of the stars and their 'panoramic glide' on a clear night in December. Nothing seems to have excited more exquisite responses in him than the sight and texture of tender leaves in May: in *The Return of the Native* (VI. i) those of the birch are as 'delicate as butterflies' wings' and 'diaphanous as amber' in the sunset light; in *The Woodlanders* (xlvii) it is the beeches which unfold 'large limp young leaves of the softness of butterflies' wings'. In 'Afterwards', a poem written when Hardy assumed he had not much longer to live, he recalls, among other prized observations, 'the full-starred heaven that winter sees', and the dewfall-hawk crossing the shades at dusk 'like an eyelid's soundless blink' to alight on 'the wind-warped upland thorn'; but pride of place goes to those tender memories of spring:

> When the Present has latched its postern behind my tremulous stay,
>   And the May month flaps its glad green leaves like wings,
> Delicate-filmed as new-spun silk, will the neighbours say,
>   'He was a man who used to notice such things'?

4 Chance, Choice, and Charity

Possibly no other single book made a greater immediate impact on Hardy than *The Origin of Species*. In numbering himself among its 'earliest acclaimers', he seems to imply that its conclusions were not altogether surprising. The subject may have been familiar to him from Tennyson's *In Memoriam*, but almost undoubtedly he recognised the truth of Darwin's presentation of nature from the evidence he had seen for himself on the heath, and in the woods, adjacent to his home at Higher Bockhampton.

The evidence of the woodlands near his home may have been intended for the story Hardy planned in 1874 but postponed until 1885. This was *The Woodlanders*, a novel in which the Darwinian view of Nature is prominent and indivisible from the principal theme. Observations of the heath were recalled in the circumstances of Mrs Yeobright's tragic death. A younger person would have been exhausted by the long walk she took in intense heat on an exposed heath, but the 'torrid attack' was too much for her. She was overcome with lassitude before she reached Alderworth; when she turned back grief-stricken, she was soon faint and in need of water. There was none fit to drink. The sun was like 'some merciless incendiary, brand in hand, waiting to consume her'. Cruelty to one species, however, may be ideal for another, and it is interesting to note that, after describing Mrs Yeobright's exhaustion in the pitiless heat, Hardy continues: 'all visible animation disappeared from the landscape, though the intermittent husky notes of the male grasshoppers from every tuft of furze were enough to show that amid the prostration of the larger animal species an unseen insect world was busy in all the fulness of life'.

The 'nicely balanced forces' of destruction and survival in nature excited a sense of wonder in the more dispassionate Darwin. He found 'grandeur' in evolution from the struggle for existence, 'from famine and death'; and consoled himself 'with the full belief' that 'the war of nature is not incessant, that no fear is felt, that death is generally prompt, and that the vigorous, the healthy, and the happy survive and multiply'. Hardy could not share such sentiments; from his childhood he had been haunted by the sight of a starved, half-frozen bird that had fallen dead when his father idly tossed a stone at it. How he reacted to the Darwinian world of survival and extinction is expressed in that most tragic of all his close-ups, those strange Arctic birds over

Flintcomb-Ash, in whose eyes are to be seen the endurance of Tess
(see pp. 29–30). It is no wonder that he associates 'the Frost's decree'
(and its wider, human implications) with the hardships of birds.

Though Hardy's views were influenced by other scientists and philosophers such as J. S. Mill, Spencer, Huxley, and Comte, they changed
very little fundamentally from 1865, a few years after he first read
Darwin. The total effect of new scientific thought is described in *Jude*:
the 'animosity of contemporary logic and vision' was 'deadly', and
Hardy could no longer believe that a Providence or God of love directed
the universe. The natural world was a set of 'nicely balanced forces',
explicable in scientific terms of cause and effect; the universe was
neutral and indifferent to man. The Cause of Things, he wrote in 1920,
'is neither moral nor immoral, but *un*moral: "loveless and hateless"
I have called it, "which neither good nor evil knows" '.

Hardy read the philosophers, but there is much evidence to suggest
that, though he accepted their main conclusions, he was confirmed in
them by writers who appealed to his imaginative reason – the Greek
dramatists, and Shelley, Carlyle, Hugo, and Swinburne, for example.
At the end of 1863, he found time once again to read a great deal, and
turned more and more to poets, among them Shelley, who remained his
favourite.

In *The Revolt of Islam* the thought of a Power created by man in
his own image ('the shade from his own soul upthrown', a phrase Hardy
uses with another connotation in the final crisis of *The Mayor of
Casterbridge*) compelled Shelley to affirm:

> What is that Power? Ye mock yourselves, and give
>   A human heart to what ye cannot know:
> As if the cause of life could think and live!
> 'Twere as if man's works should feel, and show
> The hopes, and fears, and thoughts from which they flow,
>   And he be like to them! Lo! Plague is free
> To waste, Blight, Poison, Earthquake, Hail, and Snow,
>   Disease, and Want, and worse Necessity
> Of hate and ill, and Pride, and Fear, and Tyranny![1]

In July 1893, during his vain early effort to modernize the thought of
Mrs Henniker, Hardy wrote: 'What I meant about your unfaithfulness
to the Shelley cult referred not to any lack of poetical emotion, but to
your view of things: e.g. you are quite out of harmony with this line of
his in Epipsychidion:

> "The sightless tyrants of our fate"

which beautifully expresses one's consciousness of blind circumstance
beating upon one, without any feeling, for or against.'[2]

In an essay by Carlyle, which contributed something to the creation
of Henchard, Hardy came across this sentence: 'The Soul of Man still
fights with the dark influences of Ignorance, Misery and Sin; still
lacerates itself, like a captive bird, against the iron limits which Necessity has drawn round it.'[3] Eleven days after finishing *The Mayor of
Casterbridge*, he was in London, waiting for Emma at the Marble
Arch, and watching the passers-by: 'Some wear jewels and feathers,
some wear rags. All are caged birds; the only difference lies in the size
of the cage. This too is part of the tragedy.'

One reason for Hardy's admiration of Hugo is to be seen in a passage he transcribed from *The Edinburgh Review* in 1886:

> In old romances the human will is everything, nature nothing ...
> the actors are individuals isolated from all those surroundings of
> birth, education, prejudice, by which in real life they are so power-
> fully affected. Hugo endeavours ... to be more true to reality. He
> insists on ... the powerlessness of the human will in the face of inani-
> mate forces, such as superstition, society, or nature; dogmas ...;
> religion, prejudice, or the elements. ... Man ... is a powerless unit
> in a crowd. Hugo's theme is the predestined fate of human existence,
> the struggle between man and destiny; he insists upon the compul-
> sion of circumstances, the tragic force that overrides the human will.

'The best tragedy ... is that of the WORTHY encompassed by the
INEVITABLE', Hardy wrote.

Necessity suggests determinism, but it would be a mistake to conclude that this represents his customary view of life. When he
attempted to philosophize he was not always consistent, as his unfortunate authorial comments on Tess's early tragedy illustrate on a small
scale. His views were strongly expressed, but he insisted that they
were no more than 'seemings' or impressions, 'mood-dictated' rather
than 'scientific': 'I have no philosophy – merely what I have often
explained to be only a confused heap of impressions, like those of a
bewildered child at a conjuring show', he wrote in 1920. Earlier, in the
General Preface of 1912, he stated:

> Positive views on the Whence and the Wherefore of things have
> never been advanced by this pen as a consistent philosophy. Nor is it
> likely, indeed, that imaginative writings extending over more than
> forty years would exhibit a coherent scientific theory of the universe
> even if it had been attempted – of that universe concerning which
> Spencer owns to the 'paralyzing thought' that possibly there exists
> no comprehension of it anywhere.

An examination of some of the items in the 'confused heap of impressions' which accumulated in over *sixty* years of Hardy's writing shows
that his view of Necessity was not absolute.

In 'Discouragement', a poem begun possibly in 1863 (not later than 1865), Hardy couples injustice at birth with the defects of Nature:

> Her loves dependent on a feature's trim,
> A whole life's circumstance on hap of birth,
> A soul's direction on a body's whim. . . .

There is a link with Hamlet's

> some vicious mole of nature in them,
> As in their birth, wherein they are not guilty,
> Since nature cannot choose his origin;

but the lines conjure up tragic associations in Hardy's fiction. The first, Tess, whose physical maturity and attractiveness were more advanced than her years and enlightenment; the second, the Durbeyfield family –

> six helpless creatures, who had never been asked if they wished for life on any terms, much less if they wished for it on such hard conditions as were involved in being of the shiftless house of Durbeyfield.

The third line, 'A soul's direction on a body's whim', recalls Jude's seduction. In addition, the poem has a personal note, and is probably motivated by the class resentment Hardy expressed in *The Poor Man and the Lady*. Freedom and opportunity are dependent on circumstance or chance. In 'Hap' (1866) Crass Casualty is seen in relationship with 'dicing Time'; this is the theme of 'change and chancefulness' with which Hardy's published poems appropriately begin. He recognises that these 'purblind Doomsters' are so indifferent to what befalls that his luck may be good or ill. It was good fortune (he thought at first) which took him on that fateful journey into Cornwall:

> And Devotion drops her glance
>   To recall
> What bond-servants of Chance
>   We are all.
> I but found her in that, going
> On my errant path unknowing,
> I did not outskirt the spot
> That no spot on earth excels,
> – Where she dwells![4]

There is a rather amusing sequel to this. A few months before he and Emma Gifford were married, Hardy met Helen Paterson, who illustrated *Far from the Madding Crowd*. She married the Irish poet William Allingham. 'Those two almost simultaneous weddings would have been one but for a stupid blunder of God Almighty', Hardy wrote

to Gosse in 1906. In 'The Opportunity' (a poem which in both movement and theme resembles Browning's 'Youth and Art') he recalled this
meeting forty years earlier with Helen Paterson:

> Had we mused a little space
>   At that critical date in the Maytime,
> One life had been ours, one place,
>   Perhaps, till our long cold claytime.
>
> – This is the bitter thing
>   For thee, O man: what ails it?
> The tide of chance may bring
>   Its offer; but nought avails it!

Of the rule of Chance in Hardy's fiction there are many remarkable
examples. His coincidences are sometimes unusual but never impossible. One of the most bizarre is that of the young wife in 'A Mere
Interlude' who knowingly lies between her two husbands, the corpse
of the one she had married a few days previously being in the adjacent room. 'Fellow-Townsmen' leads up to events which show the
'curious refinement of cruelty' which often proceeds from the 'whimsical god . . . known as blind Circumstance'. In *Desperate Remedies*
Hardy took pains to assert his new outlook over the conventional one.
The death of Miss Aldclyffe's father makes Cytherea stay at Knapwater House after all. Miss Aldclyffe wonders if Providence has
directed the course of events. Hardy's explanatory comment runs:

> once more in the history of human endeavour, a position which it
> was impossible to reach by any direct attempt, was come to by the
> seeker's swerving from the path, and regarding the original object
> as one of secondary importance.[5]

His most audacious comment on the idea of Providence is implicit in
the action of the villain Manston after hearing that his wife has been
burned to death; he falls on his knees and 'in a passionate outburst of
feeling' gives thanks to God. In this satirical context, all Hardy ven-
tures explicitly is a sly paraphrase: 'some Being or Personality, who in
frigid moments is dismissed with the title of Chance, or at most Law.'
There is one occasion when such an explanation does seem frigid and
inadequate. It is when Sue, distraught over the death of her children,
has said that she and Jude must submit, and that it is 'no use fighting
God'; he answers, 'It is only against men and senseless circumstance.'
Intellectually Sue assents, but only for a time. More convincing is the
substitution of 'Time and Chance' for 'Providence' at the opening of
The Mayor of Casterbridge: Susan wore the expression of one who
judged 'anything possible at the hands of Time and Chance, except,
perhaps, fair play'.

It is the weaker or less admirable characters in Hardy who blame some remote Power for untoward circumstances and events which could have been avoided. Eustacia Vye is 'one who, though willing to ward off evil consequences by a mild effort, would let events fall out as they might sooner than wrestle hard to direct them'. After her failure to act at the most crucial point in the tragedy, 'instead of blaming herself ... she laid the fault upon the shoulders of some indistinct, colossal Prince of the World, who had framed her situation and ruled her lot'. 'O, how hard it is of Heaven to devise such tortures for me, who have done no harm to Heaven at all!' she moans when she is lost in the darkness and storm on the heath, hoping (without sensible preparations) to escape to Paris. When Sergeant Troy is overcome by contrition at Fanny Robin's death, he asserts that he would have married her if Satan had not tempted him with Bathsheba's beauty and her 'cursed coquetries'. He concludes that Providence jeers at him when he finds that his first effort to show his compunction is ruined by rain. Hardy's exemplar is Gabriel Oak, who has learned to endure, and see 'the horizon of circumstances without any special regard to his own standpoint in the midst'; Bathsheba wishes she could attain such self-mastery when she knows the worst of Troy.

The question of coincidences is discussed in *Desperate Remedies*. People think it odd when 'two disconnected events ... fall strangely together by chance. ... But when three such events coincide without any apparent reason ... it seems as if there must be invisible means at work. You see, three things falling together in that manner are ten times as singular as two cases of coincidence which are distinct.'[6] So argues Cytherea, who sees the design of Providence in such a triple conjuncture. As the novel proceeds, we see it, of course, as part of Hardy's intricate design. The most impressive coincidence of this rare kind occurs at the end of *A Pair of Blue Eyes*, when Knight and Smith find that they are on the same train from Paddington to Cornwall. The reasons for this have been made so clear that the reader is hardly surprised. More singular is the discovery on reaching their terminus that they have been accompanied all the way by a 'rich and solemn' carriage bearing the coffined Elfride, whom the rivals each sought again in marriage. Even more surprising, perhaps, is it that these discoveries take place on St Valentine's Eve. There is an artistic fitness in all this, however, which lulls disbelief.

In *Far from the Madding Crowd* Fanny Robin's fate is largely determined by her mistaking the church for her wedding. This kind of chance is less credible than that of *Two on a Tower*, where the letter with its tempting annuity for life (conditional on Swithin's not marrying before the age of twenty-five) comes too late; he is already on his way to marry Lady Constantine at Bath. Had he received the letter a month earlier, and had time to reflect on it, there is no telling what might have been the stress of such a web of perplexity upon him, a young man whose love for celestial physics was second to none. But to have held before him, at the last moment, the picture of a future advantage that he had never once thought of . . . affected him about as much as the view of the horizon shown by sheet-lightning. He saw an immense prospect; it went, and the world was as before.

Character often plays a critical part in determining circumstance, and *A Pair of Blue Eyes* foreshadows *Tess of the d'Urbervilles* in 'the chance of things' whereby a devoted and too docile girl has to confront the 'logical power' of a jealous idealist. It is a 'miserable incongruity' that Elfride's second lover should not have been 'one of the great mass of bustling mankind', and that she is not more rebellious but 'proud to be his bond-servant':

> had she been a stronger character – more practical and less imaginative – she would have made more use of her position in his heart to influence him. But the confiding tenderness which had won him is ever accompanied by a sort of self-committal to the stream of events, leading every such woman to trust more to the kindness of fate for good results than to any argument of her own.[7]

The result is disastrous, just as it is for Tess. Had the latter been less passive and more worldly, she might have saved her marriage; but there were qualities in Angel Clare as well as in herself which made her second misfortune inevitable. His love was 'ethereal to a fault', and deep down, despite his confidence in his intellectual liberation, 'lay hidden' a moral intransigence, 'a hard logical deposit, like a vein of metal in a soft loam, which turned the edge of everything that attempted to traverse it'.

Some of Hardy's contrivances of Chance for the general development of his tragic plots might reasonably be regarded as rather remote possibilities. We think of the pleasure-seeking Eustacia Vye, transplanted from Budmouth to the loneliness of Egdon Heath, her Hades; it is an extraordinary fate that her only hope of escape should depend, in the first instance, on one whose high-minded altruism has made him renounce the flashiness of city life in order to educate the sparse population of his native heath. And how the scales are weighed against Tess and Jude! Tess is a victim mainly of circumstances. But for her father's celebrations, Prince would not have been killed; but for her sense of guilt over this disaster, she would not have made the sacrifice of going unwillingly to The Slopes; but for chance circumstances, she would never have thought Alec's company the lesser of two evils on the night of her rape. It is in the main plot, however, that we find the most surprising element of Chance; the antithetical extremes in the characters of Alec and Angel are obviously devised to ensure that Tess, 'once victim', is 'always victim'. The same fateful antithesis is obvious in *Jude*, where Hardy's contrivance of plot seems rather artificial. There is no real compatibility for Jude in either of his marriages, one little more than physical, the other a marriage of true minds and little more naturally.

Careful analysis would show that nowhere in Hardy is credibility more subject to strains than at the very centre of *The Return of the Native* plot. Take into account pride and obstinacy of character (all three central figures suffer rather remarkably in this respect), coincidence, and the amazing readiness of both Clym and Eustacia hopefully or resignedly to let things take their course in the whole complex of events that precipitate the catastrophe, and the slipping of Tess's letter under the carpet becomes by comparison an unexceptionable possibility.

The indivisibility of chance and character was never shown more powerfully and imaginatively by Hardy than in *The Mayor of Casterbridge*, 'a story of a man of character' based, among other literary influences, on Saul and, much less significantly, on suggestions from Carlyle's analysis of Goethe's Faust. There are many chance conjunctions which bear on the course of events, but primarily Henchard is the cause of his own downfall:

> Character is Fate, said Novalis, and Farfrae's character was just the reverse of Henchard's, who might not inaptly be described as Faust has been described – as a vehement gloomy being, who had quitted the ways of vulgar men, without light to guide him on a better way.

The contrast with Farfrae is rather like that between Boldwood and Oak, the latter a stolid example of one prepared to endure and not allow misfortune or disappointment to get the better of his practical sense. Grace Melbury's inadequacy, in the face of Fitzpiers' blandishments and her father's snobbish pressures, is the cause of her disastrous marriage; there is nothing but the characters of these three to account for the most critical event of her life.

With Marty South and Giles Winterborne the emphasis is heavily on the circumstances which compel them to endure. In *The Woodlanders* the suffering of characters (including Grace's father when he realizes the harm he has done) is artistically related to the cruelty of nature, the 'vocalized sorrows of the trees', parasitic growths, the internecine struggles of species, and sylvan death and decay. The 'Unfulfilled Intention, which makes life what it is, was as obvious' in the woods as it could be 'among the depraved crowds of a city slum'. Hardy explained his meaning several times: the Prime Cause blundered when it developed in man an emotional sensitiveness to the cruelty and suffering in life as a whole, without taking steps to remove those evils.[8]

In postulating this Cause, Hardy and the scientific philosophers of the nineteenth century presupposed the modern scientific point of view that the whole active universe in the past is contributory to anything that happens in the present. In *The Woodlanders* he alludes, in a very limited context, to the 'intangible Cause', and, more than elsewhere, demonstrates the linking of events which in life might not appear to be related. For example, but for the cutting down of a certain tree, Giles might not have lost his home and his life prematurely, and Fitzpiers might never have become involved with Mrs Charmond; but for 'a cast of the die of destiny' (character and circumstance) which made Marty South toil until three o'clock in the morning and overhear a conversation between Melbury and his wife, she might never have sold her hair; and but for this and the American Civil War, Fitzpiers might never have returned to Grace, and Mrs Charmond might have escaped an untimely end. If we could see all the links of cause and effect we should find that the Hintock events were but a minute 'part of the pattern in the great web of human doings then weaving in both hemispheres from the White Sea to Cape Horn'. Perhaps for this reason Hardy thought of the Italianized American, surely (with the fantastic baron in 'The Romantic Adventures of a Milkmaid') the most incongruous figure in all his fiction. The web image came, I believe, from John Addington Symonds' *Studies of the Greek Poets*, on which Hardy made notes in 1876 to the effect that man is part of the natural world, and that each of his acts, 'as it has had innumerable antecedents, will be fruitful of immeasurable consequents; for the web of the world is ever weaving'. Ignorance of what Shelley calls 'antecedents and consequents' in such a network can lead to untold unhappiness, as Hardy ruefully reflects in 'Self-Unconscious'. Returning to Cornwall after his first wife's death, he thinks of his self-centred failings during their courtship, and of how different the future might have been for them if only he had seen what 'God, the Elf' ('the whimsical god . . . known as blind Circumstance') now reveals:

> O it would have been good
> Could he then have stood
> At a clear-eyed distance, and conned the whole,
> But now such vision
> Is mere derision
> Nor soothes his body nor saves his soul.

In 'The Sleep-Worker' and a number of other poems we see the Prime Cause becoming the Immanent Will, automatically and unconsciously active in nature:

When wilt thou wake, O mother, wake and see –
As one who, held in trance, has laboured long
By vacant rote and prepossession strong –
The coils that thou hast wrought unwittingly;

Wherein have place, unrealized by thee,
Fair growths, foul cankers, right enmeshed with wrong,
Strange orchestras of victim-shriek and song,
And curious blends of ache and ecstasy?

In *The Dynasts* it is seen at work among warring nations, driving them
to 'demonry'. The Unfulfilled Intention is voiced by the Pities:

But O, the intolerable antilogy
Of making figments feel!

The Immanent Will remains unchanged in conception, but its presented in an unusual way. 'A new and penetrating light' shows 'the
anatomy of life and movement in all humanity and vitalized matter'
as 'one organism', activated by 'the volitions of a Universal Will',

A Will that wills above the will of each,
Yet but the will of all conjunctively.

The Will works mechanically, like clockwork. Both sets of images, the
visual and the figurative, are crude simplifications. They are redund-
ant: Hardy's views are amply expressed in other ways by the spirit of
the Years and the Spirit of the Pities. They are probably misleading,
since they seem to emphasize the permanent puppetry of man. If, as
Hardy dares to hope,

the rages
Of the ages
Shall be cancelled ...
Consciousness the Will informing, till It fashion all things fair!

and if, as Hardy asserted or implied several times over a long period,
an 'emotional sensitiveness' has evolved in human beings beyond that
of any other form of Nature, then consciousness of human suffering
can inform the unconscious collective Will only through the efforts and
influence of mankind, and not by the direction of that Will. This was
the view Hardy expressed in 'He Wonders About Himself':

Part is mine of the general Will,
Cannot my share in the sum of sources
Bend a digit the poise of forces,
And a fair desire fulfil?

A second illogicality seems to inhere in the answer of the Spirit of the
Years (which represents Hardy's neutral or philosophical view of life)

to the comments of the Ironic Spirits on the 'Immanent Unrecking':

> Your knowings of the Unknowable declared,
> Let the last picture of the play be bared.

It seems ironical that this statement should be made almost at the end of a major work in which Hardy had written much that was dogmatic and critical on what he admitted in 1920 was 'incomprehensible'. If he had been far less obsessed with the Unknowable and had dispensed with the puppetry and clockwork imagery, the reader's imagination and feelings would not have been stirred less by *The Dynasts*; rather the contrary. As it stands, it makes one sympathize with Pope's

> presume not God to scan,
> The proper study of mankind is man.

The eighteenth century was an age which knew less, but could show a greater philosophical maturity than Hardy's. A passage in Beattie's 'The Minstrel' (recalling, at first, a splendid image on the insignificance of individual human life in *Tess of the d'Urbervilles*) compares ephemeral man to a gnat, and asks what wisdom it would reveal if, with discontent and rage, it exclaimed that

> Nature hastens to decay
> If but a cloud obstruct the solar ray.

Beattie continues:

> One part, one little part, we dimly scan
> Thro' the dark medium of life's feverish dream;
> Yet dare arraign the whole stupendous plan,
> If but that little part incongruous seem . . .
> O then renounce that impious self-esteem,
> That aims to trace the secrets of the skies!
> For thou art but of dust; be humble, and be wise.

Further on we meet these lines:

> Of chance and change O let no man complain,
> Else shall he never cease to wail.

Hardy never ceased to complain of chance and change; they are the key to his work and philosophy. Yet he was too much engrossed with the teleological and incomprehensible and, to adapt the criticism of his friend Edmund Gosse, spent too much time shaking his fist at a man-made Creator who existed vaguely in his own mind.

In his more despondent moods Hardy was apt to regard man as a puppet ('my poor puppet', he calls Jude); we need to remind ourselves of the Hardy who wrote and showed in *The Mayor of Casterbridge* that 'Character is Fate'. There are times when events affecting our lives are beyond our control; there are others when, despite the limitations of our circumstances (which I take to be the meaning of 'Necessity' as used by Carlyle and Hardy), we can decide for ourselves what is the right policy. It may be argued that the decision is determined by character, and that in consequence we are surrounded by the 'iron limits' of Necessity.

This is not Hardy's view. On his birthday in 1907, during the period when he was revising Part Third of *The Dynasts*, he wrote:

> The will of man is . . . neither wholly free nor wholly unfree. When swayed by the Universal Will (which he mostly must be as a subservient part of it) he is not individually free; but whenever it happens that all the rest of the Great Will is in equilibrium the minute portion called one person's will is free . . .

The view was repeated at least three times, its most notable appearance being in the Apology to *Late Lyrics and Earlier* in 1922. Whatever the origin of the 'equilibrium' metaphor, it occurs as early as 1873 or 1874 in *Far from the Madding Crowd* (xviii), with reference to Boldwood:

> That stillness, which struck casual observers more than anything else in his character and habit . . . may have been the perfect balance of enormous antagonistic forces – positives and negatives in fine adjustment. His equilibrium disturbed, he was in extremity at once. If an emotion possessed him, it ruled him . . .

I have compared him with Henchard, the 'momentum' of whose character 'knew no patience'. Only when a person is not swayed by emotions or prejudice, when he is open to reason, is he capable of exercising freedom of choice. Swayed by love, Swithin St Cleeve is incapable of seeing reason when he receives his uncle's letter. Swayed by ambition and pride, Napoleon 'seems to have eaten on the insane root that takes the reason prisoner'; and it is significant that our first view of him is at his coronation in Milan, where all the personages taking part in this enthusiastic ceremony are seen to be activated by the Universal Will. It would be erroneous to conclude that he was a puppet to such overmastering forces all the time, but he knew, better than anyone else, how at critical junctures they had driven him on –

> Yet, 'tis true, I have ever known
> That such a Will I passively obeyed!

When nations are stirred to war by passions, 'In conclaves no voice of reflection / Is heard', and horrors and heroism follow:

> So the Will heaves through Space, and moulds the times,
> With mortals for Its fingers! We shall see

Again men's passions, virtues, visions, crimes,
    Obey resistlessly
The purposive, unmotived, dominant Thing
Which sways in brooding dark their wayfaring!

Since limited circumstances govern the lives of most people, and choice can be reasonably exercised only when they are not under great stresses, it was natural that Hardy's heart went out most to those whom Chance had given little choice. In his early novels, one thinks unequivocally of Fanny Robin. With the later, an important change seems to begin in the second half of *The Mayor of Casterbridge*. As Henchard's fortunes decline, he becomes nobler; it is his desperate need for companionship and affection which makes him instinctively selfish and dishonest. For this one error he is not forgiven by Elizabeth-Jane; and this lack of charity, from one usually so discerning, breaks his spirit. In his loneliness and self-alienation, he is befriended by the simple Whittle, who remembers that 'he was kind-like to mother when she wer here below, though 'a was rough to me'. The tragic climax of Henchard's death would have lost much of its emotional power without Whittle's devotion. In comparison Farfrae seems heartless, and Elizabeth-Jane little more than temperate. Thereafter Hardy's greatest tragic figures are the poor and lowly, who are mainly victims of circumstance. I think particularly of Marty South, Giles Winterborne, and Tess. In all three shine the virtues Hardy most admired: selflessness, devotion, fortitude – attributes of Christian charity, without which he thought civilization would fail. These positive qualities may be found in Hardy's early fiction, but they first come to the fore in the person of Lady Constantine, the heroine of *Two on a Tower* (the novel that preceded *The Mayor of Casterbridge*).

Angel Clare's lack of Tess's virtues at the crucial juncture proves fatal:

The firmness of her devotion to him was indeed almost pitiful . . . she sought not her own; was not provoked; thought no evil of his treatment of her. She might just now have been Apostolic Charity herself returning to a self-seeking modern world.

It is this spirit, as well as her being the victim of chance (in events and heredity), which justified Hardy in regarding her as 'A Pure Woman'.

In his last three novels (omitting that fantastic tale, *The Well-Beloved*) Hardy's aims were far more social than ever before, except perhaps in *The Poor Man and the Lady*. In that novel he had attempted smart satire; tragedy was now his medium. By showing the great worth that was to be found in the underprivileged, and how people were lacerated like captive birds against the iron limits of Necessity, Hardy strove to 'Bend a digit the poise of forces/And a fair desire fulfil'. As a novelist he could not ignore the problem of 'how to afford the greatest happiness to the units of human society during their brief transit through this sorry world'. These words, which echo Elizabeth-Jane's reflections on life at the end of his previous novel, occur in the preface to *The Woodlanders* with reference to the question of marriage and divorce, which Hardy took up (by implication) more dramatically and bitterly in *Jude the Obscure*. According to the conventions of society, Phillotson reflects ironically, the 'loving-kindness' of Sue and Jude is 'crude'. For Hardy there was too much truth in her consolatory remarks to Jude:

> Your worldly failure, if you have failed, is to your credit rather than to your blame. Remember that the best and greatest among mankind are those who do themselves no worldly good. Every successful man is more or less a selfish man. The devoted fail. . . . 'Charity seeketh not her own.'

Behind *The Woodlanders* and *Tess*, more than in *Jude*, one senses a writer whose intellectual background made him feel deeply that, despite the Sermon on the Mount, the meek are rewarded neither in heaven nor on earth.

On the new, non-supernatural, humanitarian religion, inherited from Comte and Mill, this is a typical Hardy point of view:

> Altruism, or the Golden Rule, or whatever 'Love your Neighbour as Yourself' may be called, will ultimately be brought about I think by the pain we see in others reacting on ourselves, as if we and they were part of one body.

Two poems enlarge on this subject. 'The Wind Blew Words' makes it clear that altruism applies to the whole of humanity, regardless of race, and to all forms of life. 'A Plaint to Man' concludes:

> The truth should be told, and the fact be faced
> That had best been faced in earlier years:
>
> The fact of life with dependence placed
> On the human heart's resource alone,
> In brotherhood bonded close and graced
>
> With loving-kindness fully blown,
> And visioned help unsought, unknown.

The last line implies that a better world will result only from man's aspirations and efforts; help which is 'visioned' or imagined from Providence will not be forthcoming.

When Sue, guilt-ridden by the death of her children, gives up Jude for Phillotson and the Church, Jude proclaims that the verses on Charity 'will stand fast when all the rest that you call religion has passed away'. That, I think, was Hardy's hope, rather than a comment on Jude's ingenuousness. In 1876 he had copied from John Addington Symonds' *Studies of the Greek Poets*:

Will not the men of the future look back with wonder on the ages in which religion, philosophy, and the science of nature were supposed to be at war, instead of being, as they will be then, one system?

In 1922, with reference to the religion of the future, he made three important points in his Apology to *Late Lyrics and Earlier*: the first, that loving-kindness, operating through scientific knowledge, would reduce pain to a minimum; the second, that poetry and essential, undogmatic religion must keep 'moving, becoming' (that is, progressing towards the truth); and lastly, that an alliance between religion and 'complete rationality' (the scientific outlook) must come 'by means of the interfusing effect of poetry' if civilization is to be saved.

Hardy's idea on the part to be played by poetry (or literature) in keeping religion alive and progressive undoubtedly came from Matthew Arnold, who believed that 'a religion without poetry, a religion which is merely ethical, or merely theological, has no power to move the soul, and is no religion at all'.[9] The idea that religion must keep 'moving, becoming' is taken straight from Arnold's 'Not a having and a resting, but a growing and a becoming, is the character of perfection as culture conceives it; and here, too, it coincides with religion.'[10] The role that poetry could play in the future had been illustrated in Greek drama; and there can be little doubt that Arnold's convictions on the subject encouraged Hardy to think of his role as a prophet of a new testament (and to write, with rather monotonous persistence, poems on Nature – the blind wounding Mother – and her unfeeling Lord). It is interesting therefore to consider why he was so critical of Arnold in 1888:

The besetting sin of modern literature is its insincerity. Half its utterances are qualified, even contradicted, by an aside, and this particularly in morals and religion. When dogma has to be balanced on its feet by such hair-splitting as the late Mr M. Arnold's it must be in a very bad way.

Hardy reacted sharply against compromise (much more, one suspects, than he would have done in his later years). Arnold believed that where Churches continued successfully to promote the true Christian spirit through outdated beliefs, it was better to temporize than not have practical Christianity at all. Similarly he felt that the retention of various forms of traditional mythology was justified by their functional power as 'poetry'. An expression such as 'the kingdom of God' in relation to its attainment on earth has meaning in the religion based on 'natural truth' which Arnold advocated. We are familiar with his reiterated hope that 'reason and the will of God' would prevail. For Hardy this terminology could do nothing but confuse the issue; he insisted, as we have seen in 'A Plaint to Man', that progress depends wholly on human resources. This was the Positivist creed; its gospel of loving-kindness and evolution may not have differed practically from that of a Church which preached that God is a spirit and God is love, but it was opposed to any supernatural, extra-mundane implication. Truth as well as humanitarianism was its goal.

Agreed though they were on this, Hardy could not be as sanguine about the future as his friend Frederic Harrison; he is quite explicit on this in the Apology. It can be seen from his *Novissima Verba* that Harrison did not underestimate the post-war problems in 1920, yet his faith in the Positivist religion of humanity, with its emphasis on education, sympathy, and humane action (Comte's 'binding up of our ideas, affections, and energies into a common harmony of life') remained unshaken. Hardy looked deeper, convinced no doubt that real progress depends as much on a change of heart as on enlightenment. The most significant feature of his later poetry is that he places responsibility for lack of progress squarely on mankind, and not on the Unknowable. Professed Christianity had brought poison-gas; instead of loving-kindness and brotherhood, he saw international rivalries and division. In 'Thoughts at Midnight' he expresses dismay at the madnesses of the human race; he condemns it for

> Acting like puppets
> Under Time's buffets;
> In superstitions
> And ambitions
> Moved by no wisdom,
> Far-sight, or system,
> Led by sheer senselessness
> And prescienceless
> Into unreason
> And hideous self-treason.

Self-treason implies human responsibility; in the *The Dynasts* a vague generalized Immanent Will was blamed for the follies of mankind. In 'We Are Getting to the End' Hardy sees the world pursuing pleasures regardless of developing disasters, just as larks sing in cages 'unthoughtful of deliverance'; he has almost abandoned hope that 'better whiles may follow worse'. Finally, as ominous notes in 'He Resolves to Say No More' confirm, he is made free by truth, and is no longer oversensitive on the score of being labelled a pessimist.

5 The Wild Duck

Ibsen's wild duck, after being wounded, dives down and holds fast to the weeds at the muddy bottom of the water, only to be brought to the surface by a dog and kept in an attic. Its natural refuge represents the world of romantic illusions in which Hjalmar Ekdal lives until he is 'rescued' by Gregers Werle, who shatters his happiness by revealing the sordid truth behind his marriage. Hardy's wild duck is not taken from its natural element; once there, it evades the predatory hawk or buzzard with dextrous energy, 'unaccountably emerging from opposite sides of the pool in succession, and bobbing again by the time its adversary reached its place'. It is too experienced for its assailant, which tires and flies off in almost perceptible dudgeon.

In an epistle to his friend J. H. Reynolds, Keats introduces a horrifying aspect of nature with these images:

> The Shark at savage prey – the hawk at pounce,
> The gentle Robin, like a pard or ounce
> Ravening a worm.

Hardy, who for more than ten years had accepted unflinchingly the Darwinian view of nature ('that red ravage through her zones/ Whereat all creation groans') makes the wild duck an emblem of his theme in *The Hand of Ethelberta*. It is the one image in the novel which assumes the proportions of a scene; placed in the forefront, it remains the most vivid at the end. Far less complex in its symbolical import than Ibsen's, it prefigures the heroine. Her story could be described as a Darwinian comedy.

When Hardy contemplated marriage in 1874 he was confronted with two major problems: how to discourage the view (which had arisen with the anonymity of *Far from the Madding Crowd* at an early stage in its serialization) that he was another George Eliot; and how to succeed financially. Once again, 'he was "up against" the position of having to carry on his life not as an emotion, but as a scientific game'.[1] When he decided to write *The Hand of Ethelberta*, he had yet to discover where his relative strengths lay. He knew that the novel of manners was the usual road to success, and he remembered Miss Thackeray's affirmation that 'a novelist must necessarily like society'. Important decisions followed: he postponed the writing of a story which became *The Woodlanders*; he spent his honeymoon in Rouen and Paris; and, after a period in Surbiton, moved to Bayswater. 'We are coming to Town for three months on account of Ethelberta, some London scenes occurring in her chequered career which I want to do as vigorously as possible – having already visited Rouen and Paris with the same object,' he wrote to his serial publisher George Smith. He was moving 'in a new and untried direction' with an energy inspired by the challenge of his new responsibilities and by the self-confidence which came from the success of *Far from the Madding Crowd*.

It was from considering life as 'a scientific game' that the leading ideas for the plot of *The Hand of Ethelberta* arose. At the outset of the novel it has to be accepted as part of the *mise-en-scène* that Ethelberta, though the eldest of a poor and numerous family, has become a member of society by virtue of her elegance in manners and appearance and a young man's unbridled infatuation. She has been 'stealthily' married, as quickly widowed, and then sent to Bonn by her mother-in-law Lady Petherwin to finish her education in a boarding-school. On her return she writes *vers de société* which are an offence to Lady Petherwin. As a result she is virtually disinherited when her mother-in-law dies, and has to start a career to maintain her social status and assist her family. Her lowly origin is unknown. The story has many improbabilities, which by and large can be accepted in a high-flown satirical comedy. At the heart of it, the 'struggle for existence' and 'natural selection' are never far apart, though the latter principle is jettisoned in the farcical conclusion. When the heroine fears for the future of her career as a professional stage story-teller, no solution remains but a wealthy marriage. Ethelberta's attractions are such that she has no dearth of suitors; the problem is to find one who is eligible and sufficiently affluent.

The one suitor with whom Ethelberta has a natural affinity is the unworldly Christopher Julian, a Hardy-like character devoted to music. Unlike her sister Picotee, she is resolved not to marry him until he is rich; yet she is afraid that 'the qualities she likes in him will make it impossible for him ever to ask her hand in marriage'. He is, in short, the kind of person who is incapable of making his life 'a scientific game'. Her determination is such that their separation is inevitable; and Julian's announcement of it to his sister ironically coincides with a description of a picture of Ethelberta she has just viewed at the Academy. Painted by her new admirer Ladywell, it shows Ethelberta in Elizabethan dress, a knight parting from her with these words:

> Farewell! thou art too dear for my possessing,
> And like enough thou know'st thy estimate.

Whether the wry ambivalence of these Shakespearian lines is lost on Julian or not, they are part of a satirical motif which is continued with the visit made by Ethelberta and some of her society friends to the tomb of Milton in Cripplegate Church. Lines from Wordsworth's sonnet addressing Milton are quoted 'with the degree of flippancy which is considered correct for immortal verse, the Bible, God, etc, in these days' and without any awareness of the poet's reason for invoking Milton's spirit as a safeguard against the ills created by wealth-seeking and ostentatious living. This ignorance is equalled by Ethelberta's apparent indifference to the import of the lines she reads from *Paradise Lost*:

The sentences fell from her lips in a rhythmical cadence one by one, and she could be fancied a priestess of him before whose image she stood, when with a vivid suggestiveness she delivered here, not many yards from the central money-mill of the world,[2] yet out from the very tomb of their author, the passage containing the words:

'Mammon led them on;
Mammon, the least erected spirit that fell
From heaven.'

Ethelberta now has two rich suitors in Ladywell and Neigh. In such a materialistic society, with 'its people of splendid momentum' and 'its abnormal, almost morbid development of the passion for position', men like Julian, loyal and virtuous but without wealth or social ambition, are of little esteem in the eyes of Ethelberta or anyone else.

The principle of natural selection and the survival of the fittest as applied to marriage in society is the subject of a number of ridiculous situations. In Julian, Ladywell, and Neigh, Ethelberta has three persistent suitors. When Julian falls out of the race, the more absurd element is free to take its course; it may be seen in the Cripplegate chapter, but it reaches its climax when the aged Lord Mountclere joins in the pursuit, and all three follow Ethelberta to Rouen. One scene here, when it is apparent that the race is to the sly jolly peer, and Neigh and Ladywell in adjacent rooms discover each other's presence as they put their heads through their windows to hear what Ethelberta and Lord Mountclere are saying down below, recalls a similar comic situation between Knight and Smith on the train which carries these jealous rivals to Cornwall at the end of *A Pair of Blue Eyes*.

In a Darwinian light, the nightmarish horror of Neigh's Farnfield estate assumes a greater congruity with the rest of the novel than it would do otherwise. Ethelberta visits it with Picotee to weigh up Neigh's economic value; as spies, they discover for themselves 'the nakedness of the land'. They see emaciated old horses kept at starvation level, and the skulls, ribs, quarters, legs, and other miasmic joints of their predecessors suspended from the lopped branches of trees in an enclosure which houses a kennel of hounds. The Neighs, they learn, have made their fortune in the knacker business and tanning. Ethelberta is horrified, and fancies that she could not marry Neigh, even if she loved him.

It is a fancy; she reasons that, as one of the *nouveaux riches*, he is too near her social level for a confession on her lineage to be 'well received by him'; however, he is handsome and rich, and she does not put him off until she finds 'a sound reason for disliking him'. The sound reason is the greater assurance of security for herself and her family in the person of the ageing but aristocratic and affluent suitor, Lord Mountclere.

One of the ironies of Ethelberta's situation is that her poverty makes her live in the house at Swanage (Knollsea) which the Hardys occupied when the novel was being finished, and that she hires a donkey to carry her to the meeting of the Imperial Archaeological Association at Corvsgate, where she is embarrassed to meet Lord Mountclere. The pride which had 'made her what she was' forbad Ethelberta to show an interest in the creature; then, thinking of her origin, 'and with a groan at her inconsistency in being ashamed of the ass, she said in her heart, "My God, what a thing am I!" ' She had already decided that she might attend the ceremony, even walk there, on the grounds that 'unconventionality – almost eccentricity – was *de rigueur* for one who had first been heard of as a poetess'. It is rather like one of Hardy's views on playing 'the scientific game' as an author. 'If you mean to make the world listen to you, you must say now what they will all be thinking and saying five and twenty years hence: and if you do that you must offend your conventional friends,' he told a young writer.[3] It was precisely because Hardy did this that he ended his career as a novelist sooner than he had intended.

For Ethelberta, 'life is a battle'. When she hears that Neigh intends to marry her, she has much to think about. Her consequent 'air of unusual stillness' is not comparable to the Wordsworthian 'silence that is in the starry sky' but like that of the astral world 'where all is force and motion'. She is not all determined calculation, however; at times she is wrung with a 'sense of disloyalty to her class and kin', and wishes that she could 'drop the name of Petherwin, and be Berta Chickerel again'. 'There is something without which splendid energies are a drug; and that is a cold heart', she feels. But she stays on course for the sake of her family, even though her father objects to Lord Mountclere; and she finds her policy confirmed by J. S. Mill's *Utilitarianism:*

> The happiness which forms the standard of what is right in conduct is not the agent's own happiness but that of all concerned. As between his own happiness and that of others, utilitarianism requires him to be strictly impartial as a disinterested and benevolent spectator.

Social criticism, high-spirited comedy, admiration of her splendid energy, and a certain topsy-turvydom of values combine to create a tolerant and even amused attitude towards the calculating, utilitarian Ethelberta. She takes advantage of folly, and the reader derives pleasure from that; but she has an endearing side. She is no Becky Sharp; she thinks at least as much for her family as for herself, and she is honest. Fortunately Lord Mountclere has known her origin for some time, and she has nothing to fear in marrying him, except jealousy and the opposition of members of her own family. The latter evokes this comment:

> The times have taken a strange turn when the angry parent of the comedy, who goes post-haste to prevent the undutiful daughter's rash marriage, is a gentleman from below stairs, and the unworthy lover a peer of the realm!

The vain efforts of Mountclere's brother, who is afraid of losing the succession to the Enckworth estate, of Ethelberta's brother, who is swayed chiefly by inverted snobbery, and of her father and Julian who wish above all to save her reputation; the outwitting of Ethelberta when she threatens to leave her husband on discovering that his 'Petit Trianon' has been reserved for a mistress – these provide a climax of high-pitched ingenuity to a theme which, despite its social satire and Ethelberta's twinges of conscience, can never be taken seriously by a detached reader.

The tone of *The Hand of Ethelberta* is very different from that of any previous Hardy novel (or any later). The self-sacrifice of Cytherea in marriage for the sake of her brother creates a crisis in *Desperate Remedies* which anticipates another in *Tess of the d'Urbervilles*. Ethelberta sacrifices her feelings, though she has no objection to Mountclere once she has asserted her conjugal rights. She ends triumphantly by force of will and character. She has no sense of loyalty to Christopher Julian, as Fancy Day has to Dick Dewy (despite succumbing to the temptation to accept the vicar's marriage offer until she sees it in the light of reason the next morning). *Under the Greenwood Tree* is a light story, but it is humorous and human. *The Hand of Ethelberta* differs in appealing even less to the heart and almost wholly to the comic perception. The tragic involvements of *A Pair of Blue Eyes* and *Far from the Madding Crowd* are left behind for social satire and absurd make-believe, in a world of artificial comedy activated by Darwinian and utilitarian principles. The application of these nineteenth-century ideas to a fictional plot may have been original and intellectually exciting in the abstract; in the event, however, they rarely appealed to the best in Hardy. *The Hand of Ethelberta* is an interesting experiment which reveals more ingenuity than genius.

Ethelberta reforms Lord Mountclere, and has the upper hand. The title, 'The Hand of Ethelberta', may imply this final disclosure. Obviously it suggests her hand in marriage, but the suggested allusion to one of the Hands – Hardy's relatives – is hardly probable (the career of his cousin Martha Sparks was not a triumphant one like Ethelberta's).[4] Its significance is more surely related to the 'scientific game' which the

heroine finds it incumbent on her to play. Judged in the spirit of the
novel, she plays it well, and Mountclere's brother, annoyed though he
may be at losing his expectations, has the sense and dignity to recognise
her finesse when he sees that his game is up: 'The best course is to leave
matters alone,' he says. 'She is a clever young woman, and has played
her cards adroitly. I only hope she never repents of the game!'

Having surmounted her initial crisis, she does not repent. It is part of
the comedy that she falls into error, but her policy succeeds. When she
has to exert her will, her 'little finger' is thicker than 'a Mountclere's
loins', and in the end she manages the viscount and his estate. The
power which she enjoys does not give her quite the exhilaration she had
felt when she discovered at Corvsgate that a landscape was being
altered to suit her whim; she uses it wisely, ensuring that her family live
in security and comfort, and that Julian is not forgotten. The romance
between him and Picotee satisfies the reader who craves a more conventional ending. Life, it is said, is like a pack of cards: much depends on
what chance deals, more perhaps on the player. In *The Hand of
Ethelberta* the game is taken one remove from life (where it would be
objectionable) and transferred with varying degrees of success to a
plane of comic ideality.

6 Mephistopheles, Satan, and Cigars

Of the books which Hardy inherited from his friend Horace Moule, three had considerable influence on his works: Palgrave's *Golden Treasury*, J. H. Bridges' translation of *A General View of Positivism* by Auguste Comte,[1] and a translation of Goethe's *Faust*.[2] Of these *The Golden Treasury* was Hardy's favourite; he must have known many of its poems by heart, and he quotes from them frequently in his fiction and letters. In the long run Comte did as much as any other writer to mould Hardy's basic philosophy of life. Goethe's *Faust* was to have a more imaginative influence on his works, the Mephistophelian element entering the novels in one form or another over a period of more than twenty years. *The Mayor of Casterbridge* (xvii) shows that his interest in *Faust* was increased by Thomas Carlyle's essays on Goethe; Henchard's character, Hardy writes, 'might not inaptly be described as Faust has been described – as a vehement gloomy being, who had quitted the ways of vulgar men, without light to guide him on a better way'.[3] It is significant that, when his difficulties with *Tess of the d'Urbervilles* made him realize the crippling restrictions imposed by Victorianism, he included *Faust* among the 'great works of the past' which 'the notions of the present day would aim to exclude from circulation, if not from publication', had they been 'issued as new fiction'.

The appeal that the Faust legend had held for generations of unlettered people must not be overlooked. Superstitions blended with incidents to create a folklore of sensational anecdotage, some of which made a memorable impression on Hardy in his boyhood. In 1911 he recalled a delightful story of his 'ancestor' (almost certainly his grandfather), who took adroit advantage of the common superstition when he was afraid of being attacked and robbed. He was walking across the heath from Puddletown one June midnight when he realized that he was being overtaken by two men he had noticed eyeing him as he left the village. Fortunately his attention had been attracted in Coomb meadow by numerous glow-worms, and he had collected several and placed them on the brim of his hat. Rolling a furze faggot into the path, he sat on it, placed his hat on his knees, stuck two fern fronds into his hair to look like horns, and began to read a letter by the light of the glow-worms. The men approached, then stopped suddenly and fled.

Soon it was rumoured that the Devil had been seen at midnight near Greenhill Pond, reading a list of his victims by glow-worm light.[4]

Two examples of the stories which prevailed in this kind are provided by Hardy in his *Life*. The first (p. 156) was told by his wife's brother-in-law, the rector of St Juliot in Cornwall:

> It was what had been related to him by some of his aged parishioners concerning an incumbent of that or an adjacent living many years before. This worthy ecclesiastic was a bachelor addicted to drinking habits, and one night when riding up Boscastle Hill fell off his horse. He lay a few minutes in the road, when he said 'Help me up, Jolly!' and a local man who was returning home behind him saw a dark figure with a cloven hoof emerge from the fence, and toss him upon his horse in a jiffy. The end of him was that on one night of terrific lightning and thunder he was missed, and was found to have entirely disappeared.

The second (p. 314) relates to the poem 'Vagg Hollow' in *Late Lyrics and Earlier*:

> Vagg Hollow, on the way to Load Bridge (Somerset) is a place where 'things' used to be seen – usually taking the form of a wool-pack in the middle of the road. Teams and other horses always stopped on the brow of the hollow, and could only be made to go on by whipping. A waggoner once cut at the pack with his whip: it opened in two, and smoke and a hoofed figure rose out of it.

The nearest approach to this kind of tale in Hardy's fiction is a story told against Jude and Sue when they are painting the Commandments in a church. Rumours of their not being married, and of Jude's divorce, have spread; and the churchwarden is reminded of 'a most immoral case that happened' in a church 'out by Gaymead', where workmen, 'about a hundred years ago' when there was 'no true religion in the country' (and no overtime pay), were allowed to have 'plenty of drink' in the hope that they would finish the regilding of the Commandments in time for the Sunday service. They put their rum-bottle and rummers on the Communion table, and 'sate round comfortable' until they finished their bumpers. They then fell senseless. A raging thunderstorm roused them, and they 'seemed to see in the gloom a dark figure with very thin legs and a curious voot, a-standing on the ladder, and finishing their work'. When it was daylight they were delighted to see that the work really was finished, and went home. The next thing they heard was the great scandal which arose after the Sunday morning service, when the congregation noticed that the Ten Commandments had been painted with all the 'Nots' omitted. The church had to be reconsecrated.

Fitzpiers is described as 'the young medical gentleman in league with the devil', and it is significant that in the previous chapter of *The Wood-landers* (ii) there is a reference to the chapbook story of Faustus, which Hardy probably heard or read in his boyhood. 'You are tempting me', Marty South tells the hairdresser Percomb when he offers her two gold sovereigns for her tresses. 'You go on like the Devil to Faustus in the penny book.' In the chapbook story the devil appears to the accompaniment of thunder and music,[5] and it seems almost indubitable that it was this background which Hardy employed for its associations of temptation and evil in the scene where the heroine of *Desperate Remedies* meets the villain Manston for the first time (viii. 4).

The 'thunder, lightning, and rain' which accompany their conversation in the old manor house are an evident extension of association which evokes the witches of *Macbeth*;[6] and the same suggestion appears in the 'unearthly weirdness' which seems to surround Cytherea in Manston's room when thunder and lightning follow his extemporization on the organ. He then plays more powerfully, and the reverberations of his music are 'heightened by the elemental strife of light and sound outside'. She is 'swayed into emotional opinions concerning the strange man before her'. He is more Satanic than Mephistophelian, but (unless they are hinted at in his vow to 'get' Cytherea, even if he has to 'move heaven and earth to do it') such overtones are limited to his first appearance. The intense 'ruby redness' of his full lips suggests a sensualist, rather like Alec d'Urberville, whose full, red lips are suitably accompanied by a swarthy complexion and a black curled moustache. Elsewhere (pp. 3–4) it has been shown that Manston was probably moulded on the villain in Wilkie Collins' *Basil*.

Hardy's attempts to present variations of a more Mephistophelian character were deferred, but it is clear that he was often reminded of the Faustus legend, and felt that it expressed interesting aspects of human nature that could not be ignored. The love of knowledge through experience which is stimulated by an eager brain (as much the subject of *Paradise Lost*, though less dramatized, as of Marlowe's *Doctor Faustus* or Goethe's *Faust*) is hinted at almost gratuitously in *The Hand of Ethelberta* (xxxi), where Hardy writes (with reference to the county members of the Imperial Archaeological Association at Corvsgate Castle and Ethelberta's exciting appearance among them) of 'spirits being so brisk as to swerve from strict attention to the select and sequent gifts of heaven, blood and acres, to consider for an idle moment the subversive Mephistophelian element, brains'. Later the designing Lord Mountclere 'looked gleeful, and shrewd enough in his own opinion to outwit Mephistopheles'. The description of reddlemen as 'Mephistophelian visitants' in *The Return of the Native* (i. ix) has no significance beyond colour, the Mephistopheles of tradition appearing in a red cloak. Diggory Venn plays a protective role, and there is obviously nothing sinister about him. As (in contrast to Christian Cantle) he is the only reliable agent Hardy has provided to solve some of his plot problems, he has an extraordinary habit of appearing in the nick of time, and this combines with the startling effect of his colour to create some slightly supernatural impressions, as Hardy acknowledges in the note on his original plan to make this 'isolated and weird' character disappear 'mysteriously from the heath, nobody knowing whither', some time after the tragic ending. As late as *The Well-Beloved* a Mephistophelian touch slides happily into the narrative when Pierston, falling in love with the grand-daughter of the Avice he had neglected forty years earlier, is overcome, after bidding her farewell, with a sudden sadness which 'swept down all the temporary pleasure he had found in the charming girl's company':

> Had Mephistopheles sprung from the ground there and then with an offer to Jocelyn of restoration to youth on the usual terms of his firm, the sculptor might have consented to sell a part of himself which he felt less immediate need of than of a ruddy lip and cheek and of an unploughed brow.

From 1880 to the opening of 1883 Hardy's continued experimentation in fiction resulted, among other things, in persistent efforts to create a Mephistophelian character. On the whole his attempt in *A Laodicean* was a failure. He was more consistently successful in a less ambitious way in *Two on a Tower*, but one suspects that his relative failure with the part in these two novels was responsible for the less human, more fantastic creation of the rather fascinating Baron von Xanten in the long short story 'The Romantic Adventures of a Milkmaid'. A brief scene in *The Return of the Native* may herald these developments, and possibly, in the garden image, further manifestations in *Tess of the d'Urbervilles*. When Eustacia's hopes of release from the heath through marriage are fading, Wildeve renews his assignations with her. Before this tempter ('tempted by the fascination that emotional smuggling had for his nature') ascertains that she is at home, and that he can catch her attention by recourse to his familiar moth-signal, he is pictured looking over her garden gate, with a cigar in his mouth (IV. iv). Smoke or smoking (particularly a cigar) is henceforth a peculiar feature of Hardy's tempters, whether vile, villainous, or romantic.

In William Dare, bastard son of an aristocrat, and villain of *A Laodicean*, Hardy has created his most depraved devil (daredevil) in the human sense. Yet the sinister aura of a Satan or Mephistopheles with which he is invested in the early stages is soon forgotten, and the main impression he leaves is of a creature who, with all his cleverness and cunning, is no more than a degenerate sample of modern civilization. After a mysterious first entry during which he remains invisible, he appears at Stancy Castle. He has a forehead like Manston's, broad and 'vertical as the face of a bastion', indicative no doubt of 'keen intellect' and determination. His looks are misleading: his face in repose suggests that of a boy; in action, that of a grown-up. As he contemplates the garden-party from his window in the castle, he is seen smoking a cigarette, a sure sign that he is engaged in some diabolical plan. His first conspiratorial steps are staged with the heightening effects of sheet-lightning and thunder (II. i). He is afraid that the wealthy chatelaine Paula, a member of the 'new aristocracy', will fall in love with the architect Somerset, and his main purpose is to defeat and discredit him, leaving the way clear for his aristocratic father, an army captain, to win her and return to his ancestral home. This is merely a means to his own ends, his supreme aim being to ensure that he is never short of money; and he is bold, resolute, and utterly unscrupulous in the prosecution of his purpose.

In his Satanic role, he is 'at home anywhere'. He is widely travelled, and will not declare his origin. He is a citizen of the world, owes no country patriotism and no king or queen obedience. 'A man whose country has no boundary is your only true gentleman,' he says; and the word 'gentleman' has overtones, as will be seen, in the literature – as well as the lore – of diabolism. In the county town this smooth-faced creature walks with a silver-tipped cane in his hand and a cigarette between his lips. Meeting his father, who asks where he comes from, he quotes the Book of Job in reply: 'From going to and fro in the earth, and walking up and down in it, as Satan said to his Maker. – Southampton last, in common speech.' The captain, after losing at cards in the church vestry, and being reminded of the way to recover his castle, tells him that he is 'quite a Mephistopheles'. When he has won the first round against Somerset, Dare sits smoking on the bole of a tree which commands a view of the castle, contemplating his next move.

The plans of this degenerate scion of an effete aristocracy are on the brink of complete success before they are ultimately dashed. Suggestions of superhuman agency are revived at the end, but not very powerfully. On the night before the marriage which is due to be solemnized between Paula and Captain de Stancy, the latter's rest is troubled like Lady Macbeth's:

> Thick-coming fancies, for which there was more than good reason, had disturbed him only too successfully, and he was as full of apprehensions as one who has a league with Mephistopheles.

When it is insisted that Dare must be arrested, he is referred to as man or boy or demon. No action is taken when his paternity is disclosed and, after setting fire to the family pictures and castle by night, he disappears as mysteriously as he had first arrived on the scene:

> Five minutes afterwards a light shone upon the lawn from the windows of the Long Gallery, which glowed with more brilliancy than it

had known in the meridian of its Caroline splendours. Thereupon the framed gentleman in the lace collar seemed to open his eyes more widely; he with the flowing locks and turn-up mustachios to part his lips; he in the armour, who was so much like Captain de Stancy, to shake the plates of his mail with suppressed laughter; the lady with the three-stringed pearl necklace, and vast expanse of neck, to nod with satisfaction and triumphantly signify to her adjoining husband that this was a meet and glorious end.

Somerset hopes that Paula will recover from the 'warp' given to her mind by her *prédilection d'artiste* for an ancient castle and aristocratic family. 'And be a perfect representative of "the modern spirit", representing neither the senses and understanding, nor the heart and imagination, but what a finished writer calls "the imaginative reason"?' she asks. Hardy may have thought that the novel he planned could embody this idea. On the whole, however, the reader is left to apply it to the *mélange adultère de tout* which may be seen in *A Laodicean*; it provides an interesting analogy but is far less integral than the main inceptive idea of *The Hand of Ethelberta*.[7]

Only at one point do story and Faustian legend unite in action. It is when Dare succeeds in making his father fall sensually in love with Paula Power, who has Grecian views on physical fitness. After plying his father with intoxicating liquor, Dare persuades him to peer into her gymnasium as the noonday sun pours down through the lantern, 'irradiating her with a warm light that was incarnadined by her pink doublet and hose'. In creating this species of 'optical poem', Hardy has adapted the scene in Goethe where Faust, after gazing voluptuously on the mirrored form of lovely woman, drinks the witch's potion, and is assured by Mephistopheles that he will soon see the model of all womankind in flesh and blood, adding (in an aside) 'With this draught in your body, you will soon see a Helen in every woman.' Hardy comes to terms with Victorian convention by clothing the attractive Paula in a costume of fleshly pink, but she has Greek associations, and for the inflammable de Stancy is another Helen.

Another parasitical member of the upper classes who is much travelled is Lady Constantine's brother Louis Glanville in *Two on a Tower*. He seems continually to threaten her romance with the young local astronomer Swithin St Cleeve whom she has secretly married. For his own selfish ends he wishes her to marry the self-important Bishop of Melchester, who clearly admires her. On discovering that she is married and with child, and unable to get in touch with Swithin, as a result of having altruistically insisted on his furthering his astronomical studies abroad without weakening his resolution by corresponding with her, Louis comes to the rescue by arranging the marriage of his ambition, which she has no choice but to accept against her principles. Glanville's Mephistophelian role is confined to that of tempter and strategist. When Viviette discovers after frantic efforts to get in touch with Swithin that it is too late, she returns home and sees a 'red coal' in the arbour. It is Louis smoking a cigar; he tells her that Swithin shall never know her position, and when she asks what can be done pretends to continue his 'Havannah'. At last his chance has come to make his sister the 'spiritual queen of Melchester'. To save her reputation and Swithin's, Lady Constantine is compelled to accept a dishonourable course:

> A tempter had shown it to her. It involved a great wrong, which to her had quite obscured its feasibility. But she perceived now that it was indeed a way. Convention was forcing her hand at this game; and to what will not convention compel her weaker victims, in extremes?

Not surprisingly this *coup d'audace* provoked much criticism, but whether this made its full impact on Hardy before he finished 'The Romantic Adventures of a Milkmaid' is uncertain. In this story the villainous role of the tempter has almost faded out, and ultimately it is he who ensures that the Victorian proprieties are respected. This extraordinary tale appears to have had few admirers. Carl Weber described it as a 'worthless trifle'. Neither of these words is admissible. For one thing the story is too long; the ending is elaborately tedious, and Hardy would have done better to conclude it (as he originally planned) without the almost phantasmagoric allegorical climax – the Baron, rather like the dying king in Tennyson's 'Morte d'Arthur', being carried on board his yacht, which 'spread her wings' and was soon 'a small shapeless phantom' out at sea. With him disappeared the romantic Margery, never more to be 'heard of in England'. Criticism of *Two on a Tower* may have persuaded Hardy to produce a more homely moral ending by extending the story; if so, he satisfied himself with an ambivalent conclusion as tantalizing as that of *A Laodicean*.

Again, it should be said on behalf of the story that the Baron and the heroine are not without their fascination, especially in the first part, which has the air of a fairy-tale for grown-ups. In attending the ball of her heart's desire by the aid of the Baron's supernatural powers, the dairymaid Margery Tucker is like a Wessex Cinderella. Her wish has been granted because she has saved him from depression and suicide. He is 'a fine dark gentleman' of mysterious origin, with black mustachios, and a very pale prince-like face'. The night grows dark as they make their long journey to the county ball in his carriage, and when they arrive the hot breath of the swarthy horses jets forth 'like smoke out of volcanoes'. At a much later point in the story the 'coal-black' steeds look 'daemonic against the slanting fires of the setting sun'. Recalling the 'thrilling beats' of the Drum Polka when she meets the ordinary Jim to whom she is engaged, Margery tells him that he is unaware of 'the world, and what a woman's wants can be'. His comment on the desire for worldly splendour she has suddenly acquired is that 'Anybody would think the devil had showed you all the kingdoms of the world since I saw you last!' The story has taken a moral turn, and 'the world' and 'a woman's wants' sum up the temptations embodied in the mysterious Baron. In this fictional blending of allegory with everyday Wessex scenes, Hardy may have been influenced by some of Hawthorne's short stories. He certainly recalled in 'the Drum-polka's booms' the 'smoky halls of the Prince of Sin' at the Argyle, as he describes them in his poem 'Reminiscences of a Dancing Man'.

On their return journey from the ball, the Baron sits on the box by the coachman as on the outward journey. This time he lights a cigar. Soon Margery is fast asleep. Unlike Tess, she is quite safe, for he represents worldly temptation (as it occurred, for example, to Eustacia Vye) at the heart of a girl, and it can go no further than her desires. She wakes when the horses are changed and, catching sight of the Baron 'against the stars', thinks, 'He watches like the angel Gabriel, when all the world is asleep!' After changing to her ordinary attire in the hollow tree where she had found her billowy white dress, satin slippers, fan, and gloves for the ball, she is agonized to see him gather twigs and set fire to all her finery. When he hears that she is engaged, he tells her that he 'wouldn't have so endangered anybody's happiness for a thousand pounds' and reprimands her sternly. In *King Lear* we read that 'the prince of darkness is a gentleman'; this dying Victorian Mephistopheles is a reformed character, not too exceptionable for conventional magazine-readers. It is true that he revives, but he overcomes temptation in the end, and restores Margery to Jim, schooling 'impassioned sentiments into fair conduct'. She is happily married, but still remembers the Baron as a magician who could move her 'as a loadstone moves a speck of steel'. Jim remains unperturbed, certain that the Baron will not come; for so had he sworn, 'and he was a man of his word'.

For the most part the adventures of Margery Tucker form a light fantastic tale, a Hardy whimsy rather than an experiment. Whatever its merits, it is more Mephistophelian than any of his novels. Only in one brief scene and its consequence does *A Laodicean* recall *Faust*; William Dare is a villain rather than a tempter. Louis Glanville in *Two on a Tower* is a tempter for a brief unsavoury episode, but he is not the outward manifestation of Lady Constantine's yearnings. Baron von Xanten's role is not wholly that of Goethe's Mephistopheles; in addition to being an agent with magical powers, he is one of the principal participants in the human story. He expresses the milkmaid's romantic yearnings in both his supernatural role and in his own temptation. In 'The Romantic Adventures of a Milkmaid' a fairy-tale Faustian romance combines with the dictates of Victorian morality and other elements to create a queer amalgam. Psychologically and imaginatively, none the less, it is Hardy's nearest approach to Goethe.

It would have been ironical and artistically absurd to have retained the same dairy vale setting for two such contrasting stories as those of Margery Tucker and Tess. Hardy therefore transferred the former to the Exe valley when he revised it for inclusion in *A Changed Man* (1913). In *Tess of the d'Urbervilles* the tempter, in being a libertine and a villain, has more in common with Manston of *Desperate Remedies* than with any of Hardy's other characters. Alec d'Urberville's role is complex; he is successively both a willing and an unwilling instrument of Tess's tragic doom. He cruelly blights her early life, but he sincerely loves and respects her later. His altruism in coming to the rescue of her family after the death of John Durbeyfield is undoubtedly a transparent cloak for opportunism, but, however selfish his philanthropy, he exerts no compulsion in Tess's 'second fall'. In the first, she is Alec's victim; in the second, the victim of circumstances. Before each occurs, he is seen as the tempter. Hardy has dispensed with all the old suggestiveness of wide travel and mysterious origins; unexpected arrivals upon the scene of events; melodramatic effects of lightning, thunder, and unusual darkness; coal-black features (beyond the facial); and strange unexplained disappearances. Influenced perhaps by Richardson's *Clarissa*, he expresses the temptation in garden scenes with reference particularly to *Paradise Lost*. Attention is given to these elsewhere (pp. 115–16). The one stage-property he has retained for his 'villain' is the cigar.

Whether 'Stoke' (his father's real name) has any link with the burning imagery which repeatedly expresses Alec's designs is an interesting but not very important question. When Tess first sees him he is smoking; before she leaves he provides her with a light luncheon. The 'skeins of smoke' which pervade his tent as she eats may hint at his scheming, or the laying of snares for women which is becoming habitual to him. She does not realize 'that there behind the blue narcotic haze was potentially the "tragic mischief" of her drama – one who stood fair to be the blood-red ray in the spectrum of her young life'. The 'cigar between his teeth' when Alec conveys Tess and her luggage to The Slopes betokens his sadistic sexuality, and his cruelty and amorousness are frighteningly revealed on the way. He nips his cigar with the tips of his large white centre-teeth, and tells her that his horse Tib has killed one 'chap', that she nearly killed him and he nearly killed her, before descending a hill at such a speed, sometimes on one wheel, that the two banks of the road which enlarge as they advance seem to divide 'like a splitting stick', 'one rushing past at each shoulder'. While waiting at Chaseborough for her companions, before falling a victim to his lust, she catches sight of 'the red coal of a cigar'; behind it Alec watches and waits for his opportunity.

Finally, at Marlott, before events compel Tess to sacrifice herself to him, his Satanic role is resumed not only with reference to *Paradise Lost* but through fire and smoke. Burning weeds on the allotment in the evening gloom, she fails to realize that her fellow-worker is not one of her family until, after catching sight of the fire-beams reflected from the steel prongs of his fork, she looks up and, in the light of a sudden flare, sees that it is Alec d'Urberville. The close association of fire with his steel prongs recalls the christening scene, when Tess, in anguish lest her child should be consigned to the nethermost corner of hell, saw 'the arch-fiend tossing it with his three-pronged fork'. The quoting of *Paradise Lost* is forced, but in general, quaint as it undoubtedly is, the Satanic role of Alec is more successful, and more appropriate to Hardy's serious fiction, than the Mephistophelian alternative with which he experimented in earlier novels.

7 Hardy's Humour

So much critical attention has been given, particularly in recent years, to the more serious aspect of Hardy's writings, and so little to his humour, that it might be considered almost negligible. Such a bias persists notably in the interpretation of a novel as light and romantic as *Under the Greenwood Tree*; it may have been shown more casually a few years ago in the selection of short stories for TV dramatization. They were popular but, as far as I remember, totally devoid of humorous relief. In consequence the view that Hardy is nothing but a gloomy and tragic author must be common. Yet his humour is considerable, as important as Fielding's or George Eliot's, or as Shakespeare's, with which it has most in common. It is in the same tradition but rarely imitative. Most of it has a quality, as all good humour has, which is peculiar to its author; but its quintessence is, to use one of Hardy's favourite expressions, as impossible to cage or capture as a perfume with a net.

It is true that his humour tended to diminish in his later novels, and that, particularly after *Two on a Tower*, tragedy rather than 'comedy' made him 'vocal'.[1] With *Jude the Obscure* such is the theme or the writer's mood that humour seems out of place, but it is notable that between the writing of *Tess* and the writing of *Jude* Hardy enjoyed a holiday of the spirit in composing *A Few Crusted Characters*, and that two of the stories in this miniature collection ('Andrey Satchel and the Parson and Clerk' and 'Absent-Mindedness in a Parish Choir') rank very high among the most delightful things he ever wrote. Like so much of the best of Hardy's humour, they relate to the Church.

The first of these short stories does not begin with a humorous situation. Pregnancy makes marriage desperately urgent for Jane, but the vicar refuses to perform the ceremony until her man Andrey is sober. She then persuades the parson to have them locked in the church tower for an hour or two until Andrey is ready; otherwise, she is afraid, 'all Van Amburgh's horses won't drag him back again'. Unfortunately both the parson and the clerk cannot resist hunting and, seeing a hunt in progress, join the chase and forget their duties. The predicament has its amusing side for the narrator, for all ends well; and good humour is engendered by his style of narration, particularly of the hunt. The excitement of the parson and the clerk infects, and creates a ready bond with the reader; it is conveyed by both comment and looks:

'Halloo!' cries the clerk. 'There he goes! Why, dammy, there's two foxes – '

'Hush, clerk, hush! Don't let me hear that word again! Remember our calling.'

'True, sir, true. But really, good sport do carry a man away so, that he's apt to forget his high persuasion!' And the next minute the corner of the clerk's eye shot again into the corner of the pa'son's, and the pa'son's back again to the clerk's. 'Hee, hee!' said the clerk.

'Ha, ha!' said Pa'son Toogood.

'Ah, sir,' says the clerk again, 'this is better than crying Amen to your Ever-and-ever on a winter's morning!'

'Yes, indeed, clerk! To everything there's a season', says Pa'son Toogood quite pat, for he was a learned Christian man when he liked, and had chapter and ve'se at his tongue's end, as a pa'son should.

Not until next morning does the clerk remember Andrey and Jane. He rushes to remind Toogood of his 'calling'. If anything has happened to the woman, it will mean the quarter-sessions and disgrace to the Church, he tells him. ' "Good God, clerk, don't drive me wild!" says the pa'son. "Why the hell didn't I marry 'em, drunk or sober!" (Pa'sons used to cuss in them days like plain honest men.). . . .'

Parson Toogood is not altogether fiction. He is based on a local hunting clergyman of the Regency period. The story conveys the 'atmosphere' of the period admirably, though Toogood belongs spiritually to the world of Chaucer. Of his original Hardy wrote:

To present that truly delightful personage as he entirely was, is beyond the power of my uncertain pen. One would like to tell of the second baptisms in old port which he used to perform on the squire's children at the christening dinner; of the bishop's descent one day upon the parsonage to convict Toogood of absenteeism, the latter's breakneck ride across country from a cocking party in consequence, and his breathless entry by his back door just in time to open his front to his visitor, whom he meekly received with a quill behind the ear, and a sermon outspread. He had several imitators in his composite calling of sportsman and divine, but no rival.

Here, perhaps, in his preface for the 1896 edition of *Life's Little Ironies*,[2] Hardy was recording a story he regrettably could not write. At a time when he was unprecedently 'overwhelmed' with invitations for stories,[3] he was incapacitated by a personal crisis which numbed his spirit and wounded him more deeply than any criticism of *Jude the Obscure* could ever have done, as poems such as 'In Tenebris' and 'The Dead Man Walking' unmistakably disclose.

'Absent-Mindedness in a Parish Choir' is for many the most entertaining anecdote Hardy ever penned. It tells of one of those events which are 'too good to be true' in such a delightful way that one feels it ought to be true. 'The best fiction', Hardy wrote, 'is more true, so to put it, than history or nature can be.'[4] His art is wonderfully concealed in this story; it shows none of the professional writer's artifice which loses its glitter with its novelty. The style seems natural to the narrator; it is lively, economical, dramatic, and masterly in the ordering. A reader avid for event may feel that the first paragraph is an impediment, but it is appropriate in its context. The local itinerant audience knew or had heard of the players, and their interest in the old story would be reawakened as soon as they and their instruments were mentioned. The culpable but involuntary irreverence of the choir which leads to their dismissal and the installation of a barrel-organ recalls the humour of 'Old Mrs Chundle', one of Hardy's best stories, published after his death by his wife Florence, much to the annoyance of her co-executor Sydney Cockerell,[5] who must have found the humour in bad taste, though the story expresses a deeper fundamental reverence than any other of Hardy's tales. The range of response in 'Old Mrs Chundle' illustrates in striking contiguity a broadmindedness and balanced outlook which are observable in most, but not all, of Hardy's fiction.

Mrs Chundle was too deaf to hear at church, and ceased to attend. A new, enthusiastic curate fixed a hearing-aid to the pulpit, consisting of a long tube with a bell-mouth at each end, one for the preacher, the other for old Mrs Chundle. It was first tried out on a fine frosty morning, and the curate had not proceeded far with his sermon before he became aware of steam rising from the tube, and obviously caused by Mrs Chundle's breathing at the lower end. Unfortunately it was accompanied by the odour of onion-stew; and eventually the curate, unable to bear it any longer, dropped the cambric handkerchief which he kept specially for Sunday morning services into the bell of the tube. Then he heard a fidgeting below the pulpit, and a hoarse whisper, 'The pipe's chokt!', which was repeated as he continued his sermon. 'Suddenly came a violent puff of warm wind, and he beheld his handkerchief rising from the bell of the tube and floating to the pulpit floor. The little boys in the gallery laughed, thinking it a miracle.' As the curate continues his sermon, asking his audience to analyse the passage he has quoted, to see how it naturally suggests three points for consideration, he detects (coincidentally with the enumeration of these points) first peppermint, then cider, then pickled cabbage, in the rising aroma with which he contends, until he can stand it no longer, thrusts his thumb into the hole, and brings his discourse to a hurried conclusion. Ironically he had just reached the subject of 'loving-kindness or grace' before doing so. A second experiment proves too much for this fastidious young preacher. He removes the apparatus from the pulpit, and soon afterwards hears that Mrs Chundle has died of over-exertion in her anxiety not to be late for church. Her will discloses her goodness of heart, and the curate, struck like Peter at the cock-crow, realizes with a shock what true godliness means. The ending of the story makes a profound impact on the reader, though its significance seems to have done nothing to allay Cockerell's fears for Hardy's reputation in 1935.

From all accounts Hardy did not display much humour in the first novel he attempted; it was heavily satirical, even heartlessly so, according to Alexander Macmillan.[6] Unlike satire, humour demands sympathy, an engaging readiness on the writer's part to enter into the mood of his characters; Hardy showed this in the rural scenes which were recommended, and subsequently adapted for *Under the Greenwood Tree*. The development of Hardy's humour in *Desperate Remedies*, his previous novel (his first to be published), and its reception by reviewers are of special interest. Not surprisingly, in days when the church was the centre of parish life, much village gossip and humour revolved around it. When the heroine Cytherea Graye first sees the old manorhouse which, she is informed, is unassociated with 'horrid stories', her driver tells her (in accordance with the author's proleptic intentions) that it is 'jest the house for a nice ghastly hair-on-end story, that would make the parish religious'. Crickett, parish-clerk and 'a kind of Bowdlerised rake', is undoubtedly Hardy's first success with comic character. In the bell-ringing scene which marks the happy ending – after a 'ghastly hair-on-end' episode of some length – he gives a hint of one kind of humour in which Hardy generally excels:

> Ah, well do I bear in mind what I said to Pa'son Raunham about thy mother's family o' seven, the very first week of his coming here, when I was just in my prime. 'And how many daughters has that poor Weedy got, clerk?' he says. 'Six, sir,' says I, 'and every one of 'em has got a brother!' 'Poor woman,' says he, 'a dozen children! – give her this half-sovereign from me, clerk.' 'A laughed a good five minutes afterwards, when he found out my merry nater – 'a did. But there, 'tis over wi' me now. Enteren the Church is the ruin of a man's wit, for wit's nothing without a faint shadow o' sin.

His best remark occurs in the cider-making scene, when Farmer Springrove expresses surprise that he could 'stand third in the list' of his wife's husbands: 'Well, 't has been a power o' marvel to myself oftentimes. Yes, matrimony do begin wi' "Dearly Beloved", and ends wi' "Amazement", as the prayer-book says.' (This is true, though not of the modern, abridged version of the Church of England marriage service.)

Hardy had been encouraged to introduce rustic humour by George Eliot's example. Two reviewers made commendatory references to their similarity, and twice comparisons were made with Dutch painters. One can see from this why Hardy wrote *Under the Greenwood Tree* and gave it the sub-title of 'A Rural Painting of the Dutch School', especially when the story of *Desperate Remedies* was judged to be 'disagreeable'.[7]

The view that the story of Dick Dewy and Fancy Day is pregnant with mischief and bodes ill for the future of the married couple is discussed elsewhere (pp. 137–8). It has soon become a literary cliché.[8] The 'possibility of tragedy lies just under the surface', Hillis Miller writes. This may mean that a situation develops to which the author could easily have given a tragic turn, but all that matters is what Hardy created and intended within the limits of his novel. There can be no doubt about the ending if all factors are considered, and they are secondary to the spirit which animates the book as a whole. One could never accuse the tranter of taking his son's falling in love over-seriously (as Melbury does the question of his daughter's marriage in *The Woodlanders*), even though he says that Dick is a 'lost man'; nor is Hardy's humour 'cynical' when he adds: 'The tranter turned a quarter round and smiled a smile of miserable satire at the setting new moon, which happened to catch his eye.' This description (amusing in its context and a worthy subject for *Punch*) reflects the rustic's traditional philosophy on marriage. When Dick tells him that he repeats what 'all the common world says', the tranter avers, 'The world's a very sensible feller on things in jineral, Dick; very sensible indeed.' The 'world' is a group of grown-ups who meet in and around Mellstock; and their point of view, handed on from one generation to another, provides the groundwork of much of the humour in *Under the Greenwood Tree*. Hardy is not an idyllic sentimentalist; on the subject of marriage he is happy to present the world's view (it is largely an affectation or stock response, the humour of which is plain) and laugh at it. With the tranter, it is none the less associated with some anxiety lest Dick is wasting his time thinking of Fancy Day, who may aim higher, as her father wishes; and it is after a hint of this fear has come from Dick himself that the tranter expresses the world's view ('When you've made up your mind to marry, take the first respectable body that comes to hand – she's as good as any other; they be all alike in the groundwork; 'tis only in the flourishes there's a difference'), then adds, in the same vein but with some paternal solicitude, his inability to understand why, 'wi' a comfortable house and home, and father and mother to take care o' thee', Dick should wish to be worse off by marrying:

> Dick looked at Smart's tail, then up the hill; but no reason was suggested by any object that met his gaze.
>
> 'For about the same reason that you did, father, I suppose.'
>
> 'Dang it, my sonny, thou'st got me there!' And the tranter gave vent to a grim admiration, with the mien of a man who was too magnanimous not to appreciate artistically a slight rap on the knuckles, even if they were his own.

The grimness of the admiration is typical of the humour.

The theme of this minor masterpiece, 'penned so lightly, even so farcically and flippantly at times', is the changes brought by time; and in this the old and new vicars are important figures, the difference in their ways affording a great subject for parish gossip. Unlike Mr Grinham, the new vicar Mr Mayhold will come 'mumbudgeting' in the middle of your work, Mrs Penny complains. She cannot empty the slops outside,

'for as sure as the sun you meet him at the door, coming to ask how you are, and 'tis such a confusing thing to meet a gentleman at the door when ye are in the mess o' washing.'

' 'Tis only for want of knowing better, poor gentleman', said the tranter. 'His meaning's good enough. Ay, your pa'son comes by fate: 'tis heads or tails, like pitch-halfpenny, and no choosing; so we must take en as he is, my sonnies, and thank God he's no worse, I suppose.'

'I fancy I've seen him look across at Miss Day in a warmer way than Christianity asked for', said Mrs Penny musingly; 'but I don't quite like to say it.' . . .

'Ah, Mr Grinham was the man!' said Mr Bowman. 'Why, he never troubled us wi' a visit from year's end to year's end. You might go anywhere, do anything; you'd be sure never to see him.' . . .

'And there's this here man never letting us have a bit o' peace . . .!'

'No sooner had he got here than he found the font wouldn't hold water, as it hadn't for years off and on; and when I told him that Mr Grinham never minded it, but used to spet upon his vinger and christen 'em just as well, 'a said, "Good Heavens! Send for a workman immediate. What place have I come to!" Which was no compliment to us, come to that.'

The end of the instrumental choir is the saddest event in the story, but even this is taken philosophically and does not cast a deep or lasting shadow. The scene where members meet the new vicar to reach a compromise is, in fact, very amusing, and none cuts a more comical figure in it than Mr Maybold. Although he proves to be Dick's most dangerous rival, he cannot be taken much more seriously than Mr Shiner, or Dick himself when he appears in black after walking four miles without overcoat or umbrella in a drizzling rain, from attending a friend's funeral on the very day of Fancy's successful début at the organ. When he departs, another figure is seen approaching Fancy Day's; he also is in black from top to toe, but he carries an umbrella. It is Mr Maybold, come to propose; and he does it as if he were in a comedy. He tells her he has struggled against his emotion continually, and implores her not to refuse him. 'It would be foolish of you – I mean cruel!' he says (and one knows that he can be taken hardly more seriously than Jane

Austen's Mr Collins). Not long afterwards he realizes that he has been 'intoxicated' into making 'the most imprudent resolution of his life'.

Rarely does one associate Emma Gifford with *Under the Greenwood Tree*. Yet before it was completed in the summer of 1871, Hardy had visited her three times in Cornwall; and some of her infectious vitality may account for the high-spirited key in which it is written. A happy recollection, with or without some petty vexation, is suspected in the introduction of the blue dress (Emma, 'the young lady in brown' of the previous March appeared 'metamorphosed' as 'a young lady in summer blue' on his second visit in August 1870) and the trial of Dick Dewy's patience:

> 'What she loves best in the world', he thought, with an incipient spice of his father's grimness, 'is her hair and her complexion. What she loves next best, her gowns and hats; what she loves next best, myself, perhaps!'

He then suffers 'great anguish at this disloyalty in himself and harshness to his darling'. Yet the motif recurs. Emma played the organ at St Juliot, and much is made of Fancy's love of attractive dress as she 'floated' down the school steps 'in a nebulous collection of colours inclining to blue', and of the profusion of curls which she had lowered to her shoulders, before she leaves Dick (in funeral black) to proceed to the church for 'the inauguration of a new order of things'. The subject is revived at their wedding:

> 'Ah!' said grandfather James to grandfather William as they retired, 'I wonder which she thinks most about, Dick or her wedding raiment!'
>
> 'Well, 'tis their nature', said grandfather William. 'Remember the words of the prophet Jeremiah: "Can a maid forget her ornaments, or a bride her attire?"'

It was not unlike Hardy to include such a reminder in his novel; he had already transferred one of Emma's remarks to the description of a scene in *Desperate Remedies*.[9]

Some of the characteristics of Hardy's humour appear full-blown at this early stage. One is the care taken to individualize his characters by visual reference to idiosyncratic movements and attitudes; in this respect Mr Spinks, once in charge of a night school, and with a reputation for learning and intelligence to maintain, makes an interesting little study whenever he seeks to say something profound and striking. Examples which come readily to mind from Hardy's later fiction are Gabriel Oak's manner of hoisting up his large watch from his waistband fob by 'throwing the body to one side, compressing the mouth and face to a mere mass of ruddy flesh on account of the exertion', and drawing it up by the chain 'like a bucket from a well'; and Hardy's cinematic delineation of a typical market-man's non-verbal expressiveness in *The Mayor of Casterbridge* (ix):

> To express satisfaction the Casterbridge market-man added to his utterance a broadening of the cheeks, a crevicing of the eyes, a throwing back of the shoulders, which was intelligible from the other end of the street. If he wondered, though all Henchard's carts and waggons were rattling past him, you knew it from perceiving the inside of his crimson mouth, and a target-like circling of his eyes. Deliberation caused sundry attacks on the moss of adjoining walls with the end of his stick, a change of his hat from the horizontal to the less so; a sense of tediousness announced itself in a lowering of the person by spreading the knees to a lozenge-shaped aperture and contorting the arms.

A gratifying second feature is the introduction of little *ad hoc* anecdotes such as that of Michael Mail's unfortunate friendly nod to an auctioneer as he passed an open window in Casterbridge and saw him inside 'stuck on his perch, a-selling off'; or of Mail again, eating fried liver and lights at the Three Mariners when a brass band struck up in the street:

> Band played six-eight time; six-eight chaws I, willynilly. Band plays common; common time went my teeth among the liver and lights as true as a hair. Beautiful 'twere! Ah, I shall never forget that there band.

If these miniature action pictures were never excelled by Hardy it is because by and large he gradually lost touch with the community which kept them alive.

More generally Hardy's humour is enriched as a result of his giving a foreground part to a group of rustics; they are clearly individualized, but it is only conjointly, in their reactions one to another in discussing a subject or brooding over it (for much of their comicality is visual) that they can express themselves most effectively. Perhaps their quaint angularity owes something to Dickens; more probably to an original humorous detachment which enabled Hardy to see rustic mannerisms and eccentricities more freshly and with greater relish after his long absence in London. They are too involved in the story to form a 'chorus', but they are the strength and stay of the novel, and contribute largely to the charm it must have had for Leslie Stephen. Not surprisingly therefore, after *A Pair of Blue Eyes*, Hardy returned to a rustic grouping in *Far from the Madding Crowd* (which Stephen had commissioned) and in later novels.

Hardy's best humour was nourished in the Dorset oral tradition. His exemplar was Shakespeare. There is a scene in *A Pair of Blue Eyes* which takes place in the vault of Endelstow Church when preparations are made for the burial of Lady Luxellian. Its humour is not of vintage quality, though it is the best in the novel; it is brought to life, partly by recollections of the gravediggers scene in *Hamlet*, but more undoubtedly by Hardy's 'romantic interest' in the story of Lady Susan and the actor with whom she eloped, and from imaginative re-creations of the vault which his grandfather had constructed for them in the church at Stinsford.

True humour has a warm or genial imaginative quality; it cannot be forced. Much of *A Pair of Blue Eyes* was written hurriedly, and one soon tires of the 'frying' in the head of a caricature like Worm, Lickpan's pig-killing stories, and Mr Swancourt's teasing habit of breaking off a story which has never got under way because (as he claims) his present company makes it inadmissible. The most amusing moment in the novel arrives with comical acuteness, and has none of the lingering quality of good humour; it is when the two jealous lovers, each secretly endeavouring to anticipate the other, look out of adjacent windows and find they are travelling on the same train to Cornwall with the same intent. In *A Laodicean*, another novel with a setting remote from the Dorset Hardy knew, there is little humour, and it is soon forgotten. The originating idea of this novel, like that of *The Hand of Ethelberta*, belongs to the realm of ideas. Neither was given time to mature. The latter is described as 'a comedy in chapters'; its entertainment springs from social satire and farcical situations rather than from character and humour.

The Trumpet-Major offers a good deal of entertainment. Hardy worked hard in its preparation, and his preoccupation with extensive researches in the British Museum and Dorset may have tired his imaginative spontaneity. Another restraint could have been his laudable policy of writing a historical novel with ordinary people as its principal protagonists. Whatever the reason, no great characters emerge, and most of the comic relief is nearer caricature than life. It is both unreal and conventional; Festus is a cowardly braggart, a *miles gloriosus* descended from ancient comedy, and his miserly uncle Benjy is equally a stereotype. Their actions are as predictable as the twitchings of puppets, though their appearances may sometimes cause a surprise. Festus becomes rather too objectionable to be really amusing. Tricks played on him tend to be jejune or juvenile, and the highest reach of humour at his expense is created by Cripplestraw, who after hearing of a French landing torments him with hints of the terrible woundings which will inevitably befall a man of his great valour, and then, discovering what Festus is intent on (and enjoying the prospect), gives ironical commendation to his proposed 'honourable retreat' in the cause of gallantry, telling him to 'hoard up' his valour for 'a higher class of war – the defence of yer adorable lady'. More sympathy is felt for Benjy's efforts to outwit his nephew (and they are often amusing), but they belong to an archaic world of make-believe which keeps them at a distance from the reader and prevents that interpenetration of delight and real sympathy which is indispensable for true humour. When Corporal Tullidge twists his arm to produce an audible crunching of bones smashed in the battle of Valenciennes he provides more sensational or excruciating effects. There is comedy in the Matilda Johnson episode from the moment Bob the sailor announces by letter his intentions of marrying his new lady-love at once and at home, 'that his father might not be deprived of the pleasure of the wedding feast'. Her arrival imparts life to the action, but the best literary gain that results is a conversational gem in a Jane Austen (or Anne Brontë) style which is nugatory at every point, from her need to conceal and her having little in common with country folk:

'You get the sea-breezes here, no doubt?'
'O yes, dear; when the wind is that way.'
'Do you like windy weather?'
'Yes; though not now, for it blows down the young apples.'
'Apples are plentiful, it seems. You country-folk call St Swithin's their christening day, if it rains?'
'Yes, dear. Ah me! I have not been to a christening for these many years; the baby's name was George, I remember – after the King.'
'I hear that King George is still staying at the town here. I *hope* he'll stay till I have seen him!'
'He'll wait till the corn turns yellow; he always does.'
'How *very* fashionable yellow is getting for gloves just now!'
'Yes. Some persons wear them to the elbow, I hear.'
'Do they? I was not aware of that. I struck my elbow last week so hard against the door of my aunt's mansion that I feel the ache now.'

The kind of 'Ha-ha!' label which Hardy attaches to characters in *The Hand of Ethelberta* – Ladywell, Neigh, Menlove, Yore (archaeologist), Breeve (organist) – is found in the names of a number of people referred to in *The Trumpet-Major*: Rootle (dentist), Timothy Titus Philemon (bishop), Lt Knockheelmann, Cornet Flitzenhart, and Capt. Klaspenkissen ('thrilling' members of the York Hussars). This well-worn kind of instant humour (in Thackeray's style) is more expressive of caricature than of individual human nature, and would have little significance were not Benjy and his nephew Festus Derriman foreground figures of the same class; 'Derriman' is almost certainly from 'derring-do'. A more typical Hardy name such as 'Leaf' or 'Poorgrass' has almost a poetic appropriateness, the former suggested perhaps by the 'trembling leaf' in Shelley's 'Song', 'Rarely, rarely, comest thou/ Spirit of Delight'.

Whatever its merits as a novel, there can be no doubt that *The*

Trumpet-Major provided an excellent magazine story, a blend of the sad and the comic. The more heroic levels reached in some of the later scenes serve to underline the rather hackneyed and unimaginative quality of much in it that passes for humour. The drilling scene was copied, and Hardy's reading when he was at work on the novel (it included Smollett and later eighteenth-century literature) may have helped to create a comic atmosphere which is not altogether Wessex. Genuinely humorous effects are rather incidental. Hardy's imagination is recognisable in the description of the night wind blowing through a beacon-watcher's few teeth 'as through the ruins of Stonehenge', or in his sympathetic account of the effect of the arriving road-waggon on the congregation of All Saints', Casterbridge:

> the rattle, dismounting, and swearing outside completely drowned the parson's voice within, and sustained the flagging interest of the congregation at precisely the right moment. No sooner did the charity children begin to writhe on the benches, and adult snores grow audible, than the waggon arrived.

Even Festus says something which is enjoyable and humorous, when John Loveday tells him that it was he who had beaten him. Festus answers that he cannot challenge him in cold blood, and, when asked who he supposed had attacked him, replies:

> I can't reveal; it would be disgracing myself to show how very wide of the truth the mockery of wine was able to lead my senses. We will let it be buried in eternal mixens of forgetfulness.

It is his greatest moment of magnanimity.

Had Hardy planned the comic relief of *The Trumpet-Major* more in terms of the Wessex yokels familiar to his imagination, he could have tapped a richer vein. Such seems to be the evidence of scenes with the same historical and geographical setting in Part First of *The Dynasts*; and it is further highlighted when we think of Grandfer Cantle in *The Return of the Native* and the exploits which he proudly wishes to recall of 'the Bang-up Locals' in and around Budmouth at the time of the French invasion scare. Festus Derriman is undoubtedly a development from him, but not nearly as genial and welcome. In fact he and Benjy seem rather alien to the Wessex which proved to be the surest source of Hardy's most living humour.

The truth of this conclusion seems to be borne out when we turn back (chronologically) to *Far From the Madding Crowd*. Nobody would suggest that Hardy's rustics are copies from life, for humour (like the best fiction) is 'more true ... than history or nature can be'. It is imaginative: it selects and transmutes; or it is wholly creative. Yet there can be no doubt that the main cause for the resurgence of Hardy's humour after *A Pair of Blue Eyes* was his second return to Dorset after a period

in London, and his consorting with farm-labourers and studying their
mannerisms and occupations in response to Leslie Stephen's challenging
invitation to write a novel rather like *Under the Greenwood Tree* but
with more incident.[10] If any of Hardy's novels surpasses *Under the
Greenwood Tree* in humour, it must surely be *Far from the Madding
Crowd*.

Spry notes of facetious detachment at the expense of Gabriel Oak
are appropriate to the opening episode before misfortune makes the
young shepherd more serious and dignified; except in the intervals they
would be out of key after the first of the tragic movements has begun
with the introduction of Fanny Robin. The humour of the minor
rustics is never discordant, however; the difference, broadly speaking,
is between critical amusement (rather like laughing at a character) and
amusement which derives from empathy (rather like laughing with a
character). Joseph Poorgrass is sometimes a fool, but one does not wish
him otherwise; criticism is out of place because it would destroy his
credibility. And the author's underlying sympathy for such a weak
creature creates no sense of discord with the tragic course of the plot
when Poorgrass stops at the Buck's Head. On the other hand, a kind of
suppressed snigger at the well-meaning young Oak's self-assurance may
be detected in the description of the startling effects he achieves, after
using all his hair-oil, in the hope of captivating Bathsheba, till his 'dry,
sandy, and inextricably curly hair' is deepened to 'a splendidly novel
colour between that of guano and Roman cement', and sticks to his
head 'like mace round a nutmeg, or wet seaweed round a boulder after
the ebb'. As Oak reaches the cottage where Bathsheba lives with her
aunt, Hardy continues in this high-spirited vein, fancying scandal and
rumour to be the staple topic of the sparrows on the eaves no less than
of those under them, and describing the rare bark of Oak's dog (uttered
'with an absolutely neutral countenance') as 'a sort of Commination-
service, which, though offensive, had to be gone through now and then
to frighten the flock for their own good'. This kind of authorial humour
is noticeable occasionally at later stages. When Oak reaches Weatherbury and asks about a lodging, the bailiff moves away 'as a Christian
edges past an offertory-plate when he does not mean to contribute';
and Laban Tall laughs at one of his wife's mortifying remarks with 'a
hideous effort of appreciation' reminiscent of the good humour of a
parliamentary candidate subjected to 'ghastly snubs'.

Far from the Madding Crowd provides a rich variety of rustic
humour. It comes from a group of labourers, most of whom play significant minor individual roles at some point or other in the story.
In gossip and reminiscence they often use choice turns of expression.
'Ah, stirring times we live in – stirring times', says one (before the main
drama is under way), when he hears that Dicky Hill's wooden cider-
house is pulled down and Tompkins' old apple tree 'that used to bear

two hogsheads of cider' has been rooted up. 'Boundless love; I shouldn't
have supposed it in the universe!' murmurs Joseph Poorgrass ('who
habitually spoke on a large scale in his moral reflections') after hearing
Coggan state that the love of Bathsheba's father, Farmer Everdene,
was such that he used to light the candle three times a night to look at
his wife. His manner of keeping in love with her and resisting the temptation of a wandering heart makes memorable gossip at Warren's Malthouse but is judged 'a most ungodly remedy' by Poorgrass. Coggan,
Mark Clark, Joseph Poorgrass, Henery Fray, and Laban Tall have
characters as unforgettable as their names. One cannot fail to com-
miserate with Laban Tall who enjoys music but dare not stay to hear
it for fear of his wife. Jan Coggan loves to recall how the free ale
'would slip down – ah, 'twould slip down sweet!' at Farmer Everdene's,
and is so grateful to Parson Thirdly for giving him a sack of seed
potatoes when his own were frosted that he must stay in the Church
even though his chances of Heaven are not as great as if he were one
of the 'chapel-folk'. Perhaps Joseph Poorgrass's remarks deserve most
notice. Everyone remembers his bashfulness and his fear that the tale
will be told of his being unable to find his way in Yalbury Wood, calling
out 'Man a-lost! man a-lost!', and answering 'Joseph Poorgrass of
Weatherbury, sir!' to an owl's 'Whoo-whoo-whoo!' Partiality for liquor
soon gives him a 'multiplying eye' which makes him see two of every
sort as if he were 'some holy man in the times of King Noah and entering into the ark'. His ready quoting of the Scriptures is perhaps his
most humorous trait, though this may not always be appreciated by
readers more than a century after his first appearance.[11]

Of the principal characters in the drama of *Far from the Madding
Crowd* only two are left in the end to pursue 'the noiseless tenor of
their way'. Quaintly idiosyncratic though the rustics are, they represent
their community and, like groups in subsequent Hardy novels, create by
their changelessness a sense of stability and continuity where all in the
foreground is subject to violent or sudden change. Time congenially
spent at Warren's Malthouse with this fraternity gives a broad view of
background, focuses attention on principal characters, and promotes
narrative interest in past and present. In their comments here, the
rustics perform the role of the Greek chorus in a style which has its
parallel in the best of Shakespeare's light relief but which is Hardy's
own. Wisely, as in *The Return of the Native*, he gives them ample and
varying scope before the tragic plot gets under way. Whether the Egdon
rustics are quite as entertaining is doubtful; they do not include as
many distinctive characters, though Grandfer Cantle and his simpleton
youngest son Christian are in Hardy's best vein. Yet their gaiety around
the bonfire in the surrounding gloom makes their first appearance one
of his most entertaining scenes. If they offer less in humour, they gain
considerably in functional importance, bringing the story into focus,

telling us dramatically what has happened and what can be expected in the immediate future.

The meeting of the choir which provides the main group of commentators in *Two on a Tower* may be less well known. Once again the story is promoted by a humorous company, and Hardy's long familiarity with the Church inspires some choice recollections, such as that of the blushing of Parson Wilton's bride when the choir sang 'His wife, like a fair fertile vine, her lovely fruit shall bring' at their wedding, or that of Hezekiah Biles's rejection for Confirmation because, when examined by the parson and asked what were the articles of his belief, he answered, at the instigation of his mischievous neighbour Blount Constantine, 'Women and wine.' Hardy uses this small rustic group most artistically at the crucial point of revelation in the early romance of the young astronomer hero:

'But the young man himself?'
'Planned, cut out, and finished for the delight of 'ooman!'
'Yet he must be willing.'
'That would come soon. If they get up this tower ruling plannards together much longer, their plannards will soon rule them together, in my way o' thinking. If she've a disposition towards the knot, she can soon teach him.'
'True, true, and lawfully. What before mid ha' been a wrong desire is now a holy wish!'
The scales fell from Swithin St Cleeve's eyes as he heard the words of his neighbours.

'What before mid ha' been a wrong desire is now a holy wish!' – the language is unmatchable and unforgettable.

The Mayor of Casterbridge suggests a reappraisal of the role of rustics in supplying what may be conveniently generalized as 'comic relief'. We have only to think of 'Old Mrs Chundle' to realize Hardy's deep Christian respect for the poor and humble; yet, for the sake of entertainment, he had repeatedly made rustics not merely a rich source of humour but objects of pleasant ridicule. It had been his habit to include a simpleton like Thomas Leaf and Christian Cantle or a laughingstock like Poorgrass in his leading group. For artistic purposes this was defensible, but it posed an ethical question. Hardy could never be classified with writers of the eighteenth-century tradition who tended to regard rustics as 'low' or beneath serious consideration and easy targets for mirth, but his motives were open to misinterpretation. His more serious view of the yokel (which *The Mayor of Casterbridge* represents, for its lower-class representatives live on the edge of a small agricultural town and have immediate access to the country) stems from the defence of Hodge which he had undertaken in 1883 (midway between *Two on a Tower* and *The Mayor*) and which was renewed in *Tess of the d'Urbervilles*.[12]

One must also take into account the agricultural depression of the period (at the end of the 1840s) in assessing the rather subdued tones of the Three Mariners *habitués*. In the words of Christopher Coney,

> we be bruckle folk here – the best o' us hardly honest sometimes, what with hard winters, and so many mouths to fill, and God-a'mighty sending his little taties so terrible small to fill 'em with. We don't think about flowers and fair faces, not we – except in the shape o' cauliflowers and pigs' chaps.

Hard times explain Christopher's action in digging up the four ounce pennies used for closing Mrs Henchard's eyes on her decease, and spending them at the Three Mariners. 'Faith,' he said, 'why should death rob life o' fourpence?' Country laughter is heard, particularly from Mrs Cuxsom (whose smiling countenance is like 'a circular disc reticulated with creases'). She has no wish to remarry. 'How's this?' asks Solomon Longways:

> 'Here's Mrs Newson, a mere skellinton, has got another husband to keep her, while a woman of your tonnage have not.'
> 'I have not. Nor another to beat me. . . . Ah, yes, Cuxsom's gone, and so shall leather breeches!'

Like Coney's unanswerable question, Mother Cuxsom's last statement has a proverbial ring. She remembers a party at old Dame Ledlow's, farmer Shinar's aunt at Mellstock – 'she we used to call Toadskin, because her face was so yaller and freckled'. Prodding Solomon's shoulder with her finger-tip 'while her eyes twinkled between the crevices of their lids', she asks if he remembers how Joan Dummett was 'took bad' when they were coming home, and Jack Griggs was forced to carry her through the mud,

> 'and how 'a let her fall in Dairyman Sweetapple's cow-barton, and we had to clane her gown wi' grass – never such a mess as 'a were in?'
> 'Ay – that I do – hee-hee, such doggery as there was in them ancient days, to be sure! Ah, the miles I used to walk then; and now I can hardly step over a furrow!'

Such reminiscences have a universality or timeless quality which recalls Shakespeare's Shallow. But the greatest speech of Mother Cuxsom relates to Mrs Henchard's death and reads like poetry.

An even greater elevation of the humble may be seen in Whittle. He is not a member of the 'choric' group, but he is a simpleton, and abominably made to look a fool by Henchard; and yet it is Whittle who in the end proves to be more loyal of heart than Farfrae or even Elizabeth-Jane. Like the fool in *King Lear* he follows Henchard to the

heath, where he tends him in his dying moments, and describes his end
in a moving vernacular which plays a major part in giving *The Mayor
of Casterbridge* perhaps the most successful of Hardy's tragic conclusions. Thereafter, as never before, Hardy draws his leading tragic
characters from the lower classes: Giles Winterborne and Marty South;
Tess Durbeyfield; Jude Fawley. The labourer still provides humour, but
he is never again made to look a simpleton.

There is sufficient humour in *The Woodlanders* and *Tess of the
d'Urbervilles* to support the view that Hardy, like Shakespeare, never
supposed that light relief was inimical to tragedy; it reflects a sense of
proportion or 'relativity', a recognition of 'cakes and ale in the world',
of 'laughter' as well as 'tears' and 'human misery beyond tears' (*Life*,
226). If his bent was towards tragical issues in his more mature years,
it was because he felt, deep down, as a Positivist, that imaginative literature could help by arousing sympathy for the less fortunate. Until his
last years he was, and professed to be, a 'meliorist' who believed 'that
if way to the Better there be, it exacts a full look at the Worst'. His
philosophical outlook was not gloomy; by and large he believed that
the 'purblind Doomsters' of chance bestowed 'blisses' as readily as pain.
Temperamentally he was subject to black moods, and in *Jude the
Obscure* his outlook was undoubtedly darkened by his own matrimonial
unhappiness. It is atypical, the one Hardy tragedy in which enjoyable
laughter is not heard, only the laughter of bitterness and despair. Here
it is worth remembering that Hardy could not bear *Wuthering Heights*;
in 1924 his wife Florence reported that he would not listen to it; he had
read parts of it and disliked it intensely 'for its unrelieved ugliness'.

Yet the humour of *The Woodlanders* and *Tess* differs from that of
the great scenes at the maltster's and on the heath in *Far from the
Madding Crowd* and *The Return of the Native*. It is less dissociated
from tragedy. Giles Winterborne's Christmas party has its amusing
features, and nobody forgets the crowning remark, 'God forbid that a
live slug should be seed on any plate of victuals that's served by Robert
Creedle', or the circumstances giving rise to it. There is a time when
laughter is a defence against setbacks, but here the issues are too great
and heartfelt for Giles; he knows, and the reader is left in no immediate
doubt, that the party is a disaster for him, and can accept the consequences only with stoical fortitude. At the end of the novel, when
Melbury and his men take respite at an inn, after the man-trap scare
and the long search for Grace which takes them to Sherton Abbas, the
talk turns to the deceptiveness of women after matrimony and in courtship. 'I know'd a man and wife', begins Farmer Cawtree; and the bark-
ripper caps his story with this:

I knowed a woman, and the husband o' her went away for four-and-
twenty year. And one night he came home when she was sitting by

the fire, and thereupon he sat down himself on the other side of the chimney-corner. 'Well', says she, 'have ye got any news?' 'Don't know as I have', says he; 'have you?' 'No,' says she, 'except that my daughter by the husband that succeeded ''ee was married last month, which was a year later after I was made a widow by him. 'Oh! Anything else?' he says. 'No', says she. And there they sat, one on each side of the chimney-corner, and were found by the neighbours sound asleep in their chairs, not having known what to talk about at all.

Even here the humour is soured a little by the mingled disgust and resignation of Melbury (which the reader shares) over Grace's reconciliation with an untrustworthy husband. None the less, it is significant that this light relief immediately precedes and counterpoises the elegiac ending (from one who is faithful). In such a mood, through Grammer Oliver, Hardy can make play with words which express the main article of his belief: 'without charity we be but tinkling simples'. (His humorous use of scriptural quotations was not confined to Joseph Poorgrass.)

Writing to J. B. Priestley in 1926, Hardy said that George Meredith, 'when aiming to represent the "Comic Spirit"', did not discover 'the tragedy that always underlies comedy if you only scratch it deeply enough'. Tragedy is rarely forgotten in *Tess of the d'Urbervilles*; most, perhaps, in the entertaining story at the dairy-farm of fiddler William Dewy's escape from a bull by the magic power of Christmas music (xvii). The broad comedy of John Durbeyfield's special 'market-nitch' celebration when he hears of his descent from an ancient and knightly family loses its edge for the reader when it brings shame to Tess; and Hardy uses humour at Talbothays to recall her sorrow and precipitate its renewal. The story of Jack Dollop was 'a humorous narration' to her companions; 'none of them but herself seemed to see the sorrow of it; to a certainty, not one knew how cruelly it touched the tender place in her experience' (xxi). Its sequel provokes laughter, but makes Tess resolve to confess her past. 'What was comedy to them was tragedy to her'; it was 'as if people should laugh at martyrdom' (xxix). The tragicomedy she hears, when she returns to Marlott after her disastrous wedding and asks the turnpike-keeper for news, makes her 'so sick at heart' that she could not 'go home publicly in the fly with her luggage and belongings' but went on alone by a back lane:

Marlott is Marlott still. Folks have died and that. John Durbeyfield, too, hev had a daughter married this week to a gentleman-farmer; not from John's own house, you know; they was married elsewhere; the gentleman being of that high standing that John's own folk was not considered well-be-doing enough to have any part in it, the bride-groom seeming not to know how't have been discovered that John is a old and ancient nobleman himself by blood, with family skillentons in their own vaults to this day, but done out of his property in the time o' the Romans. However, Sir John, as we call 'n now, kept up the wedding-day as well as he could, and stood treat to everybody in the parish; and John's wife sung songs at The Pure Drop till past eleven o'clock.

The improvident 'Sir John' is most amusing just before his sudden death, when he thinks of inviting all 'the old antiqueerians in this part of England' to subscribe to a fund for his maintenance:

I'm sure they'd see it as a romantical, artistical, and proper thing to do. They spend lots o' money in keeping up old ruins, and finding the bones o' things, and such like; and living remains must be more interesting to 'em still, if they only knowed of me.

It must be confessed that the majority of Hardy's short stories contain little humour, and none that is memorable. Some outstanding exceptions have been discussed, and mention should be made of 'The Distracted Preacher', a rather delightful smuggling story of some length which J. M. Barrie not surprisingly found 'very amusing'. It would be a mistake to overlook the humour in 'The Three Strangers', one of Hardy's greatest short stories; but the farcical absurdity of the Tony Kytes tale in *A Few Crusted Characters* may be too incredibly simple for repetition.

Reference has been made to Wessex scenes in *The Dynasts*; one on Durnover Green (Part Third, v. vi) is particularly amusing. A rustic enters 'at a furious pace', in shirt sleeves, with a smock-frock on his arm, having hurried all the way from Stourcastle in the expectation of seeing Napoleon burned alive. His vehement indignation at finding it is merely his effigy, and the perpendicular spitting of the pipe-smoking vicar, when he expresses surprise that anyone should be 'so inhuman in this Christian country as to burn a fellow-creature alive',[18] and again when news arrives of Napoleon's escape from Elba, are unforgettable.

Few of Hardy's poems are completely humorous. Two of the most noteworthy were written as early as 1866. 'The Bride-Night Fire' relates a Wessex tradition in dialect and with verve; its rustic humour is reminiscent of Fielding and belongs to a type which is perennially popular with men. 'The Ruined Maid', one of Hardy's most finished poems, is more subtle; it is dramatized, and the innocent questioning of the country girl who meets her bedizened friend in town awakens an ironical humour; but the poem as a whole is fiercely satirical. It is one of those 'satires of circumstance' which are far more successful than any of the fifteen sketches collected under that title, or 'In the Days of Crinoline', which tells the kind of scandal one might expect to hear narrated over a glass of ale. In justification, Hardy insisted that the last poem told a true story; its appeal for him lay partly in the peculiar satisfaction he derived from a joke against the Church (as with the fooling of the bishop in *Two on a Tower*), as well as in the formal fascination he found in life's little ironies. More ingenious, but still a satire prompted by the Spirit Sinister, is 'Ah, Are You Digging on My Grave?'. The irony of 'A Curate's Kindness' is tragi-comic; it is the kind of story which would excite a laugh at a stag-party, but as it is told by the frenzied victim its tragic implications seem grim. More gruesome is 'Her Second Husband Hears Her Story', 'a cool queer tale' which Hardy could not resist. Some readers will find it distasteful, and yet there is a piquant humour in the irony of the situation which is dramatically unfolded.

In 'The Homecoming' there is a happy sureness of dramatic tone which combines with the subject to make this one of Hardy's most humorous poems. The wind may growl gruffly on Toller Down, but the husband is kind, and all bodes well at the end. For some of the best of Hardy's humour, however, we turn to poems where serious subjects, or subjects which would appear serious to most people, are presented in a whimsical or fantastic way. Comparison with 'A Night of Questionings' suggests that Hardy could not have written 'Channel Firing' after the First World War as he did in April 1914, before its outbreak. His denunciation of man's folly is unequivocal – 'All nations striving strong to make/Red war yet redder' – but how remarkable that he could make God a humorist in the expression of his views to the awakened dead, after the sound of the guns and the shattering of windows in the chancel have led them to think that the Day of Judgement has arrived, and made them sit up in their coffins and observe the effects of terror on creatures in and around their church! The dramatized fantasies of 'Aquae Sulis' and 'The Levelled Churchyard', though less serious, will equally repay attention. The amusing features of the latter are more sharply defined in the hymnal form it takes and in its closing echoes of the Church Litany. More exquisite are the ways in which Hardy expresses the characters of the dead in 'Voices from Things Growing in a Churchyard'. Lady Gertrude's pride, for example, is to be seen in the laurel in which she now lives; its leaves shine as did her 'satins superfine'. Eve Greensleeves, fitly named for her promiscuity ('the handsome mother of two or three illegitimate children'), now climbs ironically as 'innocent' withwind, coiling and clinging amorously, kissed night and day 'by glowworms and bees', as she had been 'by men from many a clime/Beneath sun, stars, in blaze, in breeze'.

Hardy's lack of squeamishness is exemplified in a humorous cellar scene which shows the grim realities of the retreat to Corunna in Part Second of *The Dynasts*. He was hampered by the prudery of his age; the woman who rudely rejected Christian Cantle's proposal could never have called him a 'maphrotight fool' in a Victorian serial. Nevertheless, there is nothing in Hardy's humour to suggest a taste for bawdy such as Shakespeare enjoyed. Nor does it aspire to the wit of a Congreve or Meredith. Like George Eliot's, it depends very much on recollections of country life, and is more vigorous in the early novels. Its revival corresponds with periods when he was able to renew acquaintance with Dorset countrymen. Humour appealed to him, and he could have made more of it had he chosen. What we have is considerable and diversified. Most of it is engaging and distinctive; it is free from quirkiness, and is very English in character; it has an intimate, almost charismatic quality, showing, like Shakespeare's, the virtues of good nature and tolerance – even the rake-hell Ralph Blossom is remembered with charity.[14]

8 The Frost's Decree

Although Hardy was inconsistent in various points of view or 'seemings', and became less confidently rationalistic in his later years, in one respect at least he seems to have remained constant: he felt that too much in life is ruled by chance. His heart went out to those to whom chance had offered little choice; and it is with the misfortunes of such – deprivation, hardship, suffering, and tragedy – that Hardy's poetical imagination often associated the severities of winter. Although he used the phrase 'the Frost's decree' only once, there can be no doubt that it epitomizes every kind of misfortune for which chance is responsible, and that it is one expression of more generalized imagery which acquired a symbolical significance for Hardy very early in his writing career, and assumed a variety of wintry overtones in novels and poems over a period of more than sixty years.

My first illustration is a minor poem, 'Before Knowledge'. Its subject is a transitory and perhaps common thought, which Hardy expresses in an unusual way:

> When I walked roseless tracks and wide,
> Ere dawned your date for meeting me,
> O why did you not cry Halloo
> Across the stretch between, and say:
>
> 'We move, while years as yet divide,
> On closing lines which – though it be
> You know me not nor I know you –
> Will intersect and join some day!'
>
> > Then well had I borne
> > Each scraping thorn;
> > But the winters froze
> > And grew no rose;
> > No bridge bestrode
> > The gap at all;
> > No shape you showed,
> > And I heard no call!

It is the mathematical vision that makes a commonplace thought arresting – a variant, I suppose, of 'Never the time and the place/And the loved one all together'. The rose of love is conventional; the wintry image is readily understood. The prospect would have been less bleak had the poet known what good fortune lay ahead.

For a weightier example of 'the Frost's decree' I turn to Hardy's fiction. Perhaps he reached his peak as an imaginative writer in *The Woodlanders* and *Tess of the d'Urbervilles*. Often in these novels the human situation and the writer's philosophy of life are reflected so effectively in natural scenes that his thought is communicated wholly in imagery. This kind of transmission is poetic.

At Flintcomb-Ash, where Tess, the victim of ill-chance, is reduced to a manual slave, her stoical passivity is expressed in the sky and landscape. The swede-field has a 'desolate drab' appearance; it wears a complexion which is featureless. In another colour, the sky is similar, 'a white vacuity with the lineaments gone':

> So these two nether and upper visages confronted each other all day long, the white face looking down on the brown face, and the brown face looking up at the white face, without anything standing between them but the two girls crawling over the surface of the former like flies.

The simile suggests the insignificance of Tess and her companion Marian in the general moil of chance, but its implications can hardly be dissociated from the lines in *King Lear* which Hardy quotes in his preface to the novel: 'As flies to wanton boys are we to the gods;/ They kill us for their sport.' There is a hint of this when Tess is hanged: the President of the Immortals 'had ended his sport with Tess'.

The contrast between this scene and the Valley of the Great Dairies, 'that happy green tract of land where the summer had been liberal in her gifts', where Tess had revived in the rays of Angel's love, is obvious; and it is recalled by the two girls. They endure, but hope is not extinguished; and Hardy adds, 'So the two forces were at work here as everywhere, the inherent will to enjoy, and the circumstantial will against enjoyment.' On the first of these Hardy wrote this note:

> Thought of the determination to enjoy. We see it in all nature, from the leaf on the tree to the titled lady at the ball. . . . It is achieved, of a sort, under superhuman difficulties. Like pent-up water it will find a chink of possibility somewhere. Even the most oppressed of men and animals find it, so that out of a thousand there is hardly one who has not a sun of some sort for his soul.[1]

The circumstantial forces against enjoyment show the effects of Hardy's Immanent Will in the natural world, including man. Nature is blind, working by rote, regardless whether creatures are victims or not. This is the implication of Hardy's 'Unfulfilled Intention': natural laws have produced in man a creature far developed 'beyond all apparent first intention (on the emotional side), without mending matters by a second intent and execution, to eliminate the evils of the blunder of over-doing'.[2] Such is the effect of Darwinism on Hardy's thought. Adverse circumstances can be alleviated by society and scientific knowledge, but nature operating in and outside the human species is responsible for chance misfortunes which are inevitable. This is the significance of the 'circumstantial will against enjoyment', and its significance is synonymous with 'the Frost's decree'.

After Tess has been hacking swedes 'in the morning frosts and afternoon rains', the great winter arrives with those 'strange birds from behind the Pole' – 'gaunt spectral creatures with tragical eyes' which had beheld inconceivable Arctic horrors.[3] In this correlative image Hardy concentrates the sufferings and endurance of Tess, all a consequence of mischance and deprivation.

This larger, non-literal sense of the frost image in Hardy is to be found in 'The Frozen Greenhouse', a poem which recalls Emma Gifford's dismay at St Juliot on discovering that the greenhouse stove had been forgotten the previous evening and her plants killed by the frost. It voices even more Hardy's sense of bereavement after her death:

> The frost is fiercer
> Than then to-day,
> As I pass the place
> Of her once dismay,
> But the greenhouse stands,
> Warm, tight, and gay,
>
> While she who grieved
> At the sad lot
> Of her pretty plants –
> Cold, iced, forgot –
> Herself is colder,
> And knows it not.

So in 'Standing by the Mantelpiece', where Hardy's friend Horace Moule is imagined speaking before his suicide:

> To-night. To me twice night, that should have been
> The radiance of the midmost tick of noon,
> And close around me wintertime is seen
> That might have shone the veriest day of June!

It was with reference to Henchard's loss of the will to live that Hardy animadverted on 'the circumstantial will' at odds with human wishes, as he was to do in the passage already quoted from *Tess of the d'Urbervilles*. 'But the ingenious machinery contrived by the Gods for reducing human possibilities of amelioration to a minimum – which arranges that wisdom to do shall come *pari passu* with the departure of zest for doing' prevented Henchard from making a new start in life. Once again, though only incidentally, Hardy links the conflict of the two wills, the thwarting of enjoyment, with frost. Henchard reflects:

> Here and everywhere be folk dying before their time like frosted leaves though wanted by their families, the country, and the world; while I, an outcast, an encumberer of the ground, wanted by nobody, and despised by all, live on against my will!

At the end of January 1899 Hardy wrote to Mrs Henniker, 'Frost has always a curious effect on my mind, for which I can never account fully – that something is imminent of a tragic nature.'[4] Such an association is to be found in Hardy's works. For example, when Tess on her fruitless mission reached Emminster vicarage, the shrubs on the lawn 'rustled uncomfortably in the frosty breeze', and so nipping was the wind that the ivy leaves 'had become wizened and gray'. Hardy wrote this more than twenty years after 'Neutral Tones', which begins:

> We stood by a pond that winter day,
> And the sun was white, as though chidden of God,
> And a few leaves lay on the starving sod:
> – They had fallen from an ash, and were gray.

The poem concludes:

> Since then, keen lessons that love deceives,
> And wrings with wrong, have shaped to me
> Your face, and the God-curst sun, and a tree,
> – And a pond edged with grayish leaves.

In *Two on a Tower* Lady Constantine is a victim of chance. News comes to her that her husband has died abroad much later than she had previously been informed, so much so that her secret marriage to the young local astronomer Swithin St Cleeve has been illegal. Then, on discovering that by marrying her he had forfeited a substantial annuity and his career prospects, she insists that, as he is legally unmarried, he accept the terms of his uncle's will and travel to further his professional ambition. She has made it a condition that he does not allow his resolve to weaken by writing to her. It is at such a juncture that she finds she is pregnant and his ship has sailed. Her first consideration is whether she will have the courage to 'meet her impending trial singly, 'despising the shame' until he returns at twenty-five to marry her, as the will allowed. Then, with the realization that she would be thirty-five and 'fading to middle-age and homeliness', a 'fear sharp as a frost settled down upon her, that in any such scheme as this, she would be building upon the sand'. An almost identical expression, 'fear fell upon me like frost', occurs in the poem 'Family Portraits'. At the conclusion of 'The Marchioness of Stonehenge' (in *A Group of*

Noble Dames), the view is expressed that 'Lady Caroline's history afforded a sad instance of how an honest human affection will become shamefaced and mean under the frost of class-division and social prejudices'.

The link between frost or winter and hardship or loss is found in other authors. There is a parallel to the winter–June imagery of 'Standing by the Mantelpiece', for example, in *Jane Eyre*, after the heroine's marriage hopes have been dashed. The midsummer and June of the passage are not to be taken literally:

> A Christmas frost had come at midsummer; a white December storm had whirled over June; ice glazed the ripe apples, drifts crushed the blowing roses; on hay-field and corn-field lay a frozen shroud: lanes which last night blushed full of flowers, to-day were pathless with snow; and the woods which twelve hours since waved leafy and fragrant as groves between the tropics, now spread, waste, wild and white as pine-forests in wintry Norway. My hopes were all dead –. . .[5]

Frost imagery occurs at a poignant juncture in Richardson's *Clarissa*: 'All my prospects of felicity, as to this life, are at an end. My hopes, like opening buds or blossoms in an over-forward spring, have been nipt by a severe frost!' And an echo of Wolsey in Shakespeare's *Henry the Eighth* can be heard in this. Frost imagery connoting the death of hope is so common, in fact, that it would not merit this attention unless it had a special personal and philosophical significance for Hardy.

There is evidence that it had tragic associations for him throughout the greater part of his life. The last volume of his poems, not completely prepared for the press when he died, was *Winter Words*; and it contains his most pessimistic statements on the future. One of his earliest recollections was

> being in the garden at Bockhampton with his father on a bitterly cold winter day. They noticed a fieldfare, half-frozen, and the father took up a stone idly and threw it at the bird, possibly not meaning to hit it. The fieldfare fell dead, and the child Thomas picked it up and it was light as a feather, all skin and bone, practically starved. He said he had never forgotten how the body of the fieldfare felt in his hand: the memory had always haunted him.[6]

Another startling boyhood experience remained in his mind as a horrible spectacle of nature's indifference to life. He had been playing second violin to his father, at a 'gentleman-farmer's' party, and they were returning home at three o'clock in the morning: 'It was bitterly cold, and the moon glistened bright upon the encrusted snow, amid which they saw motionless in the hedge what appeared to be a white human figure without a head.'[7] It was a ghastly sight for Thomas, but his father, apprehensive for another reason, went to the rescue of the 'very tall thin man in a long white smock-frock, leaning against the bank in a drunken stupor, his head hanging forward so low that at a distance he had seemed to have no head at all'. Had he been left, he might have frozen to death.

Nevertheless, it is questionable whether the application of wintry imagery to life would have been as marked in Hardy's writing had it not been confirmed by literary influences. Two brief lyrics which could have played a part in this are Keats's 'In a drear-nighted December' and Shelley's 'When the lamp is shattered', the latter with reference to love:

> Its passions will rock thee
> As the storms rock the ravens on high;
> Bright reason will mock thee,
> Like the sun from a wintry sky.
> From thy nest every rafter
> Will rot, and thine eagle home
> Leave thee naked to laughter
> When leaves fall and cold winds come.

It is significant that the first four of these lines are bitterly quoted by Miss Aldclyffe as she remembers her cruel betrayal in love,[8] and that the tragic theme of *A Pair of Blue Eyes* is announced in the singing of the previous four by the ill-starred heroine Elfride:

> O Love! who bewailest
> The frailty of all things here,
> Why choose you the frailest
> For your cradle, your home, and your bier?

In adapting parts of *The Poor Man and the Lady* (first written in 1867) for the composition of 'An Indiscretion in the Life of an Heiress', Hardy undoubtedly kept the chapter epigraphs for the main episodes of his magazine story. One of them consists of the two lines 'Bright reason will mock thee/Like the sun from a wintry sky.' Its context confirms an early imaginative fixation in Hardy of Shelley's mocking wintry sun in association with the wrecking of love, and suggests that the poem 'Neutral Tones' could have developed from the imaginative fusion of Shelley's image with an actual wintry scene. Shelley's influence on Hardy was great, and to understand why this was so with reference to wintry imagery, we have to consider in what respects their thinking was comparable.

In the 1860s Hardy had the courage and integrity to relinquish traditional ideas on Providence in favour of the new scientific views on heredity and evolution, and on the universe at large and in geological time. He recognised that we are in a Darwinian world of imperfection, struggle, and cruelty, where events impinge and proceed by the laws of nature, and where personal choice is determined by the limitations of chance. These include hereditary characteristics as well as external circumstances. It is not wholly a deterministic philosophy but, in the aggregate of things, it often falls very little short of it, since people and nations in crises are actuated by passions and prejudices rather than by reason. As chance falls unequally on people, it is the duty of society and its leaders to remove social and economic injustices, and to use scientific knowledge for the benefit of the human race.

Such thinking permeates Shelley's poetry from *Queen Mab* to *Prometheus Unbound*. It is an essential part of the background to Hardy's most serious writing in fiction, drama, and poetry. Over the years it may have been subject to developments and changes of emphasis, but it never differed radically from the creed of Auguste Comte which had influenced Hardy indirectly in his late twenties through the writings of Mill and Spencer, and directly in his early thirties, if not earlier, through translations.

Before returning to Shelley and what may be regarded as the main literary source for Hardy's frost imagery, I propose to glance at its association with the kind of outlook I have just outlined. The principal topic of the poem 'Discouragement', which he began as early as 1863 (or 1865), is the chance of being handicapped by heredity. The thought suggests frost twice, once as it were on the threshold of consciousness in 'chill' and 'blain'. Nature is distressed that her plans for the ideal are marred by forces beyond her control. 'Over her purposed genial hour' there is a 'chill'; 'upon her charm of flawless flesh a blain'. Her loves (and Hardy is thinking of the human) are

> dependent on a feature's trim,
> A whole life's circumstance on hap of birth,
> A soul's direction on a body's whim,
> Eternal Heaven upon a day of Earth,

and the thought of such natural injustices

> Is frost to flower of heroism and worth,
> And fosterer of visions ghast and grim.

Reference will be made later to winter images in *The Woodlanders*. They are related to two of the dominant features of the novel. The first is the juxtaposition of glimpses of Darwinian nature and the misfortunes of Marty South, Giles Winterborne, Grace Melbury, and her father; Darwinian overtones are more frequent in this novel than anywhere else in Hardy. It goes far to illustrate the working of the imperfect, conscienceless Will, the Unfulfilled Intention, in the Hintocks; and its events are 'part of the pattern in the great web of human doings then weaving in both hemispheres from the White Sea to Cape Horn'. This web of events is the second feature, and Hardy displays great care

in the ramifications of his plot to show how cause and effect are linked
on an extensive and complex scale, so that, for example, but for the
American Civil War and the enforced sale of Marty's tresses, Mrs
Charmond's life might have been prolonged and Grace spared her
reunion with her untrustworthy husband. In *Tess* and *Jude* the web is
less complicated. Heredity plays an important part with each central
character, but much depends on the extraordinary chance that each
has the misfortune to become in turn attractive to, or attracted by,
rather extreme and antithetical types of the opposite sex.

Urged by his modern, Positivist and scientific philosophy, Hardy in
1893, almost at the outset of their long friendship, advised Mrs Henniker that to succeed as a novelist she must 'say now' what the world
would be thinking 'five and twenty years hence'. He regretted that she,
'pre-eminently the child of the Shelleyan tradition', 'should have
allowed herself to be enfeebled to a belief in ritualistic ecclesiasticism'.
The postscript to his next letter ran: 'What I meant about your
unfaithfulness to the Shelley cult referred not to any lack of poetic
emotion, but to your view of things: e.g., you are quite out of harmony
with this line of his in Epipsychidion:

> "The sightless tyrants of our fate"

which beautifully expresses one's consciousness of blind circumstances
beating upon one, without any feeling, for or against.'9 The 'sightless
tyrants' are the forces whereby, to quote 'Discouragement' again,
Nature is 'racked and wrung by her unfaithful lord', so that her role
is that of a 'subaltern':

> – 'I would not freeze thee, shorn one,' cried
>   The North, 'knew I but how
> To warm my breath, to slack my stride;
>   But I am ruled as thou.'10

In 'Epipsychidion', a few lines after 'the sightless tyrants of our fate',
comes the phrase 'the wintry forest of our life'. The ideas in these two
expressions are inseparable; they constitute 'the Frost's decree'. It
appears that Hardy used to read from *Queen Mab and Other Poems*
to his fellow architects at Blomfield's in London.11 The other poems
included 'Alastor', *The Revolt of Islam*, and *Prometheus Unbound*.
In *Queen Mab* Shelley illustrates Nature's ruthlessness from the
'ceaseless frost' of the Polar regions, and stresses its complete indifference to human fate:

> Spirit of Nature; all-sufficing Power
> Necessity! thou mother of the world!
> Unlike the God of human error, thou
> Requir'st no prayers or praises; the caprice

> Of man's weak will belongs no more to thee
> Than do the changeful passions of his breast
> To thy unvarying harmony ...
> No love, no hate thou cherishest ...
> ... all that the wide world contains
> Are but thy passive instruments, and thou
> Regard'st them all with an impartial eye,
> Whose joy or pain thy nature cannot feel,
>> Because thou hast not human sense,
>> Because thou art not human mind.

Hardy wrote, 'the said Cause is neither moral nor immoral, but *un*moral: "loveless and hateless" I have called it, "which neither good nor evil knows" '. He often presents Nature as 'the Mother', blind and insentient. Shelley's note on the passage from *Queen Mab* bears a striking similarity to Hardy's thought and to modern scientific philosophy (see p. 152).

In *The Revolt of Islam* we voyage figuratively to 'the warm home of human destiny'; and 'warm' is opposed to 'winter' in Shelley's imaginative thought. If a happier civilization is to be created, it can come only through man's efforts. Why place one's hopes on an unknown power that is responsible for

> Blight, Poison, Earthquake, Hail, and Snow,
> Disease, and Want, and worse Necessity
> Of hate and ill, and Pride, and Fear, and Tyranny!

The theme is the forerunner of *Prometheus Unbound*. The key to the future is 'Gentleness, Virtue, Wisdom, and Endurance'; 'to love and bear'; all that Hardy sums up in Christian 'charity'. The hope expressed in *The Revolt of Islam* is the faith which inspires *A Defence of Poetry*, that 'poets' – great thinkers, statemen, artists, writers – will create progressive ideas for the future. The idea dramatically conveyed in Shaw's *Saint Joan* is expressed by Shelley in this way:

> The good and mighty of departed ages
>> Are in their graves, the innocent and free,
> Heroes, and Poets, and prevailing Sages,
>> Who leave the vesture of their majesty
>> To adorn and clothe this naked world; – and we
> Are like to them – such perish, but they leave
>> All hope, or love, or truth, or liberty,
> Whose form their mighty spirits could conceive,
> To be a rule and law to ages that survive.

The same idea appears in imagery of the seasons:

The blasts of Autumn drive the wingèd seeds
  Over the earth, – next come the snows, and rain,
And frosts, and storms, which dreary Winter leads
  Out of his Scythian cave, a savage train;
  Behold! Spring sweeps o'er the world again . . .

O Spring, of hope, and love, and youth, and gladness
  Wind-wingèd emblem! . . .
Virtue, and Hope, and Love, like light and Heaven,
  Surround the world. . . .
  Lo, Winter comes! – the grief of many graves,
The frost of death, the tempest of the sword,
  The flood of tyranny, whose sanguine waves
Stagnate like ice at Faith the enchanter's word,
And bind all human hearts in its repose abhorred.

The seeds are sleeping in the soil. . . .[12]

These ideas are familiar from Shelley's 'Ode to the West Wind':

Drive my dead thoughts over the universe
Like withered leaves to quicken a new birth!
And, by the incantation of this verse,

Scatter, as from an unextinguished hearth,
Ashes and sparks, my words among mankind!
Be through my lips to unawakened earth

The trumpet of a prophecy! O, Wind,
If Winter comes, can Spring be far behind?

There is good reason to think that Hardy in 1866–7, before he left London, was more political, and more optimistic about reform, than he was in his later years. Nevertheless, there is no doubt that in his last three great novels, he set himself more and more to write imaginative stories that would move readers to press for a more liberal and humane society. He sensed, as Philip Sidney demonstrated in his *Apologie for Poetrie*, that a moving story would have more appeal than exhortation or reasoning. That such was his aim may be seen in the 1895 preface to *The Woodlanders*, where he refers to the question of 'how to afford the greatest happiness to the units of human society during their brief transit through this sorry world' (the last phrase almost an exact echo of words in the tragic conclusion of *The Mayor of Casterbridge*). It appears in the poem 'A Plaint to Man', where the hypothetical God affirms that human welfare depends on 'the human heart's resource alone', on 'brotherhood' and 'loving-kindness', and nothing outside human scope. This was the philosophy Hardy had learnt in the 1870s from the writings of the French philosopher Comte.

Hardy's association of winter and frost with obstacles in the way of human happiness, or with the failure of 'the will to enjoy' in the struggle with 'the circumstantial will against enjoyment', seems very decided in his early poetry and fiction. It appears in the poem he wrote for his employer, probably just before he left London. A footnote indicates that it was composed in 1867 at 8 Adelphi Terrace. The poem, 'Heiress and Architect', is contrived with such cunning that one must assume that Hardy wrote the fair copy of the completed poem at Blomfield's offices. Whatever her expectations, the heiress's plans can never be fulfilled. The house of her dreams is life, and – as Hardy was to write much later – 'Life offers – to deny!' The architect is an archdesigner, and in him Hardy's Prime Cause or Shelley's 'all-sufficing Power, Necessity' is dramatically personified. What he signifies is manifest when he counters her first expectations:

> 'An idle whim!'
> Broke forth from him
> Whom nought could warm to gallantries:
> 'Cede all these buds and birds, the zephyr's call,
> And scents, and hues, and things that falter all,
> And choose as best the close and surly wall,
> For winters freeze.'

'Neutral Tones' was also written in London in 1867. It is not certain that the 'pond edged with grayish leaves' is in any way associated with Rushy Pond, but it is worth noting that the fickle lover's song 'I Said and Sang Her Excellence' was written by the side of it. The frosty tones of the poet in the first certainly contrast with the insincerity of the lover in the second:

> 'She moves a sylph in picture-land
> Where nothing frosts the air',

but the poem recalls 'Heiress and Architect' even more:

> I sang of her in a dim old hall
> Dream-built too fancifully.

On leaving London for Dorset, Hardy set to work on his first novel *The Poor Man and the Lady*. It was romantic, but also political, and too bluntly satirical to find a publisher. His first published novel was *Desperate Remedies*, an ingenious but crudely sensational story, with admirable poetry in some of its texture. In particular it reveals the crystallization of wintry imagery with the bleak philosophical outlook that won Hardy's approval in Shelley's earlier work. The context is the prospective marriage between the heroine Cytherea and the (as yet undisclosed) villain Manston. Like the more tragic Tess, she sacrifices herself in marriage (legalized in this instance) for the sake of her family (her brother, the only survivor, who, it is feared, needs expensive medical treatment for a long period). On the night before her wedding,

Cytherea is disturbed by the rattling of a tree below her window; in the morning she finds that there has been a hoary drizzle, and that trees and shrubs are laden with icicles 'to an extent such as she had never before witnessed'. Boughs are bent to the earth; many have snapped off. She could never have believed that 'trees would bend so far out of their true positions without breaking' or that she could 'so exactly have imitated them'. She has a sudden access of hope: perhaps the weather will make it impossible to hold the wedding-service; perhaps it is 'a scheme of the great Mother to hinder a union of which she does not approve'. It is strange that Hardy should have referred to Nature as the 'great Mother' in a novel which was intended to be popular, but its conjunction with severe wintry condition is consistent with their association in his poems; and it is quite possible that these emblematic wintry scenes in *Desperate Remedies* were transferred and developed from *The Poor Man and the Lady*, first written in the latter half of 1867, not long after Hardy's two-year immersion in poetry and the writing of poetry.

Unfortunately there is a change of weather, and the wedding does take place. The hero Edward Springrove, 'who had stolen her heart away, and still kept it', arrives too late, and by chance he and Cytherea meet before her departure. They are separated by a river; over it hangs a large dead tree, thickly robed in ivy and 'considerably depressed by its icy load'. The imaginative tones are obvious; in this severing scene the frost is ancillary to the river, which is indifferent (like the great Mother) and flows on 'as quietly and obtusely as ever'.[13] There were severing scenes in Hardy's life more than twenty years after the publication of *Desperate Remedies*. The first of the 'In Tenebris' poems begins:

> Wintertime nighs;
> But my bereavement-pain
> It cannot bring again:
> Twice no man dies.
>
> Flower-petals flee;
> But, since it once hath been,
> No more that severing scene
> Can harrow me.
>
> Birds faint in dread:
> I shall not lose old strength
> In the lone frost's black length:
> Strength long since fled!
>
> Leaves freeze to dun;
> But friends can not turn cold
> This season as of old
> For him with none.

Hardy may have alluded to this period in 'The Something that Saved Him':

> In that day
> Unseeing the azure went I
> On my way
> And to white winter bent I,
> Knowing no May.

The ruined garden of Shelley's 'The Sensitive Plant' presents an emblem of the world as it is. When winter comes, only the 'loathliest weeds' prosper –

> thistles, and nettles, and darnels rank,
> And the dock, and henbane, and hemlock dank;

by the end of the winter

> The Sensitive Plant was a leafless wreck;
> But the mandrakes, and toadstools, and docks, and darnels,
> Rose like the dead from their ruined charnels.

When Cytherea's helplessness in the circumstances which compelled her marriage struck her, she stood with Manston in a meadow by 'the fragment of a hedge – all that remained of a "wet old garden" –... It was overgrown, and choked with mandrakes, and she could almost fancy she heard their shrieks.' In *Far from the Madding Crowd* when Bathsheba discovers Troy's treachery she leaves home and wakes up by a swamp dotted with fungi and rotting tree-stumps; with the red and yellow leaves in her lap Hardy reminds us of Shelley's 'Ode to the West Wind'. Late autumn and winter draw on apace, and soon she is left to ponder 'what a gift life used to be'. Eustacia Vye attempts her escape from Egdon Heath on a night of funereal gloom when she is full of a sense of the injustice of her lot. It is November, and she stumbles over 'twisted furze-roots, tufts of rushes, or oozing lumps of fleshy fungi, which at this season lay scattered about the heath like the rotten liver and lungs of some colossal animal'. In the woods, when all goes ill for Grace Melbury, the scene is more Darwinian, but fallen leaves, bright fungi, and rotting stumps confront her. These passages suggest that Hardy had adopted Shelley's imagery, and was in danger of resorting to it almost automatically.

The Woodlanders presents wintry touches in close association with tragic situations, but perhaps the dominant climatic feature is the fog which Hardy uses with Norse overtones to reinforce the theme of unfulfilment. Yet it should not be overlooked that the novel opens on a winter's day, and with Marty South, who continues to learn uncomplainingly the lesson of self-denial and endurance; that the first wintry dawn is sunless, the bleared visage of the day emerging like a dead-born child; and that the tragic hero is Winterborne, his name indicative of mischance and suffering. 'When the sun shines flat on the north front of Sherton Abbey – that's when my happiness will come to me', he concludes.

Six consecutive poems in *Poems of the Past and the Present* relate to 'the Frost's decree'. Nearly all are about birds; and birds in Hardy frequently symbolize man or woman (nearly always the latter) trapped and suffering through the workings of chance. Three of the poems may seem literal, but the subject of 'The Puzzled Game-Birds' ('The Battue' in the Wessex Edition) is clearly indicated in a poem written by Hardy as early as 1866: 'That Sportsman Time but rears his brood to kill.' Similar human overtones will be found in the two other triolets in this group: 'Birds at Winter Nightfall', and 'Winter in Durnover Field' with its repeated lament: 'Throughout the field I find no grain:/The cruel frost encrusts the cornland.' In 'The Last Chrysanthemum' the question is raised:

> Had it a reason for delay,
> Dreaming in witlessness
> That for a bloom so delicately gay
> Winter would stay its stress?

Hardy comments:

> – I talk as if the thing were born
> With sense to work its mind;
> Yet it is but one mask of many worn
> By the Great Face behind.

The Great Face is inscrutable; God moves in a mysterious way.

The first and last of the six poems raise the question whether people know more about the nature of things than do the lesser creatures. 'The Caged Thrush Freed and Home Again' concludes:

> They cannot change the Frost's decree,
> They cannot keep the sky serene;
> How happy days are meant to be
>
> Eludes great Man's sagacity
> No less than ours, O tribes in treen!
> Men know but little more than we
> How happy days are meant to be.

In 'The Darkling Thrush' Hardy is even more modest. No other poem expresses his pessimism more admirably through imagery. At the end of the year and of the century, everything in the scene reflects his outlook. The frost is 'spectre-gray'; the weakening daylight is made desolate by 'Winter's dregs'; the landscape appears like the 'Century's corpse':

> The ancient pulse of germ and birth
> Was shrunken hard and dry,
> And every spirit upon earth
> Seemed fervourless as I.

Suddenly there breaks into his wintry musings the 'full-hearted even-song' of 'An aged thrush, frail, gaunt, and small/In blast-beruffled plume' among 'the bleak twigs overhead'. So great is the contrast and so inexplicable the bird's happiness that Hardy wonders if, after all, he has drawn the wrong conclusions about life.

There is no point in saying that Hardy quarrelled with Providence; he could not believe in it. He must have reflected often on the happier outlook of his immediate predecessor, the Dorset poet William Barnes, whose Christian faith no adversity could extinguish and who, in a poem with the philosophical title 'Rivers Don't Gi'e Out', wrote:

> An' yet, while things do come an' goo,
> God's love is steadvast, John, an' true;
> If winter vrost do chill the ground,
> 'Tis but to bring the zummer round,
> All's well a-lost where He's a-vound,
> Vor if 'tis right, vor Christes seäke
> He'll gi'e us mwore than he do teäke, –
> His goodness don't gi'e out, John.

So great was Hardy's sense of imperfection and unmerited suffering in the whole living world that he could sympathize with those who pre-sumed that man could have planned the universe more wisely than the Creator. Yet we must not take the poem 'Could I but Will' too seriously:

> Even half-god power
> In spinning dooms
> Had I, this frozen scene should flower,
> And sand-swept plains and Arctic glooms
> Should green them gay with waving leaves,
> Mid which old friends and I would walk
> With weightless feet and magic talk
> Uncounted eves.

The last lines show that this 'song' was no more than a day-dream. Elsewhere we can see that Hardy had no time for the 'self-glamourer' whose 'trustful daring undoubt' made him count his

> springtime-day's
> Dream of futurity
> Enringed with golden rays
> To be quite a summer surety,

but who, though he believes his dreams have come true, can never be quite certain of the future:

> My years in trusting spent
> Make to shape towardly,
> And fate and accident
> Behave not perversely or frowardly.
> Shall, then, Life's winter snow
> To me be so?

If Hardy indulged in 'some blessed Hope', it was surely when he came to the closing lines of *The Dynasts*. The 'consciousness' which he thought might inform the Will 'till It fashions all things fair' was that of mankind, the most important part of 'the general Will'. Then came the First World War, which made Hardy regret that he had ever voiced such optimism. 'By truth made free', he preferred 'a full look at the Worst'. His belief in altruism and the brotherhood of man continued to receive setbacks in the post-war years; the prevailing lack of 'far-sight'[14] made him return to the view that man was swayed not by reason but by some 'demonic force'.[15] It is interesting to see that his blame falls less on some Ultimate, whom he had come to acknowledge as 'unknowable', than on man, for his 'hideous self-treason', his failure to behave sensibly for the sake of the human race in general:

> We are getting to the end of visioning
> The impossible within this universe,
> Such as that better whiles may follow worse,
> And that our race may mend by reasoning.

Significantly he concluded his last volume of poetry with two of his most pessimistic utterances, and gave the whole collection the title *Winter Words*.

9 Hardy and Myth

Myth has become such a mazy academic subject, and the term is used and misused with such a variety of meaning that it is essential at the outset to state its implications for the present subject. I assume that myths are religious in origin, and relate to gods or similar personalized powers, that they were thought to reveal inescapable truths about the universe and nature, and that, even though their narrative features are fictitious, they can be used imaginatively by virtue of their original significance to reinforce or symbolize aspects of life.

I propose to discuss the functioning of images from four mythologies in four of Hardy's novels: Greek mythology in *The Return of the Native*, Norse in *The Woodlanders*, Christian in *Jude the Obscure*, and Hardy's own mythology in *Tess of the d'Urbervilles*. The question implicit in the Greek mythology of *The Return of the Native* is revived in *Tess* and *Jude*, but Norse mythology with non-literal, human overtones is confined to *The Woodlanders*, and Christian to *Jude the Obscure*. Though Hardy did not make his own mythology explicit until he had renounced prose fiction for poetry, he alludes to it several times in his novels. He refers to the First Cause under one name or another, and once at least, rather egregiously, to Nature as 'the great Mother'. It is only, I believe, in certain episodes of *Tess of the d'Urbervilles* that his mythical interpretation of the universe assumes a creative role, becoming an indissoluble part of the narrative, or directing and permeating a dramatic action.

* * *

Eustacia Vye's Greek associations are well known. Much is made of them in that overcharged, extra-dimensional chapter 'Queen of Night'. Her father was Greek by birth, a native of Corfu: 'Where did her dignity come from? By a latent vein from Alcinous' line, her father hailing from Phaeacia's isle?' Elsewhere he is referred to as 'a romantic wanderer – a sort of Greek Ulysses'. Hardy describes Eustacia as Clym's 'Olympian girl'. The spot which forms on her arm from Susan Nonsuch's needle jab appears 'like a ruby on Parian marble'. In a dim light her 'general figure' recalls Greek goddesses:

> The new moon behind her head, an old helmet upon it, a diadem of accidental dewdrops round her brow, would have been adjuncts

sufficient to strike the note of Artemis, Athena, or Hera respectively, with as close an approximation to the antique as that which passes muster on many respected canvases.

She is 'the raw material of a divinity' and, with a little preparation, would have done well on Olympus.

Unfortunately Eustacia is on Egdon, and Egdon is her Hades. Her second misfortune is that she lives in a world of day-dream, and falls in love with Clym Yeobright before she sees him. The 'iris-hued embowment' with which she envisions him (to use Hardy's later expression for the illusion of a lover's dream) proceeds from the perfervid hope that he will be her means of escape to the gaiety and splendour of Paris. As she has no other choice for the fulfilment of her aspirations, it is a confounding irony of chance that the imaginary saviour returns to his native heath completely disillusioned with the vanity and flashiness of city life, and haunted by a sense of 'the whole creation groaning and travailing in pain'. All for 'plain living and high thinking', he is happy on Egdon, and wishes above all to be of service to his fellowmen. When her prospects of life and happiness in Paris recede, she thinks of the flight of time; as the sand in her hour-glass slips away, the moon's eclipse grows. The altruism of Clym Yeobright conflicts with the hedonism of Eustacia.

Her protest against the restrictions of circumstance is manifested symbolically in her bonfire, the brightest of all those lighting up the heath as the pagan ritual is renewed at the onset of winter. This ritual is described as 'Promethean', and its parallel in Eustacia is clear: she has 'Pagan eyes, full of nocturnal mysteries'. Her essence is 'flame-like'; her 'smouldering rebelliousness' against Egdon gives her a 'true Tartarean dignity'. Not until her marriage to Clym does she realize that there is no hope of changing his purpose. When she is stung to protest against his submission in adversity, he replies:

> Now, don't you suppose, my inexperienced girl, that I cannot rebel, in high Promethean fashion, against the gods and fate as well as you. I have felt more steam and smoke of that sort than you have heard of. But the more I see of life the more do I perceive that there is nothing particularly great in its greatest walks, and therefore nothing particularly small in mine of furze-cutting. If I feel that the greatest blessings vouchsafed to us are not very valuable, how can I feel it to be any great hardship when they are taken away? So I sing to pass the time.

The result is that Eustacia battles against depression, and goes to a gipsying, an outdoor dance, with Wildeve; she floats round and round on his arm in pagan ecstasy.

In the theme-chapter which introduces the novel, Hardy tells us that

Egdon spells endurance, and that only a 'most thorough-going ascetic'
(like Clym) could feel a 'natural right' to wander there. The heath is
one of those places 'wearing a sombreness distasteful to our race when it
was young' but appealing to 'a more recently learnt emotion' than
'that which responds to the sort of beauty called charming and fair'.
With thoughts akin to these Hardy wrote in January 1887: 'Nature is
played out as a Beauty,... The "simply natural" is interesting no
longer ... – it is ... the style of a period when the mind is serene and
unawakened to the tragical mysteries of life.' The pagan ecstasy which
Eustacia savours with Wildeve is a reminder of an earlier civilization to
whom the sombreness of 'haggard Egdon' would have seemed repug-
nant. The main theme of *The Return of the Native* is the irreconcilability of Hellenism with the modern Positivist philosophy which
Hardy hoped would form the basis of 'the new religion': an alliance
between Christian ethics and the best of modern science, its intellectual
aim truth, its moral aim altruism.

There can be little doubt that Hardy was much influenced by the
essay on Winckelmann in Walter Pater's *Studies in the History of the
Renaissance* (1873). Pater, and Arnold after him, contrasted Greek
sensuousness and Christian asceticism; but the deep impact Pater made
on Hardy was due to his success in formulating the dilemma of the
modern artist. In the 'bewildering toils' of immutable laws operating
through the universe and within the individual, how could one attain
the Greek ideal of 'balance' and 'serenity' in presenting tragic issues?
Jude the Obscure shows that the tragic consequence of natural laws
may be inherent (from the chance of heredity and circumstance), or
may arise from their incompatibility with the *mores* of a particular
society. This is the kind of context which explains why the contrast
drawn by Pater between Hellenic and advanced modern philosophy
found a permanent lodgement in Hardy's mind. He alluded to it not
long before his death in the introductory note to his last volume of
poetry.

'The longer we contemplate that Hellenic ideal, in which man is at
unity with himself,' writes Pater, 'the more we may be inclined to regret
that he should ever have passed beyond it, to contend for a perfection
that makes the blood turbid, and frets the flesh, and discredits the actual
world about us.' In Clym one can see the 'parasite' thought 'ruthlessly'
at work; it is 'a disease of the flesh', and indirectly he 'bore evidence
that ideal physical beauty is incompatible with emotional development
and a full recognition of the coil of things'. After the death of Eustacia,
he knows this coil from his own involvement and inadequacy, and he
remains quite unfitted by philosophy and experience to share the
'instincts of merry England' and participate in Maytime revels deeply
rooted in pagan impulses.

The latent dichotomy of a note made by Hardy in 1876 from John

Addington Symonds on the Greek philosophy of life, 'What Clough described as a "Stoic-Epicurean acceptance" of the world', probably gave greater emphasis to Clym's thematic role as the protagonist who endures. Arnold's essay 'Pagan and Mediaeval Religious Sentiment' undoubtedly influenced Hardy's modification of Eustacia. When he read this essay, at least fifteen chapters of *The Return of the Native* had been completed,[1] but he replanned and rewrote much of what had been written before he produced the novel as we know it. Its first seven chapters were not finished until the end of August 1877, nearly five months after he had completed the fifteen chapters of the first version.

When Arnold writes on the 'ideal, cheerful, sensuous, pagan life' that is not 'sick or sorry', or the 'gay sensuous pagan life' that had gone when St Francis stirred 'the heart and imagination' of the poor, he comes nearer the hedonistic side of Hardy's subject than Pater does; and it is significant that, in speaking of Heine's reaction against Christian asceticism and his championship of 'the warm and glowing motions of sense', he comments: 'That is Heine's sentiment, in the prime of life, in the glow of activity, amid the brilliant whirl of Paris.' Paris and 'the warm and glowing motions of sense' cannot be dissociated from Eustacia.

Clym's asceticism is not Arnold's 'mediaeval sentiment'. In his face could be seen 'the typical countenance of the future' as Hardy foresaw it. He thought that the view of life 'as a thing to be put up with, replacing that zest for existence which was so intense in early civilizations', must ultimately change the facial expression of advanced nations. This view of life, in attuning Clym to Egdon, makes him incompatible with Eustacia; his humanitarian aims soon make him impatient with her 'sentiment on the wisdom of *Carpe diem*'.

> The truth seems to be that a long line of disillusive centuries has permanently displaced the Hellenic idea of life, or whatever it may be called. What the Greeks only suspected we know well; what their Aeschylus imagined our nursery children feel. That old-fashioned revelling in the general situation grows less and less possible as we uncover the defects of natural laws, and see the quandary that man is in by their operation.

The reference to 'natural laws' shows the writer's philosophical kinship with Pater. Clym's views coincided with those of Hardy and J. S. Mill. Discussing Rousseau in his treatise *On Liberty* (which Hardy had known 'almost by heart'), Mill maintains that 'The superior worth of simplicity of life, the enervating and demoralizing effect of the trammels and hypocrisies of artificial society, are ideas . . . needing to be asserted as much as ever, and to be asserted by deeds, for words, on this subject, have nearly exhausted their power.' The 'Sermons on the Mount' which Clym delivered on Rainbarrow were not restricted to Christian ethics;

sometimes they were secular, sometimes religious. He sought to promote the enlightenment and progress of his fellow-men, altruism or 'the eleventh commandment'[2] being the key to the religion of the future. 'He was a John the Baptist who took ennoblement rather than repentance as his text. Mentally he was in a provincial future, that is, he was in many points abreast with the central town thinkers of his date.'[3]

Here Hardy was probably thinking of men like Mill, to whom he had listened in London.[4] There can be no doubt that Hardy had thought seriously of what he could do for mankind. He had been interested in political reform; he was interested in education; before being converted to Mill's 'religion of the future', he had aspired to be a country parson like William Barnes (writing poetry in his spare time); and his later writings show more and more openly the critical boldness of his altruism. Towards the end of his life, when he was losing faith in mankind, he asked himself why he went on writing, and decided that he must continue to write as long as he lived in a world of pain.[5] That is how Clym Yeobright felt; he could not live for his own ease and pleasure in a world 'groaning and travailing in pain'.

If therefore Eustacia's self-seeking may be regarded as in any way Promethean (as Hardy suggests), it is polarized by the idealism of Clym as a Promethean light-bringer to a people in darkness. Yet he fails to carry conviction. Clym, like Eustacia, is a dreamer, but they live in two different dream-worlds. Her wish to escape from Egdon or the harsher realities is dramatized in the storm scene on the night of her death. The storm is Egdon's lover, and the wind its friend.[6] Clym is at home there, but is too sanguine about man's readiness for enlightenment, and fails to realize that most people prefer material advancement to 'plain living and high thinking'. Hardy had noticed that the 'religious sincerity' of Mill's speech 'was jarred on by his environment – a group on the hustings who, with few exceptions, did not care to understand him fully, and a crowd below who could not', though they were not wholly unimpressed. Nor does Clym quite convince the reader; and the reason for this, I believe, is that, while the pagan and hedonistic Eustacia appealed to Hardy's imagination, his response to Clym was primarily intellectual and idealistic. In the gathering gloom at the beginning of the novel Eustacia makes a more impressive figure on Rainbarrow than Clym in the daylight at the end. A degree of anticlimax was inevitable in the conclusion of *The Return of the Native*, whatever happened to Diggory Venn.

*   *   *

The theme of *The Return of the Native* is summed up in the words, 'That old-fashioned revelling in the general situation grows less and less possible as we uncover the defects of natural laws . . .'. They could serve as the epigraph to *The Woodlanders*. This novel, like Yell'ham

Wood, signifies a 'thwarted purposing'; 'Life offers – to deny!'[7] The key to the dominant idea and feature of the novel is supplied in this passage:

> On older trees ... huge lobes of fungi grew like lungs. Here, as every-where, the Unfulfilled Intention, which makes life what it is, was as obvious as it could be among the depraved crowds of a city slum.

Hardy argued that, as man's awareness has evolved so far by natural law, it is unfortunate that the Creator has not mended matters 'by a second intent and execution', the elimination of evil in nature. If natural law had consciousness, 'how the aspect of its creatures would terrify it, fill it with remorse!'[8] In *The Woodlanders* he continually presents glimpses of the outer Darwinian world to reinforce the tragedy of the human situation:

> They halted beneath a half-dead oak, hollow and disfigured with tumours, its roots spreading out like claws grasping the ground. A chilly wind circled round them, upon whose currents the seeds of a neighbouring lime-tree, supported parachute-wise by the wing attached, flew out of the boughs downwards like fledglings from the nest. The vale was wrapped in a dim atmosphere of unnaturalness, and the east was like a livid curtain edged with pink.

Here we have description at three levels. The descent of the winged lime-seeds shows the observation of the poet; the distant scene is pre-monitory, hinting at disaster (Grace realizes, and her father is begin-ning to suspect, Fitzpiers' treachery); and the consumption at the heart of the oak (sharpened by the image of roots like claws) accentuates the cruelty of fate.

Grace Melbury is the victim of circumstances, of her father's ambition particularly, and of her own inherited weakness of will. Both characters are central to the suffering of the novel, but in the end one's sympathies remain unequivocally with Giles Winterborne and Marty South, both thwarted and unfulfilled in their lives, the stoic victims of chance. It is with them that images from Norse mythology are signifi-cantly linked.

The novel presents sunny woodland scenes and one particularly bright landscape, but its prevailing tone is sombre. Characteristically it opens in a 'tomb-like' silence on a winter's day. The first dawn has a 'bleared white visage' which emerges 'like a dead-born child'; soon 'the regular dripping of the fog from the plantation boughs around' is heard. Sunlessness, fog, winter, decay and death, in addition to images revealing the cruelty of nature, are important features of scenes which mirror the human situation.

The network of chance or causality is particularly elaborate. If there had been no American Civil War, and if Marty South had not had beautiful hair, Mrs Charmond would not have died as she did. Hardy seems to make a point of showing that the 'lonely courses' of Little Hintock inhabitants 'formed no detached design at all, but were part of the pattern in the great web of human doings then weaving in both hemispheres from the White Sea to Cape Horn'. It was 'but a cast in the die of destiny' that Marty South should be cutting spars late into the night. When she finished at three o'clock in the morning, she looked out:

> The night in all its fulness met her flatly on the threshold, like the very brink of an absolute void, or the ante-mundane Ginnung-Gap believed in by her Teuton forefathers.

The 'ante-mundane Ginnung-Gap' (the void before the earth was created, according to Norse mythology) expresses the emptiness or bleakness of Marty's life.

After hearing that Giles Winterborne is not for her, she cuts off her long locks of hair for the guineas and her invalided father. She has accepted her self-sacrificial role. Her hair lay on the 'pale scrubbed deal' of a coffin-stool table like 'waving and ropy weeds over the washed white bed of a stream'. She would not turn to the looking-glass, 'knowing what a deflowered visage would look back at her, and almost break her heart; she dreaded it as much as did her own ancestral goddess the reflection in the pool after the rape of her locks by Loke the Malicious'.

The next Norse reference occurs after the Unfulfilled Intention passage. Giles follows Melbury and Grace in the wood.

> They dived amid beeches under which nothing grew, the younger boughs still retaining their hectic leaves, that rustled in the breeze with a sound almost metallic, like the sheet-iron foliage of the fabled Jarnvid wood.

Hardy may have been familiar with the Jarnvid wood image in Arnold's *Balder Dead*, a poem which probably suggested the symbolic application of the last and most important Norse reference in *The Woodlanders*. This is to Niflheim, Hela's gloomy realm, where the sad spirits of those who have died of sickness or old age, the unfulfilled, as opposed to those who lived and died heroically, were doomed to remain.

One strangely fascinating feature of Hardy's story arises from the tree which appears to have a hold on John South's life. The source of this animistic belief seems to be no more than local tradition:

> The shape of it seems to haunt him like an evil spirit. He says that it is exactly his own age, that it has got human sense, and sprouted up when he was born on purpose to rule him, and keep him as its slave. Others have been like it afore in Hintock.

South had intended chopping it down when it was small and he was a boy. It had never forgiven him, he believed, 'And at last it got too big, and now 'tis my enemy, and will be the death of me.' This mania is driving him demented: 'As the tree waved South waved his hand, making it his fugleman with abject obedience.'

To spare his torments and save his life, Giles is persuaded to lop off the lower boughs. As he worked upwards one afternoon it grew dark and misty. In the evening gloom and thickened fog, he was no more than 'a dark grey spot on the light grey zenith' when Grace returned to tell him they were still close friends despite her acquiescence in her father's will. Giles, however, like Marty, had accepted his fate. He remained aloft till the fog and the night completely obscured him from Grace's view. If only he had come down immediately, 'something might have been done' (Hardy says) which would have raised his hopes. 'But he continued motionless and silent in that gloomy Niflheim or fogland which involved him, and she proceeded on her way.'

It might be thought that the fog represents the ignorance in which Giles works. He does not know how Grace feels; he does not know that by lopping off the boughs to save South's life he is helping, in Hardy's proleptic phrase, to fray it away. Nor is he aware that his action is the first step towards his own doom. Yet the emphasis at this point is on the blanketing-out of Winterborne's hopes, and the loss of Grace; this is confirmed by the synonymous linking of 'fogland' and 'Niflheim', to express the resignation or gloom of one who remains unfulfilled, like the spirits of Hela's realm.

*   *   *

Although he returned to it time and time again over a long period, Hardy never seemed quite satisfied with his plan for *Jude the Obscure*. Perhaps he was attempting too much; perhaps at the crucial period he had neither the time nor the calm of mind to achieve all that he aimed at. It contains some of his most dramatic and poignant scenes, probably not a far cry from his own matrimonial dilemma. Undoubtedly the idealization of Mrs Henniker and her refusal to be emancipated by his arguments against 'ritualistic ecclesiasticism' and 'retrograde superstitions' had much to do with the final recasting of the plan for his novel.[9]

Paradigmatically, taking the unformalized marriage of Jude and Sue as the point of intersection, it is a cross. Disaster makes Sue give up her modern emancipated outlook for 'ritualistic ecclesiasticism'. Jude's course is the reverse; after studying for the Church, he burns his books and adopts contemporary rationalistic views, regarding Sue's return to conformity and Phillotson as the effect of 'retrograde superstitions'.

When Hardy told Edmund Gosse that 'the plot is almost geometrically constructed', he seems to have had this cruciformity of design

in mind. He claims that it was not consciously planned; 'the characters
necessitated it, and I simply let it come'. In choosing to call Oxford
'Christminster', however, there can be no doubt that he was thinking
of the Crucifixion, and it is significant that the doomed sufferers first
meet in Christminster 'at the cross in the pavement which marked the
spot of the Martyrdom', and that Jude begins his 'ministry' at Melchester at the age of thirty, 'an age which much attracted him as being
that of his exemplar when he first began to teach in Galilee'.

The name 'Jude' is linked with Judah and Jerusalem. When the boy
Jude first sees Christminster, distance lends it enchantment; it is a city
of light like the New Jerusalem.[10] Heaven lies about us in our infancy,
but the 'gleam and glory' of its lights seem dubious at close view.
Allusions to 'Intimations of Immortality' link experiences which are
years apart. There is no moonshine when Jude finds the colleges; they
are decrepit, with unillumined corners, and many shadows cast by contemporary lights around them. This is the first step of disillusionment
towards the prospect of Sarcophagus College, 'silent, black and window-
less' with 'four centuries of gloom, bigotry, and decay'.

Merged dramatically in this story is the debate between Hellenism
and Christian asceticism. Sue's views are Heine's, and when Jude rejects
Christian theology, the two resolve 'to make a virtue of joy'. When they
are happy, she says, 'I feel we have returned to Greek joyousness, and
have blinded ourselves to sickness and sorrow.' 'The ideal, cheerful,
sensuous pagan life is not sick or sorry', Arnold wrote.

When Jude reaches Christminster with Sue and his children it is
'Remembrance Day'. The parallel between Commemoration Week at
Oxford and the week of the Passover is made evident when Sue speaks
of coming up to 'Jerusalem' to see the 'festival', and describes 'leaving
Kennetbridge for this place' as 'like coming from Caiaphas to Pilate'.
She loses her children, is smitten with a sense of sinful indulgence in
the past, and decides to mortify the flesh ('the terrible flesh – the curse
of Adam'), take to ritualistic ecclesiasticism, and accept conformity and
(as Jude sees it) a 'fanatic prostitution' to Phillotson.

Both Sue and Jude are slowly crucified during the subsequent year.
We are reminded of the Crucifixion when Jude first accepts her loss:
'Then let the veil of our temple be rent in twain from this hour', he
says. And when she is faced with the duty of self-sacrifice to her licensed
husband, she does not wish the cup to pass from her but will drink it
'to the dregs'. As Mrs Edlin says, her re-wedding is like a funeral.
So too is Jude's. When he realizes that Sue still loves him, he makes no
effort to live. His request for water recalls the Johannine account of the
Crucifixion. The sounds of 'Remembrance games' as Jude is dying are
another reminder of the Passover festival.

References to the Crucifixion and events leading up to it are not
mythological in themselves, yet, as one quotation has already hinted,

they are ancillary to the myth of Adam and sin and Redemption. Twice Sue asserts that her children have died to save her from sin, and in fact Little Father Time takes the lives of the other two children and his own to spare the parents. The sight of the three hanging children is a ghastly travesty of the Crucifixion:

> The boy's face expressed the whole tale of their situation. On that little shape had converged all the inauspiciousness and shadow which had darkened the first union of Jude, and all the accidents, mistakes, fears, errors of the last. He was their nodal point, their focus, their expression in a single term. For the rashness of those parents he had groaned, for their ill-assortment he had quaked, and for the misfortunes of these he had died.

Here matrimonial incompatibilities and their hereditary effects are vaguely linked to the Christian myth of sin and redemption. 'For the rashness of those parents he had groaned' alludes unmistakably to Milton's *Paradise Lost* and to the Crucifixion. Hardy seems to be obsessed to the point of morbidity with this imaginative motif. He prepares us for it very slightly by presenting Little Father Time as a 'Divinity', though 'enslaved and dwarfed by his mortal condition'. 'A ground swell from ancient years of night seemed now and then to lift the child in this his morning-life, when his face took a back view over some great Atlantic of Time, and appeared not to care about what it saw.'

This seems to hint at hereditary disposition and outlook, but there is nothing in the presentation of the story to make the death of Sue's children convincing, or to explain it completely with reference to Hardy's statement that the novel was concerned, not with 'the marriage question' but with 'the tragic issues of two bad marriages, owing in the main to the doom or curse of hereditary temperament peculiar to the family of the parties'. What we hear on this doom is almost peripheral – hints and reminders; nowhere is it felt to be a living or essential part of the tragic action. Before his involvement with Sue, Jude reflects that, 'were he free, in a family like his own where marriage usually meant a tragic sadness, marriage with a blood-relation would duplicate the adverse conditions, and a tragic sadness might be intensified to a tragic horror'. Here are united the 'three enormous reasons' against his being intimate with Sue, and a hint from the author of the hanging designed for Jude's children. Nothing in their relationship seems to make such a doom inevitable. Personally and spiritually they are a remarkable match, 'almost the two parts of a single whole'; only sexually are they incompatible. Sue is 'quite unfitted by temperament and instinct to fulfil the conditions of the matrimonial relation with Phillotson, possibly with scarce any man'. Hardy is more explicit in a letter to Gosse (*Life*, 272):

there is nothing perverted or depraved in Sue's nature. The abnormalism consists in disproportion, not in inversion, her sexual instinct being healthy as far as it goes, but unusually weak and fastidious ... one of her reasons for fearing the marriage ceremony is that she fears it would be breaking faith with Jude to withhold herself at pleasure, or altogether, after it; though while uncontracted she feels at liberty to yield herself as seldom as she chooses. This has tended to keep his passion as hot at the end as at the beginning, and helps to break his heart. He has never possessed her as freely as he desired.

It is fear of losing Jude to Arabella, and a false, almost hysterical passion, that makes Sue no longer withhold herself. Self-compulsion against her instinctive nature creates nervous anxieties, and it is for this reason that she dreads the thought of a marriage contract (v. iv). Hardy uses the occasion to remind the reader of a matrimonial disaster in the family, and Sue has a presentiment of 'tragic doom'.

Little Father Time has grown up to feel that he is unwanted by his mother and her family, and a nuisance to Jude and Sue and her family: 'I troubled 'em in Australia, and I trouble folk here. I wish I hadn't been born!' Sue hoped to lift 'the cloud' from his mind, but, as rumours of her being unmarried spread, 'a cloud' settled on her family. The boy was the 'nodal point' of the misfortunes of Jude's first union with those of his second. Yet this hardly validates the extreme form the nemesis takes; and the result is that the major tragedy or double 'crucifixion' which follows is the less convincing, since it is the direct consequence of a 'tragic horror' which lacks inevitability.

The hanging episode seems to have originated, like 'The Church-Builder', in one of Hardy's 'In Tenebris' moods, when his belief that our nursery children feel what Aeschylus imagined coincided with thoughts on abnormal heredity and perhaps on Malthusianism. This horror is unacceptable on realistic grounds, and achieves little imaginative coherence with the remainder of the novel. It seems to have been introduced for the sake of the myth, but the mythical context of the Crucifixion parallel (with its overtones of sin and redemption) is out of proportion to the circumstances of this tragical climax, and an example of that 'mental bombast' which Coleridge defined as 'thoughts and images too great for the subject' – adding, 'This, by the bye, is a fault of which none but a man of genius is capable.' Any parallelism is, in fact, inchoate and incapable of extension, since the myth ends happily. In the *Jude* sequel Hebraism conquers Hellenism: Sue chooses self-abnegation, Sacerdotalism, and mortification of her flesh. She has submitted to the world she had condemned with Swinburne (II. iii):

> Thou hast conquered, O pale Galilean:
> The world has grown grey from thy breath!

*   *   *

Almost at the end of 1875 Hardy noted in Schlegel, 'The deepest want and deficiency of all modern Art lies in the fact that the Artists have no mythology.' This means, I suppose, a set of beliefs or religion which is regarded as the key to life and the universe by both the artist and his public. Hardy's own philosophy was rooted in Comte's Positivism. In a world of imperfection created by natural law, no God could be regarded as omnipotent. Since 'man is entirely subordinate to the world', progress depends on co-operation for the common good. Comte stresses the importance of altruism. In Hardy it appears also as 'charity' or 'loving-kindness'. Its spirit animates some of his finest characters, none more than Tess:

> she sought not her own; was not provoked; thought no evil of [Angel's] treatment of her. She might just now have been Apostolic Charity herself returning to a self-seeking modern world.

It was, I think, predominantly with this spirit of self-sacrifice for others in mind that the Positivist Frederic Harrison described *Tess* as Hardy's 'very beautiful book'. 'To me it reads like a Positive allegory or sermon', he wrote to Hardy.

Hardy described Positivism as 'the new religion'. He agreed with J. S. Mill that Jesus was 'excellently fitted to aid and fortify that real, though purely human religion, which sometimes calls itself the Religion of Humanity'. In *The Positive Evolution of Religion* (1913) Harrison said that the acceptable part of Christianity was in no way higher than the religion of humanity, but that the religion of the future could not be limited to it, for Jesus was only one of many Messiahs. Hardy's thought is similar in his poem 'Unkept Good Fridays'.

There are incidental echoes of Comte in *Tess of the d'Urbervilles* (in references to fetichism, for example). More interesting, however, are two passages which are not so much allegorical (in Harrison's moral sense of the word) as the merging of the human narrative and the mythology which Hardy constructed on the basis of scientific human-ism. In this he was considerably helped and fortified by the writing of intermediaries, J. S. Mill in particular. Hardy's mythopoeic period begins very early with the poetry he wrote in London from 1865 to 1867. The opening lines of 'Discouragement' –

> To see the Mother, naturing Nature, stand
> All racked and wrung by her unfaithful lord

– contain the essence of many poems in *Poems of the Past and the Present* (1901) which Hardy intended as a kind of preparatory course for the religion of the future and, more immediately, for the great mythological presentation of *The Dynasts*.

The first of the passages in *Tess* which relate the human situation to the universal 'Cause of Things' merges with the Christian mythology of *Paradise Lost* and is less effective than the second, probably because it contains little action. It occurs after Tess's arrival at The Slopes. Mrs d'Urberville is kindly and well-meaning, but ineffective. She is blind and remote, unaware of what is going on; and she makes only one appearance (and that a brief one). In her secondary, mythic role, she is 'The Lacking Sense' or Nature, working to immutable law:

> Ah! knowest thou not her secret yet, her vainly veiled deficience,
>   Whence it comes that all unwittingly she wounds the lives she loves?
> That sightless are those orbs of hers? – which bar to her omniscience
>   Brings those fearful unfulfilments, that red ravage through her zones
>   Whereat all creation groans.

She is also 'The Sleep-Worker':

> When wilt thou wake, O Mother, wake and see –
> As one who, held in trance, has laboured long
> By vacant rote and prepossession strong –
> The coils that thou has wrought unwittingly;
>
> Wherein have place, unrealized by thee,
> Fair growths, foul cankers, right enmeshed with wrong,
> Strange orchestras of victim-shriek and song,
> And curious blends of ache and ecstasy?

Appropriately the image we associate with blind Mrs d'Urberville is the 'large, four-post bedstead hung with heavy damask curtains' in the room where Tess performs the strange task of whistling to her caged bullfinches. She is absent when danger threatens:

> Once while Tess was at the window where the cages were ranged, giving her lesson as usual, she thought she heard a rustling behind the bed. The old lady was not present, and turning round the girl had an impression that the toes of a pair of boots were visible below the frieze of the curtains.

The interloper is, of course, Alec d'Urberville. The caged birds are a reminder of the human condition: all people are caged birds, Hardy wrote in 1885. For 'the Mother' we turn to the poem 'The Bullfinches':

> All we creatures, nigh and far
> (Said they there), the Mother's are;
> Yet she never shows endeavour
>   To protect from warrings wild
>   Bird or beast she calls her child.
>
> Busy in her handsome house
> Known as Space, she falls a-drowse;

> Yet, in seeming, works on dreaming,
> While beneath her groping hands
> Fiends make havoc in her bands.

Alec has already been associated with the arch-fiend Satan in the scene which is carefully placed before the suggestion of menace in the bedroom. The old house and garden which are the home of his blind mother's pet poultry are surrounded by a wall, with only one door for entrance. Thick ivy conceals Alec before he springs from the coping of the wall into the plot, as Milton's Satan entered Eden:

> One gate there only was, and that looked east
> On the other side: which when th' arch-felon saw,
> Due entrance he disdained, and in contempt
> At one slight bound high overleaped all bound
> Of hill or highest wall, and sheer within
> Lights on his feet.

The Satanic role of Alec d'Urberville is reinforced later, when he is seen in the smoke of the bonfire in the Durbeyfield garden at Marlott, and quotes from the Tempter's speech in *Paradise Lost*, a less convincing technique than the allusive one just sketched.

After Tess's 'fall' there came her spring revival, happiness and love in the summer, a marriage mockery, and a cruel winter at Flintcomb-Ash. So we come to the second scene. 'It is', as Hardy writes, 'the threshing of the last wheat-rick at Flintcomb-Ash Farm' on a March day. By the stack stands 'the red tyrant' that the women have 'come to serve'; a little way off is the engine which is to act as 'the *primum mobile* of this little world'. It has a sinister, Tophet-like or Plutonic appearance. By Farmer Groby's orders Tess has to stand by the man who feeds the thresher, unfasten the sheaves, and pass them in steady succession so that the machine can be fed evenly and continuously (an indescribably hard task when sheaves were fastened with tough bands of corn):

> for Tess there was no respite; for, as the drum never stopped, the man who fed it could not stop, and she, who had to supply the man with untied sheaves, could not stop either, unless Marian changed places with her, which she sometimes did for half an hour in spite of Groby's objection that she was too slow-handed for a feeder.

As Tess could not turn her head, she did not observe the arrival of Alec d'Urberville.

When dinner-break came she 'left her post, her knees trembling so wretchedly with the shaking of the machine that she could scarcely walk'. She would avoid d'Urberville by having her meal out of sight, alone, on the stack. He came up the ladder, and they talked. Sensual and selfish he may have been, but he was in love with Tess, and would have done anything to save her from servitude; his protest to Farmer Groby showed the courage born of conviction. His jibe against Tess's legal husband Angel Clare is justified; but she has been plagued by Alec long enough, and the taunt is too truthful for her endurance. The hereditary d'Urberville temper flares up and, without the slightest warning, she picks up one of her leather gloves, and swings it by the gauntlet hard in his face. The blow fetches blood:

> 'Now, punish me!' she said, turning up her eyes to him with the hopeless defiance of the sparrow's gaze before its captor twists its neck. 'Whip me, crush me; you need not mind those people under the rick! I shall not cry out. Once victim, always victim – that's the law!'

Alec is angered by Tess's ingratitude, and warns her that he will be master. By force of circumstances he is; Tess has to submit for the sake of her family. She admits that he is good to her and to them, but spiritually she is dead, a corpse drifting with the current.

To the Positivist in Hardy here was Tess, her one life ruined. Analyse the poem 'Discouragement' and the novel carefully, and you will find that she is the victim of chance – of heredity, physical and temperamental; of the position she was born into, and all the other factors that impinge on her life. She could not be held responsible for them; she was, in Hardy's words, 'a pure woman'.

Her victimization by chance is expressed in the threshing scene. In the pre-Copernican era, the universe was imagined in terms of concentric spheres. It was created for man, and he was at the centre. Round the earth turned the sphere to which the moon was fixed; beyond that, in turn, the spheres which held the sun and the planets; beyond them, the sphere containing the stars. Outside, giving movement to all within, was the Primum Mobile, which was inseparable from the Empyrean and God. Just as the Primum Mobile connoted God in medieval philosophy, so the term was used for the Prime Cause in Positivist philosophy. In *The Positive Evolution of Religion* Frederic Harrison describes the 'first Cause' as 'a kind of *Primum Mobile*'.[11] Tess has no choice; she is the victim of chance; she is the slave to a machine driven by an engine, and that engine is the *primum mobile* of her little world. In the words which open the After Scene of *The Dynasts*:

> Thus doth the Great Foresightless mechanize
> In blank entrancement now as evermore.

*   *   *

Ultimate causes are indefinable; they need a mythology to express them. In the last scene Hardy has succeeded in expressing his view of life through the dramatic integration of narrative and myth. *The Return of the Native* presents two opposing points of view, one in some respects Hellenic; mythological references reinforce the antithesis, but they never endow action with a concurrent, symbolical import as in the threshing scene; they are no more than incidental illuminations of a theme. The Norse references in *The Woodlanders* are much rarer, but they are just as incidental, providing a slight intensification of mood, outlook, and theme. The hanging of Jude's three children lacks sufficient credibility to support a myth which has universal significance; nor do the features of the novel give coherence to the myth of sin and redemption as it is applied to this event. The threshing episode in *Tess* shows Hardy's imaginative thought working harmoniously and powerfully; the hanging scene in *Jude* suggests either a failure in critical judgement or a failure to raise performance to the level of earlier imaginative thinking. As Hardy's unresolved matrimonial discords became seriously aggravated after the completion of *Tess*, he was probably unable to give *Jude* as much attention as he had devoted to the former novel. Something more than false modesty lies in his remark to Gosse, 'You have hardly any idea how poor and feeble the book seems to me, as executed, beside the idea of it I had formed in prospect.' When we consider why Hardy abandoned novel-writing, we are apt to forget conditions at Max Gate. They were not always conducive to that 'balance', that 'unity with one's self' which Pater thought a prerequisite for art, particularly in the 'perplexed light' of the modern world.

10 *Tess* and *Clarissa*

Intenser scenes in the later, more tragic phases of *Jude the Obscure* are predominantly dramatic, the dialogue of the lovers reaching at times a pitch of agony and despair never equalled in Hardy. Those of *Tess* tend to be poetic, both the background and theme in major movements of the novel being conducive to a descriptive enrichment of style which is hardly ever approached in the whole of *Jude*. Several features in *Tess* were nourished and developed (perhaps conceived) in accordance with a literary tradition which stimulated a poetic rather than a realistic presentation. For Hardy the most important link in this tradition was Samuel Richardson's *Clarissa*, a novel of inordinate length and hauntingly moving and imaginative scenes, the theme of which was influenced very evidently by *Paradise Lost* and less importantly by Shakespeare's *The Rape of Lucrece*. The influence of all three works can be seen in *Tess of the d'Urbervilles*.

The image of white as a symbol of virtue in *The Rape of Lucrece* is found in a variety of forms in Richardson's novel and Hardy's, as is that of a snared bird for the victimized heroine. Shakespeare's antithesis of an 'earthly saint' adored by a 'devil' recurs endlessly throughout *Clarissa*, but Tess is a more human, less sentimentalized creation than Richardson's heroine, and for the 'angelic' half of the concept in Hardy's novel we have to turn to her idealization of Angel Clare. Both Lucrece and Clarissa are regarded as 'immaculate and spotless' in mind after being ravished. Neither is inclined to 'accessary yieldings', and in this respect each is a prototype of Tess. Hardy's heroine is cast in a less heroic mould than Lucrece; she is less idealized than Clarissa. Neither of her predecessors wishes to prolong her life on earth after the defilement of her body; Tess recovers and does not lose the will to live or the 'appetite for joy' until events have victimized her beyond endurance. Her emblematical association with the legendary white hart of Blackmoor Vale (ii) was prompted no doubt by Shakespeare's image of the 'white hind' pleading in a wilderness

> To the rough beast that knows no gentle right,
> Nor aught obeys but his foul appetite.

The most significant feature of *The Rape of Lucrece* for Hardy, however, may well have been its emphasis on the misfortunes created by 'Opportunity' or chance; and it is noteworthy that the line which

Hardy utilizes with reference to the rape of Tess (xii, 'the serpent hisses where the sweet birds sing') occurs in Shakespeare's introduction to this theme.

Richardson's influence on the development of *Tess* was much greater than Shakespeare's. It is clear from his remarks in 'The Profitable Reading of Fiction' that Hardy was impressed with *Clarissa*, and especially by Richardson's constructive skill:

> However cold, even artificial, we may, at times, deem the heroine and her companions in the pages of that excellent tale, however numerous the twitches of unreality in their movements across the scene beside those in the figures animated by Fielding, we feel, nevertheless, that we are under the guidance of a hand which has consummate skill in evolving a graceful, well-balanced set of conjectures, forming altogether one of those circumstantial wholes which, when approached by events in real life, cause the observer to pause and reflect, and say 'What a striking history!' ... No person who has a due perception of the constructive art shown in Greek tragic drama can be blind to the constructive art of Richardson.

This was written early in 1888, when Hardy was probably engaged in the initial planning of *Tess of the d'Urbervilles*. Notes which he made in the second half of the year and subsequently (*Life*, 213ff.) provide pointers to features of his novel, but disclose nothing relative to the story except a generalization (p. 221) which seems to have a direct bearing on the murder of Alec d'Urberville. The principal idea for *Tess* probably sprang to mind from a reading of *Clarissa*.

Even insignificant features in Richardson's novel could have contributed largely to the story of *Tess*. The surprising fact that Clarissa could be a 'most elegant dairy-maid' when she stayed with her grandfather, and showed proficiency 'in all the parts of dairy management', may have suggested Tess's period of happiness as a dairymaid at Talbothays. A mere comment on one of Lovelace's minor manifestations of hypocrisy – 'But what, dear, will become of us now? – Lovelace not only reformed, but turned preacher; – What will become of us now?' – may have weighed with Hardy in working out Alec's role after Tess's desertion by Angel Clare.

The White Hart inn at which Lovelace lodged when he stagemanaged the circumstances which tricked Clarissa into leaving her home and accepting his treacherous protection probably reminded Hardy of the white hind image in *The Rape of Lucrece*, and prompted the poetic association of a heroine born in Blackmoor Vale with the beautiful white hart slain there (according to legend) in the reign of Henry III.

Even in the most tedious commentaries with which Richardson thought fit to moralize his epistolary novel and slow down the action for long intervals, significant details catch the eye as a result of italicization. They are apt to recur, and it is probable that, though Hardy's familiarity with the Bible was exceptional, Belford's repeated use of 'Devils believe and tremble' with reference to Lovelace accounts for Alec d'Urberville's application of it to himself when he meets Tess after his religious conversion (xlvi). Another comment (unitalicized), 'since what is done is done, and cannot be undone' is echoed in Mrs Durbeyfield's 'what's done can't be undone' (xxxviii).

Over and over again in *Clarissa* we meet the maxim of the libertine, 'Once subdued, always subdued'. Hardy adapts it with dramatic fitness in the scene which symbolizes Tess's oppression by the Prime Cause (see above, pp. 116–17). 'Now punish me!' she cries after striking Alec d'Urberville under provocation: 'Whip me, crush me; you need not mind those people under the rick! I shall not cry out. Once victim, always victim – that's the law!'

More than in any other novel by Hardy, bird imagery is used in *Tess* to present the plight and suffering of the heroine. Her lot is paralleled in sleeping birds which are doomed (xi), and in those bleeding and dying from man's cruelty (xli). She whom the sight of a bird in a cage had often made cry is caught 'during the days of her immaturity like a bird in a springe' (xxxi) and, at Flintcomb-Ash, 'like a bird in a clap-net' (xliii). Clarissa likewise, under inhuman pressures at home, before she falls into the hands of Lovelace, finds herself entangled 'like a poor silly bird'. He spreads his snares like a cunning fowler and, making reformation his stalking-horse, has her in his 'gin' with 'springes close about her'. Having caught her, he thinks of her sadistically as his caged bird, and he imagines it beating and bruising itself against the wires until it is exhausted and lies panting at the bottom of the cage, where it bemoans its fate until it is reconciled to its new surroundings and begins to sing. The motif of the snarer and the captive bird is recurrent through the greater part of *Clarissa*, and its poignant association with the heroine's cruel wrongs undoubtedly influenced Hardy in the imaginative presentation of Tess.

Clarissa's virtue is emphasized in the whiteness of her lustring nightgown and in the 'snowy hand' which she waved with 'moving oratory' in addressing her 'destroyer' with 'the consciousness of an innocent sufferer'; in the white flowing robes which illuminate the dark and squalid bedchamber where she is imprisoned, 'her linen beyond imagination white'; or again in the 'virgin white' of her dress, and her hands 'white as a lily' just before her death. Similarly Tess wears the white muslin dress of the club-walking scene when she leaves home and entrusts herself to Alec, and again on the night of her rape; in her long white nightgown, while she baptizes her child, her countenance is transformed into 'a thing of immaculate beauty, with a touch of dignity' which is almost 'regal'; subsequently, in times of duress, even after the murder of Alec, her facial whiteness is an oblique reminder of her essential innocence.

Clarissa is almost unexceptionally the model of rectitude and Christian piety. She is noble, but too supremely an example to be quite of this world. Tess has hereditary weaknesses, but her conscience is unusually sensitive, and again and again her concern for others is the main source of her tragedy. She is never 'angelic' like Clarissa, but she is pure of heart, admirable in her altruism and self-sacrifice. Though tending to drift and accept her fate, she has the Christian virtues. 'She might just now have been Apostolic Charity returned to a self-seeking modern world', Hardy writes (xxxvi). Inspired by deeply moving episodes in Richardson's story, and by critical reflection, he may have made it his aim in *Tess* to create a woman who was 'pure' but more human and convincing than Clarissa.

Richardson continually alludes to the analogue of *Paradise Lost*; Clarissa is regarded as an angel, and Lovelace as Beelzebub or Satan. He enters her garden in disguise, and is described as 'a wall-climber'. Her one rash act is to commit herself to his protection, to avoid a compulsory marriage which has been arranged by her family; it is rather like Tess's committing herself to Alec in order to avoid Car Darch's fury: 'Out of the frying-pan into the fire.' Frequently references to her rashness recall Milton's Eve:

> So saying, her rash hand in evil hour
> Forth reaching to the fruit, she plucked, she eat.

After her fancied escape Clarissa is indignant at Lovelace's deceit; 'here, sir,' she says, 'like the first pair (I, at least, driven out of my paradise) are we recriminating'. Like Milton's Satan he rejoices in being actuated predominantly by pride and revenge; he is regarded as a 'reptile' and 'serpent'. Alec d'Urberville's role as Satan is discussed elsewhere (see pp. 65–6). Whether Hardy in his antithetical characterization of Angel Clare owed anything to Richardson's antithetical idealization of Clarissa is conjectural. The name assumes a relevance from Tess's idealization of him, and Hardy has daringly presented him as a harp-player. The instrument and execution are poor, however; 'the relative is all', Hardy comments. Tess is drawn towards the player 'like a fascinated bird', and she discovers his inadequacies too late.

At The Slopes there is a garden where Tess tends a 'community of fowls' belonging to Mrs d'Urberville. Like Milton's paradise, it is surrounded by a wall which has only one door; Alec d'Urberville's entrance is reminiscent of Satan's vaulting into Eden (see p. 116). Yet the leading features of Hardy's garden are not found in Milton. They are the fowls – 'Hamburghs, Bantams, Cochins, Brahmas, Dorkings, and such other sorts as were in fashion just then'; the old thatched cottage; and the ivy which cloaks the wall and overruns the house, 'its chimney being enlarged by the boughs of the parasite to the aspect of a ruined tower'. The characteristics of the scene are adapted from the garden and grounds in which the disguised Lovelace secretly meets Clarissa, after one of his hirelings has supplied him with a key to a remote back-door. In the frequented parts there is a 'wood-house' with its lowest timbers rotted away; by it is a poultry yard, where Clarissa tends 'bantams, pheasants, and pea-hens', her favourite birds because they were her grandfather's gift; in a coppice, much nearer the back-door, Lovelace finds a natural shelter in 'the great overgrown ivy, which spreads wildly round the heads of two or three oaklings'. The 'parasite' which cloaks the entrance of the 'wall-climber' Alec affords a clue to Hardy's symbolism; the 'defects of natural laws' extend to mankind.

Richardson's moral sense at this juncture is more evocatively conveyed in a footnote. The grounds adjoining the back-door by which Lovelace eventually persuades Clarissa to leave her 'paradise' are pathless and lonesome. Some ruins, the remains of a chapel (which seems to have the same overtones as Eliot's in *The Waste Land*), stand in the midst of a coppice, with 'here and there an overgrown oak, surrounded with ivy and mistletoe, starting up, to sanctify, as it were, the awful solemnness of the place'. The spot is haunted, and feared by children and maid-servants. In conjunction with the oaks, the pagan associations of mistletoe may have flashed upon Hardy's imaginative eye the scene of Tess's violation amid the 'primeval yews and oaks of The Chase'.

Lovelace is annoyed that he cannot 'fasten an obligation' on Clarissa. Nothing, he has found, 'more effectually brings down a proud spirit, than a sense of lying under pecuniary obligations'. He offers her money and raiment, therefore, in the hope of making her more agreeable and accommodating, just as Alec gives presents to Tess after wronging her. Less exemplary than Clarissa, Tess has to learn from experience; when she realizes Alec's motives, and her folly in accepting his gifts, she loathes herself and returns home immediately. She makes clothes for her brothers and sisters 'out of some finery which d'Urberville had given her, and she had put by with contempt'.

Some of the influences which have been suggested above are inevitably conjectural, but the evidence as a whole makes it reasonable to conclude that *Clarissa* was important in the shaping of *Tess of the d'Urbervilles* in both detail and ample proportions. Hardy's indebtedness does not show weakness or failure in inspiration; his artistic instinct made him realize the possibilities of enrichment from a literary tradition. He was not a mere borrower; it was often a critical response which made him creative, as several of his poems show. Though presented as 'a pure woman', Tess differs from Clarissa in being

not too bright or good
For human nature's daily food.

A comparison of the death-wish incidence in *Clarissa* and *Tess* affords another instance of Hardy's critical reaction. When Richardson's heroine has escaped from captivity, and is secure, her thoughts are devoted to preparations for life after death. Like Shakespeare's Lucrece, she has no wish to live (as her medical adviser testifies). Though she has never stooped to folly, she shares the view expressed in Goldsmith's lyric that the only decent course left for a dishonoured woman is to die. This is a lofty sentiment, which has rarely seemed in accord with human nature. Most people wish to live,[1] and with Tess a resurgence of vitality and hope leads to enterprise and a period of happiness so great that she fearfully wishes it could last for ever. Her marriage destroys that happiness. Angel's self-centred, unimaginative weakness at this critical juncture and his desertion of Tess form the cruellest and most abiding disaster in her short life. Yet she remains loyal and hopeful. Her outbreak against d'Urberville in the threshing scene is indicative of the strain created by growing insecurity and fading hope. Only when she consents to live with him for the sake of her indigent family after her father's death does she lose the will to live. When Angel returned, 'he had a vague consciousness of one thing, though it was not clear to him till later; that his original Tess had spiritually ceased to recognize the body before him as hers – allowing it to drift, like a corpse upon the current, in a direction dissociated from its living will'. His unexpected return is the climactic trick played by fate against Tess. It is too much for her; in murdering Alec she strikes out against the situation into which she has been betrayed. After her brief period of happiness with Angel, reality returns, and she is ready for death.

11 A Pure Woman

To judge by Hardy's reactions, the two expressions in *Tess* which caused most contemporary agitation and misunderstanding were the sub-title 'A Pure Woman' and the Aeschylean reference at the end: ' "Justice" was done, and the President of the Immortals . . . had ended his sport with Tess.' They are related, and they still seem to be misunderstood. Occasionally a critic writes as if Hardy believed in a malevolent Deity or Cause of Things, and more often critics write of Tess's relations with Alec d'Urberville as if purity and innocence were irrelevant criteria.

For many readers Tess's sin was at least doubly compounded; whatever might be said about her 'fall', she was a kept mistress and a murderess. To some the sub-title must have seemed not so much a gauntlet thrown in the face of Grundyism as a meaningless piece of cynical arrogance. *Melius fuerat non scribere*, Hardy wrote in the additional prefatory note for the 1912 edition. In the face of hostile criticism he was willing to back down or make excuse; and nowhere is such weakness or ready accommodation more regrettable than here. Had he written in like vein on the President of the Immortals passage he would have had greater justification. He defended it, with complete logicality, as a figure of speech summing up 'the forces opposed to the heroine' (*Life*, 243–4), without reference to philosophical or religious implications which the Victorians accepted with equanimity in Greek drama. Hardy's mildly Swinburnian bravado was inevitably provocative; the 'personality' in which 'the forces opposed to the heroine' were unobjectionably 'allegorized' in *The Graphic* had been 'Time, the Arch-Satirist'. If Hardy had said that Tess had been repeatedly tricked by Fate, or victimized by circumstances which had finally proved beyond her endurance, he would have conveyed what he meant without panache and without offence. On the question of the sub-title, however, he should never have given the impression of compromising one iota; 'A Pure Woman' is the *leit-motiv* of the novel.

The validity of such a conclusion depends on two sets of factors, the first of which may be regarded as negative, the second positive (though actually they are inseparable). On the one hand, Tess is a victim of chance: in crucial situations, her character being what it is ('a cast in the die of destiny' like Marty South's), she can do no other than she does. On the other, her character shows moral and spiritual qualities (especially in the ultimate version of the novel)[1] which qualify her admirably to be a tragic heroine in accordance with Hardy's finest conception of tragedy: 'The best tragedy – highest tragedy in short – is that of the WORTHY encompassed by the INEVITABLE.'

It is Tess's extraordinary and unfortunate chance that her fate is bound up with such unreliable opposites as Alec d'Urberville and Angel Clare, a parallel in all major respects to Jude's misfortune with Arabella Dunn and Sue Bridehead, and as extreme as the lot of Eustacia Vye in fondly hoping that the unknown and somewhat Rousseauistic Clym Yeobright will be her means of escaping to the city of her dreams. Tess herself is rather an unusual character; her conscience makes her readily shoulder blame and guilt which more rightly belong to her feckless parents, who happen to be the most improvident but well-meaning pair of 'waiters on Providence' in all Hardy's fiction (a good springboard for a 'Positivist' novel). For them she consigns herself unwillingly to Alec and employment at The Slopes. He is a libertine; her beauty and a physical maturity beyond her experience and worldly knowledge make her immediately attractive to him. An accession of panic delivers her into the hands of her betrayer. Much later, after her father's death, she submits to the degradation of living with Alec simply because she has no other choice.

Ethereally Shelleyan, Angel Clare had imagined that in wooing Tess and 'giving up all ambition to win a wife with social standing, with fortune, with knowledge of the world' he would secure 'rustic innocence'. So convinced is he of her perfection that he discounts her fears and unwittingly reinforces her proneness to let things take their course until it is too late. His confession on the evening after their marriage leads to hers, and a wave of antipathy immediately washes away his idealizing sentiment. His vision is 'mocked by appearances'; and his affection proves to be 'less fire than radiance':

> Within the remote depths of his constitution, so gentle and affectionate as he was in general, there lay hidden a hard logical deposit, like a vein of metal in a soft loam, which turned the edge of everything that attempted to traverse it. It had blocked his acceptance of the Church; it blocked his acceptance of Tess.

The characters of Angel and Tess are very dissimilar from those of Knight and Elfride in *A Pair of Blue Eyes*, but the parallel between the two pairs of lovers in the crunch of crisis is remarkable. Once more the tragic situation created by irresolution, confession, irreconcilability, and submission is 'the chance of things'. Against the 'keen scrutiny and logical power' of Knight, Elfride's 'docile devotion . . . was now its own enemy. . . . A slight rebelliousness . . . would have been a world of advantage to her. But she idolized him, and was proud to be his bondservant' (see p. 41). If only Elfride could be 'the woman she had seemed to be', Knight reflects; 'but that woman was dead and buried, and he knew her no more'. He leaves London for the Continent, just as Angel departs for Brazil. In dramatic fashion the sleep-walking scene shows how for Angel the Tess of his vision was also dead and buried. It never occurs to Knight that he owes Elfride 'a little sacrifice for her unchary devotion in saving his life'. In both men the head has developed at the expense of the heart; in both the springs of charity are blocked. This defect of nature (rather than an allusive Shelleyan resonance) is probably the true explanation of Angel's name: 'Though I speak with the tongues of men and of angels, and have not charity, I am become as sounding brass or a tinkling cymbal.' In a book which is imaginatively endowed to appeal above all to charity, it is Tess who is the exemplar.

This does not mean that she is perfect. Her intentions are good, but her willingness to endure is sometimes another aspect of her weakness of resolve in the clutch of circumstances arising from her early misfortune. She is pure of heart; conscious-ridden from the outset of her tragic career, and ready to abnegate her own wishes and interests for the sake of others. Her last act, in choosing the Stone of Sacrifice for her resting-place before her surrender, dramatizes symbolically the role she has chosen to play in one crisis after another. Clare had known that she loved him, 'but he did not know at that time the full depth of her devotion, its single-mindedness, its meekness; what long-suffering it guaranteed, what honesty, what endurance, what good faith'. When he turned adamantly against her, 'she sought not her own; was not provoked; thought no evil of his treatment of her. She might just now have been Apostolic Charity herself returned to a self-seeking world.'

In arguing for the abandonment of their marriage before it had begun, Angel's concern for his reputation and what might happen to their hypothetical children if the past became known (as it must, he insisted) had been too much for her distressed mind:

> She had never truly thought so far as that, and his lucid picture of possible offspring who would scorn her was one that brought deadly conviction to an honest heart which was humanitarian to its centre.

The thought of what could happen makes her decide unselfishly to leave Angel free and return home:

> though nobody else should reproach me if we should stay together, yet somewhen, years hence, you might get angry with me for any ordinary matter, and knowing what you do of my bygones you yourself might be tempted to say words, and they might be overheard, perhaps by my own children. O, what only hurts me now would torture and kill me then! I will go – to-morrow.

Whereas another woman might have protested, wrung and re-won his heart,

her mood of long-suffering made his way easy for him, and she herself was his best advocate. Pride, too, entered into her submission – which perhaps was symptom of that reckless acquiescence in chance too apparent in the whole d'Urberville family – and the many effective chords which she could have stirred by an appeal were left untouched.

Young and independent-minded, Angel Clare has much to learn before he realizes what humanly, not ideally, is required to make a moral man or woman: 'The beauty or ugliness of a character lay not only in its achievements, but in its aims and impulses; its true history lay, not among things done, but among things willed.' 'No prophet had told him, and he was not prophet enough to tell himself, that essentially this young wife of his was as deserving of the praise of King Lemuel as any other woman endowed with the same dislike of evil, her moral value having to be reckoned not by achievement but by tendency.' Readers familiar with Proverbs xxxi and I Corinthians xiii will have realized that here and in passages quoted earlier Hardy has said that Tess was an honourable woman in whom could be found the leading Christian virtues.

Controversy about Tess's purity must concentrate on her relations with Alec while she was at The Slopes and later at Sandbourne. Many critics have written of her 'seduction' by Alec, who is presented as a tempter before her first and her final degradation. Undoubtedly he wished to seduce her before and after her 'fall'; but she is the innocent victim of rape, and Hardy deliberately associated *Tess of the d'Urbervilles* with *The Rape of Lucrece* and *Clarissa* for this very reason.

Though Hardy had to draw a prudent (rather than a prudish) veil over what happened in the Chase, he leaves the reader in no doubt. Alec was ruthless: 'Doubtless some of Tess d'Urberville's mailed ancestors rollicking home from a fray had dealt the same measure even more ruthlessly towards peasant girls of their time.' There is no question about the ruthlessness; it is a matter of degree. News spreads among the agricultural labourers until we hear at harvest-time, 'There were they that heard a sobbing one night last year in The Chase; and it mid ha' gone hard wi' a certain party if folks had come along.' And Tess, frenzied by the return of Angel after she has consented to live with Alec, alludes to his cruel compulsion on this occasion. She herself supplies evidence incidentally: 'suppose your sin was not of your own seeking?' she asks the itinerant text-painter. Nor is there any reason to think she hides anything from her mother, who advises her not to tell Angel everything, 'specially as it is so long ago, and not your

Fault at all'. When Tess finally rejoins Angel, she tells him she has killed Alec, and that she had feared she might do it some day 'for the trap he set me in my simple youth'. Alec's admissions are more consistently explicit. When she is on her way home from The Slopes, he admits he has done her wrong; at Flintcomb-Ash he expresses his wish to marry her, 'to make the only reparation I can make for the trick played you'; she had remained 'unsmirched in spite of all', he says, and for that reason he had never despised her; 'I saw you innocent, and I deceived you', he recalls when he thinks of her 'grand revenge' in being the unintentional means of making him renounce his Evangelical faith and mission. Angel Clare's testimony (found in his maturer reflections after discussing 'the sorrowful facts of his marriage' with a stranger in Brazil) is quite unequivocal:

> His inconsistencies rushed upon him in a flood. He had persistently elevated Hellenic Paganism at the expense of Christianity; yet in that civilization an illegal surrender was not certain disesteem. Surely then he might have regarded that abhorrence of the un-intact state, which he had inherited with the creed of mysticism, as at least open to correction when the result was due to treachery. A remorse struck into him.

Hardy's comment on Tess when she makes her way to Flintcomb-Ash more than eight months after Clare had left her seems conclusive:

> Inside this exterior, over which the eye might have roved as over a thing scarcely percipient, almost inorganic, there was the record of a pulsing life which had learnt too well, for its years, of the dust and ashes of things, of the cruelty of lust and the fragility of love.

Ultimately it is Hardy himself who is most to blame for the uncertainty and confusion which have grown around this issue. Three reasons for this have become clear. The first is that Hardy's conception of Tess changed and, as J. T. Laird has demonstrated, the various stages of his revision show a progression towards the ennoblement of her character. The second is that at certain critical points the text suffers from an ambivalence which Hardy parsimoniously contrived, to ensure that it served for both the emasculated serial version and the later book publication. Had he not lost interest in his novels when he turned to poetry, he might have given them less perfunctory revision for new editions, and have clarified those passages in *Tess* the vagueness of which seems to convey implications which are quite inconsistent with the remainder of the evidence for either of the above reasons.[2] The third source of bewilderment is to be found in some of the authorial comments in the novel on Tess's violation and its consequences.

Controversy is centred mainly in the relations between Alec and Tess at The Slopes after 'the disastrous night of her undoing'. The 'first layer' of the manuscript shows an insertion after the following passage in the scene (xii) where he overtakes Tess on her way home:

> 'You are not going to turn away like that, dear? Come!'
> 'If you wish', she answered indifferently. 'See how you have mastered me!'
> She thereupon turned round and lifted her face to his, and remained like a marble term while he imprinted a kiss upon her cheek – half perfunctorily, half as if zest had not quite died out.

The addition occurs at this point, and is deleted; it runs, 'for only a month had elapsed since she had ceased to defend herself against him'. Not surprisingly this has been taken to mean that Tess was Alec's mistress for a month,[3] but such an interpretation lacks supportive evidence, and Hardy may have realized its misleading possibilities when he deleted it. There is no reason to suppose that more is implied than in the word 'mastered' which he retained. Tess had given way involuntarily and passively to Alec's demand for a final kiss, and it was half perfunctory. By this time, even he, as he complains a little later, had begun to realize that she could not love him. He had sought to appease and win her round, and he had learned, as he said years after, to respect her because she remained 'unsmirched'.

Perhaps it should be pointed out that the expression 'making love' in Hardy never had the connotation it has acquired nearly a century later. In the 1970s it generally suggests sexual intercourse. When Hardy implied sexual intercourse, he did not hesitate to make his meaning clear: Charles Bradford Raye on his western circuit wins Anna 'body and soul', just as Eustacia gave herself 'body and soul' to Wildeve in the 1895 version of *The Return of the Native*. 'Love-making' in Hardy implies no more than courting. The Platonic Pierston of *The Well-Beloved* asks the second Avice to forgive him for 'making love' to her (II. xiii); before they reach the Chase, Alec asks Tess if he has offended her 'often by love-making'; and the 'ethereal' and highly shockable Angel is reassured, after Tess has told him that she cannot marry him, by the thought that 'she had already permitted him to make love to her'. Soon afterwards he remarks, 'I know you to be the most honest, spotless creature that ever lived' (xxviii).

Tess tells Alec in their encounter on her way home that she has never loved him, and that if she did love him she had 'the best o' causes' for letting him know it. A more critical passage occurs when Hardy summarizes her feelings and reflections after her mother had said she ought to have 'got' d'Urberville to marry her:

> Get Alec d'Urberville in the mind to marry her! He marry *her*!...
> She had never wholly cared for him, she did not at all care for him now. She had dreaded him, winced before him, succumbed to adroit

advantages he took of her helplessness; then, temporarily blinded by his ardent manners, had been stirred to confused surrender awhile: had suddenly despised and disliked him, and had run away. That was all.

The novel shows clearly that Alec had set out to attract Tess and partially succeeded, that she had allowed herself to be kissed (admitting his 'mastery' to this extent, since she feared him), and accepted gifts from him, after her violation. She admits that she had been temporarily 'dazed' by him, and that she loathes and hates herself for this weakness; if she continued to accept more from him she would be his 'creature'; 'and I won't!' she adds. That was the extent of her 'confused surrender'. She had discovered that she was being tempted by Alec's seductive wiles, and it was the horror of this self-discovery that made her pack and leave with secret dispatch: 'I made up my mind as soon as I saw – what I ought to have seen sooner.' As Alec attested much later, she had remained 'unsmirched in spite of all; you withdrew yourself from me so quickly and resolutely when you saw the situation'. Whether the summing-up in 'That was all' is Tess's or Hardy's can make hardly any moral difference; it indicates no serious indiscretion, nothing beyond what was venial in the circumstances.

In *The Graphic* serialization of *Tess* the heroine was tricked into a bogus marriage with Alec; there was no rape (of course), and no child was born. Preparing a text which as far as possible would serve for both the serial and the book, Hardy frequently took the short cut of contrived ambivalences, sometimes with regrettable results. It accounts for such euphemisms as 'trick' and 'deceived', and seems the only explanation of 'grief at her weakness' (end of xiii), and 'succumbed to adroit advantages he took of her helplessness' (above). Yet it throws no light on the inexplicitness of 'the whole unconventional business of our time at Trantridge' (xlvi), when the converted Alec, after hearing of Tess's child, takes upon himself the 'whole blame' for fouling her 'innocent life'. This blurred phrase was substituted in the 1902 edition for 'the whole blackness of the sin, the awful, awful iniquity', which occurs in both the manuscript and *The Graphic*.[4] The language here does not seem excessive for the self-condemnation of an evangelist preacher, and is undoubtedly more satisfactory than Hardy's unfocused revision.

It has been argued with reference to the 'That was all' passage that Hardy's view accords with Tess's sufficiently to regard them as identical. Some of his authorial comments, however, fail signally to do this, and can do nothing but add to the confusion which obscures the purport of the sub-title. Such comments are not only an irrelevance; they probably constitute the greatest flaw in Hardy's greatest novel. These extraneous assertions illustrate the validity of D. H. Lawrence's generalization, 'Never trust the artist. Trust the tale.'[5] Hardy asks, for example, whether Tess, alone on a desert island, would have been greatly wretched at what had happened to her, and answers, 'Not greatly. . . . Most of the misery had been generated by her conventional aspect, and not by her innate sensations.' Such a hypothetical Tess is not the Tess of the novel. Hardy has detached himself from the imaginative world of his creation, and is considering a question which is more in the abstract. To adapt Lawrence, he is showing his 'idealistic halfness' rather than his artistic integrity.

Less exceptionable, perhaps, but still detached, are Hardy's statements that 'but for the world's opinion' her misfortune might have been the beginning of 'a liberal education' for her (xv), and that 'Tess's corporeal blight had been her mental harvest' (xix). There could be an allusive link here with the innocence of the girls in white at the Marlott 'Cerealia' (ii) and the harvesting scene (xiv); but how far Tess's fall contributed to her spiritual development is not clear, though one might conclude it made her more charitable. The 'world's opinion' is found to be deep-rooted in Angel Clare, despite his progressive ideas and highly prized 'intellectual liberty'; and much suffering and liberalizing experience are required before he reaches his 'mental harvest'.

Only a Hardy who stood outside his novel could say with reference to Tess when she is bearing a child that 'the world is only a psychological phenomenon', and that her conventional fears were a mistaken fancy, 'a cloud of moral hobgoblins by which she was terrified without reason'. In her social environment she had much to conceal; shame made her feel guilty, and years later, after her father's death, one of the reasons for her family's eviction may well have been the objections of some neighbours to their harbouring a woman of ill-fame. Tess is continually handicapped by something more real and substantial than moral hobgoblins or psychological phenomena.

It is a striking example of one of Hardy's inconsistencies that he states this view quite unequivocally in the novel where the rich fertility or 'oozing fatness' of the Froom valley is an expression of that 'irresistible law' in nature which brings Tess and Angel Clare together 'as surely as two streams in one vale'. This physical reality makes dairymaids 'writhe feverishly'; and, despite herself, Tess succumbs to it, drifting acquiescently in the end towards marriage. The brimfulness of nature breathes from her at a time 'when a woman's soul is more incarnate than at any other time; when the most spiritual beauty bespeaks itself flesh; and sex takes the outside place in the presentation'. Here more than anywhere else Hardy makes the reader aware of human physical forces which are independent of consciousness or will, and gives us glimpses of a non-psychological world more fully explored by D. H. Lawrence.

One other puzzling authorial comment may be found in Hardy's reply to hostile critics, particularly with reference to the sub-title, in his 1892 preface to *Tess of the d'Urbervilles*:

> Some of these maintain a conscientious difference of sentiment concerning, among other things, subjects fit for art, and reveal an inability to associate the idea of the title-adjective with any but the licensed and derivative meaning which has resulted to it from the ordinances of civilization. They thus ignore, not only all Nature's claims, all aesthetic claims on the word, but even the spiritual interpretation afforded by the finest side of Christianity; and drag in, as a vital point, the acts of a woman in her last days of desperation, when all her doings lie outside her normal character.

It is clear from *Jude the Obscure* and its preface that 'licensed' (for which 'artificial' was substituted in 1895) relates to marriage. 'Nature's claims', therefore, must apply to people who are drawn naturally to each other, whether they are married or not. Hardy, as can be seen in Sue Bridehead's views and such poems as 'The Christening', was attracted to the belief that the marriage bond is inimical to love, but this *sequitur* has no relevance to the question of Tess's purity, unless he has her natural antipathy to Alec in mind. Of the beginning of their association and its disastrous consequence, Hardy writes:

> Nature does not often say 'See!' to her poor creature at a time when seeing can lead to happy doing . . . Enough that in the present case, as in millions, it was not the two halves of a perfect whole that confronted each other at the perfect moment; a missing counterpart wandered independently about the earth waiting in cross obtuseness till the late time came. . . .

> why so often the coarse appropriates the finer thus, the wrong man the woman, the wrong woman the man, many thousand years of analytical philosophy have failed to explain to our sense of order.

The 'aesthetic claims' which Hardy has in mind arise from the 'beauty' which may be achieved from the presentation of nobility in action, just as one can contemplate 'the beauty of holiness'. The 'finest side of Christianity' alludes to the charity which is expounded in 1 Corinthians xiii; 'its verses will stand when all the rest that you call religion has passed away', Jude asserts; without charity or 'loving-kindness' there can be little hope for civilization, Hardy proclaims in the Apology to *Late Lyrics and Earlier*.

His reference to Tess's 'last days of desperation' is excellent, and its omission from the surviving 1895 preface is a serious loss. That Tess's powers of endurance were being exhausted by the prolongation of Angel's uncommunicative absence, the heavy toll exacted from her by the severe winter at Flintcomb-Ash, and by d'Urberville's renewed solicitations, seems clear from the threshing scene and her confession to Angel: 'I feared long ago, when I struck him on the mouth with my glove, that I might [kill him] some day for the trap he set me in my simple youth, and his wrong to you through me.' The death of her father and her family's eviction because of her return (as it seemed to her) made it incumbent on her to act for the sake of her younger brothers and sisters. The tragedy which formed the crisis of Hardy's first published novel is repeated in a more compulsive form. Cytherea Graye, at a time when she believed she was deserted by the man she loved, had no choice but to marry a libertine in order to provide the medical aid her brother desperately needed. Tess, guilt-ridden again, feels that she must act for her family, as she had done when she thought she was guilty of Prince's death. Only one way is open to her, and that is to live with Alec. She knows he will do anything to help her family provided she accepts a *de facto* marriage with him. Spiritually, like Cytherea, she does not consent. Hardy uses the same metaphor of the body dissociated from the will for each of them (see pp. 12–13). Cytherea is saved; Tess for altruistic reasons sacrifices herself physically. She is still Apostolic Charity in a self-seeking world, and her soul remains unsullied.

Alec had always said that Angel would not return, and in her desperation she had believed him. His sudden appearance unhinged her. Long-suffering had reached breaking-point, and the uncontrollable impulse of the d'Urberville temperament was fatal. Tess believed she was avenging Angel, and Hardy must have felt that there was a degree of parallelism between her frenzied behaviour and that of Lucy Ashton in *The Bride of Lammermoor*. A note written when the novel was well under way (*Life*, 221) sheds important light on Hardy's reason for thinking Tess guiltless of murder: 'When a married woman who has a lover kills her husband, she does not really wish to kill her husband; she wishes to kill the situation.' For him Tess was the victim of chance or overwhelming forces in all her crises; at the worst, her actions were excusable, her intentions good.

Hardy made what seems to me his most explicit and unexceptionable statement on his heroine in an interview with Raymond Blathwayt (*Black and White*, 27 August 1892). Blathwayt took exception to the sub-title of the novel. He could understand it with reference to Tess's first 'fall', but failed to see how it could apply to the woman who returned to Alec; he thought his murder 'absolutely unjustifiable'. After stressing that hereditary factors had much to do with it, Hardy stated:

> but I still maintain that her innate purity remained intact to the very last; though I frankly own that a certain outward purity left her on her last fall. I regarded her then as being in the hands of circum-

stances, not morally responsible, a mere corpse drifting with the current to her end.

Taking hereditary instinct into account, in addition to innate disposition and the force of circumstances, Hardy might have said that, like Napoleon in times of crises, she was swayed by the Immanent Will.

It seems impossible for Hardy not to have had Tess in mind when writing 'The Blinded Bird'. In the novel her tragic plight and suffering evoke images of trapped and suffering birds, as in Richardson's *Clarissa*, where Lovelace imagines the heroine as a caged bird bruising itself against the wires until it submits and sings. The virtues extolled in the poem belong to both heroines, and are explicitly claimed for Tess:

> Who hath charity? This bird.
> Who suffereth long and is kind,
> Is not provoked, though blind
> And alive ensepulchred?
> Who hopeth, endureth all things?
> Who thinketh no evil, but sings?
> Who is divine? This bird.

The climactic statement has its parallel in the sub-title of *Tess*. The subject of the novel is the victimization of an innocent and essentially good woman. Her weaknesses are hereditary; her misfortunes are the work of others in the context of chance. Her first disaster plagues her all her life: 'Once victim, always victim – that's the law!' Nothing further is intended in the figurative reference to the Aeschylean 'President of the Immortals'.

12 Bird Imagery

Hardy makes frequent use of bird imagery, but it never suggests the range or the expert knowledge and precision of an ornithologist. In his boyhood, no doubt, on the heath and in the woods near his home, he acquired an extensive familiarity with bird habits, colours, and song; yet, though in 'Afterwards' he includes an unforgettable image of the dewfall-hawk (the night-jar or night-hawk) crossing the shades at dusk to alight on a 'wind-warped upland thorn', nothing indicates that his ocular and aural observations of birds equalled his keen awareness of 'the full-starred heaven' in winter, or of the wind in various kinds of trees and heath vegetation. The most important aspect of Hardy's significant bird images is their function: they are not mere observations or 'pure description' (in the style of a naturalist like W. H. Hudson) but artistically employed as a comment on life, and particularly on human situations. More often than not they provide a parallel to them, functioning metaphorically, almost at times to the point of symbolism.

Since Hardy's philosophy of nature was bleak rather than sunny, and his 'instinct for expression' responded more to the tragedy of life,[1] it is hardly surprising that few cheerful notes of bird song are heard in his works. There are exceptions, two in particular. Of these, 'The Darkling Thrush' is by far the more serious. It was written at the century's end, and the English setting at the close of a mid-winter day harmonizes with the fervourless mood of the poet. The scene may be familiar but, as with other bird images in Hardy, the subject derives from literature. The poem as a whole was suggested by the hymn for the twenty-first Sunday after Trinity in John Keble's *The Christian Year*, but a heightened sense of 'joy illimited' in the bird's song against the wintry gloom came from a striking passage in W. H. Hudson's *Nature in Downland*.[2] Hardy in his wisdom wonders whether the 'aged thrush, frail, gaunt, and small,/In blast-beruffled plume' is not instinctively nearer the truth of life than he with his rather cheerless philosophical outlook:

> So little cause for carollings
> Of such ecstatic sound
> Was written on terrestrial things
> Afar or nigh around,

That I could think there trembled through
His happy good-night air
Some blessed Hope, whereof he knew
And I was unaware.

Here the situation may be seen as that of 'The Impercipient' in reverse.
In the latter poem, after commenting on the mystery of fate which has
made him give up his orthodox faith and thereby 'consigned' him to
'infelicity', Hardy asks: 'O, doth a bird deprived of wings/Go earth-
ward wilfully!'

The happiest bird song with human overtones in all Hardy is heard
at the end of *Under the Greenwood Tree*, after the wedding of Fancy
Day and Dick Dewy:

'Tippiwit! swee-e-et! ki-ki-ki! Come hither, come hither, come
hither!'

'O, 'tis the nightingale', murmured she, and thought of a secret
she would never tell.

There are those who would have us believe that Dick Dewy's future is
threatened, that the girl who could give way to temptation (though she
soon changes her mind) and promise to marry the vicar for social status,
is certain to play her husband false. *The Woodlanders* was conceived
as a contrast to *Under the Greenwood Tree*. In both we have an
'educated' heroine who loves a countryman with little or no social
veneer. Fancy Day makes the right choice; Grace Melbury, the wrong.
The ending of *The Woodlanders* clearly bodes further trouble for
Grace, as her father knows and Hardy acknowledged.[3] Fancy was never
in love with the vicar, much as he admired her; but nobody who
catches Hardy's tone through some of the final scenes of Dick Dewy's
courtship can fail to feel how genuinely she loved him and how anxious
she was not to lose him. She can be vain and trying; she will undoubtedly do much to improve Dick's social style, but she could never
bear to annoy him deeply, and it would be absurd to say that she is
not a woman of integrity. The story was penned 'lightly' and even
'farcically'; it blends comedy with romance, and the most serious reflections on life and on the principal characters are made humorously.
Shadows quickly pass, and they are never deep. A grey cloudy sky
betokens Fancy's sorrow at her father's opposition to her choice of
Dick, and the same kind of parallelism is intended in the Darwinian
reminder which is briefly heard just before Dick asks the gamekeeper
for his daughter Fancy. The cry of a small bird being killed by an owl
in the adjoining wood can by no stretch of the imagination fit any
event which is likely to develop in the future; it is no more than an
appropriate warning when a gamekeeper is intent on killing a lover's
hopes. Father and suitor lean on a piggery rail, contemplating a

'whitish shadowy shape ... moving about and grunting among the straw of the interior' when the critical question is raised. However much we sympathize with Dick, the situation cannot be taken seriously. It accords with the prevailing tone of the novel. Hardy was not a sentimental Arcadian; the course of true love never did run smooth, he reminds us, and many a woman marries and lives loyally and happily with secrets of Fancy's kind which are thought best left undisclosed. Mrs Penny seems to be a sensible judge:

> Well, 'tis humps and hollers with the best of us; but still and for all that, Dick and Fancy stand as fair a chance of having a bit of sunsheen as any married pair in the land.

The romantic song of the nightingale confirms what is hinted in the swarming of the bees just before the wedding.[4] 'A' excellent sign', said Mrs Penny, from the depths of experience. 'A' excellent sign.' And as if to confirm it twice over at the close, Hardy links the bird's happy notes with Shakespeare's song:

> Under the greenwood tree
> Who loves to lie with me,
> And turn his merry note
> Unto the sweet bird's throat,
> Come hither, come hither, come hither;
> Here shall he see
> No enemy
> But winter and rough weather.

The traditional use of bird song for ironical purposes is illustrated most movingly in an early version of Burns's 'Ye Banks and Braes o' Bonnie Doon':

> Thou'll break my heart, thou bonnie bird,
> That sings upon the bough;
> Thou minds me o' the happy days,
> When my fause luve was true.

It is a device which Hardy uses sparingly. When Bathsheba discovers Troy's perfidy, she is distraught and leaves home immediately, not knowing where she is going in the dark. She takes refuge in a thicket overhung by oak and beech trees, and is awakened by the chatter of birds, the chuck-chuck-chuck of a squirrel, and the song of an approaching ploughboy. The world goes on just the same, unaware of her sorrows, just as, after the storm which has undone the effects of his remorseful romanticism on Fanny's grave, Troy wakes to find the bright sunshine and infinite beauties in the wet sparkling foliage. Tess still grieves when, resolving to be useful, she works in the harvest-field near Marlott:

Meanwhile the trees were just as green as before; the birds sang and
the sun shone as clearly now as ever. The familiar surroundings had
not darkened because of her grief, nor sickened because of her pain.

More often Hardy harmonizes setting and mood. In his more
imaginative work the Wessex background is more than an audio-visual
representation. It expresses feelings and states of mind. Tess sets out
for her new life at Talbothays on a 'thyme-scented, bird-hatching'
morning. Her hopes mingle with the sunshine as she bounds along
against the soft south wind. 'She heard a pleasant voice in every breeze,
and in every bird's note seemed to lurk a joy.' (The qualification in
'seemed' is not an authorial intrusion; it conveys Tess's growing, but
not absolute, confidence in her prospects.) A humorous story by the
dairyman reawakens her old sorrows, and she goes out: the evening
sun appears to her like a great inflamed wound, and a solitary crack-
voiced reed-sparrow greets her from the bushes by the river 'in a sad,
machine-made tone, resembling that of a past friend whose friendship
she had outworn'. Birds are not heard singing around Tess's home until
she and her family have vacated it (liv), and yet it was the singing of
the birds which particularly caught Hardy's attention on his one recorded visit to 'Marlott'.[5]

A breach between Clym Yeobright and his mother threatens when
he falls in love; he goes out to meet Eustacia, and waits for her in a
ferny hollow. The 'machine-made foliage' connotes the same kind of
depression which is conveyed by the reed-sparrow heard by Tess; more
significantly, like the scene after his meeting with Eustacia, it expresses
Clym's gloomy 'sense of bare equality with, and no superiority to, a
single thing under the sun': 'The scene seemed to belong to the ancient
world of the carboniferous period . . . when there was neither bud nor
blossom, nothing but a monotonous extent of leafage, amid which no
bird sang.' The last three words recall the desolation of the knight in
Keats's 'La Belle Dame sans Merci'.

The full significance of the changing scene, actual and visionary,
cannot be realized unless one feels how deeply runs the current of
Clym's love for his mother; it is more profound and permanent, one
suspects at the end of the novel, than his sudden, short-lived passion for
Eustacia could ever have been. When they decide to marry in haste, he
walks six miles across the heath to secure a house. The scene which
greets him on the way to Alderworth signifies not so much the conflict
within him as the greater crises and sorrows to come. In the high gusts
of wind which lash them, wet young beeches are suffering renewed
damage 'which would leave scars visible till the day of their burning';
'convulsive sounds' come from the branches, as if pain is felt; and a
finch in a neighbouring brake, finding the gale too much for it, gives
up the attempt to sing.

In contrast to the song of the nightingale at the end of *Under the Greenwood Tree*, the ominous note of the night-hawk is heard in *The Woodlanders* when it can be seen that the heroine, thanks largely to her father's snobbishness, is destined to marry an upper-class libertine. While Fitzpiers and Suke Damson 'remained silent on the hay the coarse whirr of the eternal night-hawk burst sarcastically from the top of a tree at the nearest corner of the wood'. In a minor form it functions like the Spirit Sinister of *The Dynasts*. There is a similar hint of the unfavourable in *A Pair of Blue Eyes* when Stephen Smith, on his return from India, sits within the porch of the church for the appointment that Elfride fails to keep. When Clym Yeobright is on his journey across the heath from Alderworth to Blooms-End, hoping for a reconciliation with his mother and unaware of her abortive visit for the same purpose, a night-hawk is heard in almost every isolated and stunted thorn, signalling his presence by 'whirring like the clack of a mill as long as he could hold his breath'; three miles further on Clym catches 'a sound between a breathing and a moan', and soon discovers that his mother is dying. In 'The Romantic Adventures of a Milkmaid', when Margery Tucker, unknown to her 'young man', is waiting for her assignation with the mysterious foreign baron who is to satisfy her romantic yearnings for worldly splendour and gaiety, the night-hawk may sound a warning of temptation, but (as the sequel shows) there can be little of the sinister in it, and one wonders whether it is no more than a natural feature of the scene:

> She dressed herself with care, went to the top of the garden, and looked over the stile. The view was eastward, and a great moon hung before her in a sky which had not a cloud. Nothing was moving except on the minutest scale, and she remained leaning over, the night-hawk sounding his croud from a bough of an isolated tree on the open hill side.

The bird image here and that of the dewfall-hawk in 'Afterwards' may have been based on the same observation.

It seems probable that the incidence of bird imagery in conjunction with heroines in distress is not so much the result of observation as of a literary heritage. One example which must have appealed to Hardy occurs towards the tragic conclusion of Scott's *The Bride of Lammermoor*.[6] Pining for her absent lover, Lucy is confronted with marriage to Bucklow. After hearing her mother tell the latter that 'we must all be ready to *sign and seal*', she sinks in 'a state resembling stupor', and her younger brother enters to complain that his new falcon looks like being a 'rifler':

> '. . . she just wets her singles in the blood of the partridge, and then breaks away, and lets her fly; and what good can the poor bird do

after that, you know, except pine and die in the first heather-cow or
whin-bush she can crawl into?'

'Right, Henry – right, very right,' said Lucy, mournfully, holding
the boy fast by the hand, after she had given him the wire he wanted;
'but there are more riflers in the world than your falcon, and more
wounded birds that seek but to die in quiet, that can find neither
brake nor whin-bush to hide their heads in.'

As the tragic climax in *Desperate Remedies* approaches, the main circumstances are similar for Cytherea Graye:

> Thus terrified, driven into a corner, panting and fluttering about
> for some loophole of escape, yet still shrinking from the idea of being
> Manston's wife, the poor little bird endeavoured to find out from
> Miss Aldclyffe whether it was likely that Owen would be well treated
> in the hospital. . . .
>
> Manston once more repeated his offer; and once more she refused,
> but this time weakly, and with signs of an internal struggle. Manston's
> eye sparkled; he saw for the hundredth time in his life, that persever-
> ence, if only systematic, was irresistible by womankind.

Bathsheba is never wholly a victim of circumstances like Cytherea,
but she can show a bold and independent spirit in a crisis. It is significant that when jealousy makes her restive and rebellious after her
marriage she is compared not to a caged bird but to a caged leopard.
After learning the worst of Troy, and leaving home, she returns. 'It is
only women with no pride in them who run away from their husbands',
she tells Liddy, adding: 'if ever you marry . . . don't you flinch. Stand
your ground, and be cut to pieces.' But when Boldwood breaks the news
outside the market-house in Casterbridge that her husband is drowned,
and Bathsheba falls on hearing it,

> He lifted her bodily off the ground, and smoothed down the folds of
> her dress as a child might have taken a storm-beaten bird and
> arranged its ruffled plumes, and bore her along the pavement to the
> King's Arms Inn.

This splendid image communicates an immediate sense of Bathsheba's
trials and suffering, but it expresses even more the tender-heartedness
of a man who worshipped her. The association of a bird in distress
('the Frost's decree') is more appropriate to Fanny Robin, and Hardy
may have intended to convey as much by her name.

The most indomitable of Hardy's heroines is Ethelberta, but she lives
very largely in a rarer world of satirical comedy, created in accordance
with a Darwinian principle or two. And in this world, though she
sometimes wishes she could play a less strenuous, more humble role,

she can fend for herself (and her family). Near the opening of the novel her spirit is seen in the wild duck which eludes the hawk at prey.

Another bird image of Darwinian, but less general, import is that of the solitary thrush cracking a small snail on the doorstep; it gives a sharp point to the reader's sense of life's cruelty when Clym Yeobright, over-wrought by his conviction that Eustacia is no better than a murderess, returns home to confront her (v. iii).

In *A Pair of Blue Eyes* (xxxiv), where one might expect the image of 'a bird in a springe' to be applied to the harassed Elfride, it is psychologically interesting to find it applied by the heartless and over-virtuous Knight to himself, when he is indignant at discovering that he had fallen in love with a girl who has had previous admirers.

Two interesting bird images occur at the opening of *The Mayor of Casterbridge*. The ambitious Henchard is hampered by his early marriage, and longs for independence. He is surly, self-centred, and indifferent to his wife as they walk towards Weydon-Priors; she appears happy only when she looks down sideways at the child she is carrying:

> That the man and the woman were husband and wife, and the parents of the girl in arms, there could be little doubt. No other than such a relationship would have accounted for the atmosphere of stale familiarity which the trio carried along with them like a nimbus as they moved down the road.

The road is a very ordinary road, 'the scene for that matter being one that might be matched at almost any spot in any county in England at this time of the year'; it is dingy, dusty with use, and autumnal, and 'a weak bird singing a trite old evening song' reinforces its overtones on the commonness of stale marriages. Such a bird's song 'might doubtless have been heard on the hill at the same hour, and with the selfsame trills, quavers, and breves, at any sunset of that season for centuries untold'.

The second bird image occurs when Henchard, the worse for drink, offers his wife for sale:

> 'Well, then, now's your chance: I am open to an offer for this gem o' creation.'
>
> She turned to her husband and murmured, 'Michael, you have talked of this nonsense in public places before. A joke is a joke, but you may make it once too often, mind!'
>
> 'I know I've said it before; I meant it. All I want is a buyer.'

At the moment a swallow, one among the last of the season, which had by chance found its way through an opening into the upper part of the tent, flew to and fro in quick curves above their heads, causing all eyes to follow it absently. In watching the bird till it made its escape the assembled company neglected to respond to the workman's offer, and the subject dropped.

The escaping bird gives a foretaste of Susan Henchard's relief when the situation is no longer a joke and she is sold to the kindly-looking Newson. She has lived with her husband two years, 'and had nothing but temper'; and she is ready (as she says) to try her luck elsewhere.

In another tragic context, the heron which Mrs Yeobright sees gleaming like burnished silver as it flies towards the sun, and she lies heart-broken and utterly exhausted on Egdon Heath, embodies her wish for release from life:

> Up in the zenith where he was seemed a free and happy place, away from all contact with the earthly ball to which she was pinioned; and she wished that she could arise uncrushed from its surface and fly as he flew then.

No other novel by Hardy contains as many images or suggestions of bird-suffering as *Tess of the d'Urbervilles*. For this, as I have suggested earlier, the influence of Richardson's *Clarissa* may to some extent have been responsible. The tragic heroine of each novel has little freedom of choice, and the image of the snared or caged bird and its torments is particularly appropriate to what they have to endure. Tess, who never could bear to hurt a fly or worm, and whom the sight of a bird in a cage had often made cry (lviii), is 'caught during her days of immaturity like a bird in a springe'. At Talbothays, she is drawn to Angel despite herself; on the outskirt of an uncultivated, weed-choked garden, she stands listening to his harp, and rooted to the spot 'like a fascinated bird'. Later, when they recognise their love for each other, 'the buoyancy of her tread' is noticed; it is 'like the skim of a bird which has not quite alighted'. Honour makes her refuse his marriage proposals, but love is strong; afraid of drifting into acquiescence, she had wondered whether to 'close with him at the altar' and 'snatch ripe pleasure before the iron teeth of pain could have time to shut upon her'. (Here a mantrap such as that described at the end of *The Woodlanders* seems to be envisaged.) Their marriage is fatal; the wedding ceremony is hardly over before the iron teeth close mercilessly upon her. Long after Angel's desertion, her wretchedness and endurance are expressed in the hardships she suffers at Flintcomb-Ash. Tyrannized by the farmer, and not wishing to be recognised by the two 'Amazonian' sisters she had known at Trantridge, Tess is 'like a bird caught in a clap-net'. With no news of Angel since his departure, her endurance is almost at breaking-point when she is plagued by Alec d'Urberville. A truthful but overbold remark from him on her husband's neglect stings her to instinctive retaliation during the threshing break. When blood appears where her glove had caught his face, she looks up at him 'with the hopeless defiance of the sparrow's gaze before its captor twists its neck'. The scene epitomizes Tess's fate in her supreme crises from the beginning to the end of the novel.

Two scenes suggest parallels between Tess's fate and that of birds roosting in trees. When she lies sleeping before her violation, we are presented with a picture of 'primeval yews and oaks of The Chase, in which were poised gentle roost-birds in their last nap'. On her way to Flintcomb-Ash she has reason to be terrified (xli), and takes refuge for the night in the deep recesses of a plantation, where she makes a 'nest' of dead leaves. Her sleep is interrupted by strange sounds, like palpitations, gasps or gurgles, and heavy falls. In the morning she finds pheasants lying around, their rich plumage dabbled with blood, some dead, others 'writhing in agony', the victims of the kind of battue with which Hardy was familiar.[7] To end their torture, she 'broke the necks of as many as she could find, leaving them to lie where she had found them till the gamekeepers should come'.

Two roosting scenes in *The Woodlanders* are of interest. The first relates to the stoical hopelessness of Marty South's undying love for Giles Winterborne. She knows he is in love with Grace Melbury, and that he is thinking of her as he talks of the Christmas party he is planning; she has seen them walking together. When they finish tree-planting for the day, she notices three pheasants settling down to roost near the end of a bare horizontal branch against the glowing western sky. She observes that it will be fine on the morrow, or they would squeeze close to the trunk. Then she adds, 'The weather is almost all they have to think of, isn't it, Mr. Winterborne? And so they must be lighter-hearted than we.'

The other is not as simple, and relates to Fitzpiers. It is artfully placed between two bird images which contrast the ideality of his romantic dreams and the reality of his urge for sexual licence. After lingering by the remains of the woodman's fire and indulging an idyllic fancy that he could enjoy a simple country life, until it is twilight, and the nightingale ('the shy little bird of this dusky time') begins 'to pour out all the intensity of his eloquence from a bush not very far off', Fitzpiers sees Grace Melbury return. He helps her to find a lost purse, a present from Giles. Fitzpiers' questioning elicits answers which soon make him realize that the donor is no longer quite in favour, and he at once begins a flattering overture.

> A diversion was created by the accident of two large birds, that had either been roosting above their heads or nesting there, tumbling one over the other into the hot ashes at their feet, apparently engrossed in a desperate quarrel that prevented the use of their wings. They speedily parted, however, and flew up, with a singed smell, and were seen no more.
>
> 'That's the end of what is called love', said some one.

The speaker is Marty South, who has been trying to trace the birds – a pair of pigeons. She had no idea when she spoke that any other person was present, and the overtones of the passage can have no reference to the past. Giles has never known that Marty is in love with him, and her love for him will die only when she ceases to live. The quarrel of the birds and their parting prefigure the course of Grace's married life with Fitzpiers, and the pejorative 'called' points forward to this. The scene is followed by the ritual of the Midsummer Eve pairings, with Fitzpiers finally lured to the hay meadow by Suke Damson; and the sarcastic whirr of the night-hawk with which this series of movements begins and ends provides a loud and sustained hint of what is to be expected. The time of the nightingales is past, Hardy adds almost parenthetically.

The suffering of birds in accordance with 'the Frost's decree' represents the harshness of life. It is the subject of a number of poems immediately preceding 'The Darkling Thrush' in *Poems of the Past and the Present* (see pp. 100–101), but nowhere is it more intensely conveyed than in the imagery of the Arctic birds at Flintcomb-Ash, where Tess's plight is agonizingly reflected in their tragical eyes (see pp. 29–30). In another poem, 'The Reminder', Hardy's attention is drawn from the Christmas blaze inside his room to a thrush in the frost outside his window. Why, he asks, cannot he forget harsh reality on a day traditionally set aside for good cheer? (The thought, it should be added, is not typical of Hardy, so often is he struck by the ironical contrast between Christmas sentiments – peace on earth, good will towards men – and the practice of people and nations who call themselves Christian; examples may be found in his short stories and poems, the most apt being 'Christmas: 1924'.) The 'starving bird' of 'The Reminder' no doubt recalled the starved, half-frozen bird which fell dead at Higher Bockhampton when his father tossed a stone at it. The memory of it haunted him for life (see p. 91).

Hardy changes from the bird-in-a-springe image to that of the snared rabbit in *Jude the Obscure*, at the turning point of the story (IV. ii) when Sue and Jude hear the repeated cry of pain which expresses the plight of their separation as a result of two disastrous marriages.

An image of the bird's nest filled with snow occurs in *The Well-Beloved* (I. vii) when Pierston thinks of the migratory 'Well-Beloved' flitting from woman to woman, each in turn losing the 'divinity' and 'radiant vitality' with which she has been invested by her admirer, to become a 'mournful emptied shape' like 'the nest of some beautiful bird from which the inhabitant has departed and left it to fill with snow'. This striking parallel has a poetic aptness; it is not found elsewhere in Hardy, and could have come from Wordsworth's sonnet 'Why are thou silent?'

Hardy's imagery of the caged bird derives from two sources. One has an individual reference, and is exemplified, as already indicated, in

Richardson's *Clarissa*; the other has a more general, philosophical significance. The first is seen in the earlier version of *Tess of the d'Urbervilles*, where the heroine, before stabbing Alec, cries, 'O, you have torn
my life all in pieces ... made me a victim, a caged wretch!' Elsewhere
(p. 135) I have put forward the view that, in its dominant motif of
charity and the parallel of its conclusion to the sub-title of *Tess*, 'The
Blinded Bird' is an emblem of Tess. 'Blinded ere yet a-wing', she hopes
and endures, sacrificing herself altruistically; as a victim of chance, she
also is 'enjailed in pitiless wire'. 'The Caged Goldfinch' has no figurative overtones, as its original ending anticlimactically shows:

> True, a woman was found drowned the day ensuing,
>   And some at time averred
> The grave to be her false one's, who when wooing
>   Gave her the bird.

Henchard's caged goldfinch recalls King Lear's hope of reconciliation
when he is restored to Cordelia: 'We two will sing like birds i' th' cage.'
Hardy's hero, however, is rejected and his wedding-gift ignored until
it is too late. Like the goldfinch, Henchard is not found by Elizabeth-
Jane until he is dead.

As Hardy's more serious fiction is directed by a philosophical outlook
which did not change radically from 1865 onwards, it is not surprising
that the second type of caged bird image occurs in his novels as well as
in his more personal writings. It is a late development, none the less,
and probably originates from 'Goethe's Helena', an essay by Thomas
Carlyle to which Hardy alludes in *The Mayor of Casterbridge*. Nothing
in it could have impressed him more than this passage:

> The Soul of Man still fights with the dark influences of Ignorance,
> Misery and Sin; still lacerates itself, like a captive bird, against the
> iron limits which Necessity has drawn round it.

Hardy's views on Necessity fluctuated but, even when he uses the term
without qualification, there is no proof that he was ever quite a Neces-
sitarian. By and large they show a belief in a 'modicum of free will'.
The degree of Necessity or lack of choice depends on many factors, an
obvious one being means; or as Hardy expressed it, after observing
crowds and traffic by the Marble Arch in May 1885 (six weeks after
finishing *The Mayor of Casterbridge*), the degree of movement one is
allowed depends on the size of the cage:

> The hum of the wheel – the roar of London! ... The people in this
> tragedy laugh, sing, smoke, toss off wines, etc., make love to girls in
> drawing-rooms and areas; and yet are playing their parts in the
> tragedy just the same. Some wear jewels and feathers, some wear

rags. All are caged birds; the only difference lies in the size of the cage.

In Hardy's poem 'The Bullfinches' a hedonistic philosophy of life like that of the *Rubáiyát of Omar Khayyám* is fancifully advocated by one of the 'bulleys' who has heard from the fairies in Blackmoor Vale how little protection they can expect from Mother Nature. There is a relationship between this drowsy Mother – she is 'The Sleep-Worker' and the 'sightless' Mother of 'The Lacking Sense' – and blind Mrs d'Urberville, who is unaware of what is going on around her and in particular of the danger threatening Tess. Caged bullfinches are housed appropriately in her bedroom, where they flit 'freely at certain hours'. Like the Mother of Hardy's poems, she is kindly but incapable of doing what needs to be done for the welfare of her creatures, which had suffered neglect before Tess arrived. After her introduction to Tess, she withdraws into the background, where she remains while Alec does as he pleases. Tess, who later says that the sight of a caged bird often made her cry, tends the bullfinches and cheers them by whistling. Here Hardy introduces mythic overtones; there is a complete parallel between narrative and philosophy, which would remain unnoticed or be regarded as inadmissible were not this curious feature of Tess's life at The Slopes part of a symbolic pattern which gives the story at this juncture a deeper and more universal meaning (see pp. 115–16).

One of his last poems, and one of his most pessimistic, is 'We Are Getting to the End'. In this poem and 'He Resolves to Say No More' (both appropriately placed at the end of his last volume) Hardy's increasing despair of humanity's betterment was almost certainly due to his agonized awareness that another world war was looming. He thinks of the masses of people enjoying themselves (like the 'caged birds' of London), heedless of the tragedy around them or of the greater tragedy that is being prepared:

> We know that even as larks in cages sing
> Unthoughtful of deliverance from the curse
> That holds them lifelong in a latticed hearse,
> We ply spasmodically our pleasuring.

The caged larks sing, it may be argued, as the bullfinches are urged to do, in order to forget unpleasant realities; but the nub of Hardy's criticism is in the words which follow. 'Unthoughtful of deliverance' implies that deliverance is possible; if men heeded, something could be done to prevent a catastrophe urged on by 'some demonic force'. The madness of international wars had made him impugn a vague Ultimate called the Immanent Will; in his last years he more sensibly attributed such large-scale disasters to the folly of mankind.

13   The Influence of Shelley

It is no exaggeration to say that Shelley's influence on Hardy's thought and basic outlook was greater than that of any other writer. Philosophical views which scholars commonly ascribe to later writers such as Schopenhauer and von Hartmann had become convictions for Hardy in the mid-1860s when he read Shelley with enthusiastic assiduity in London. In his poetry he found an exhilarating freedom and intellectual intrepidity, a scientific view of the universe consistent with Darwinism, and principles for social reform which were to make him sympathetic to much in the writings of Comte and later philosophers. Shelley's ideas helped enormously to free Hardy from the shackles of convention.

He was enraptured by Shelley's lyricism, and in his later years described him as 'our most marvellous lyrist'. Some of Shelley's imagery was appropriated by Hardy's creative imagination, but his influence on Hardy's poetic style was negligible compared with that of Browning's dramatic and lyrical use of speech idiom in verse. Not surprisingly, when Hardy was on holiday in central Italy in 1887, Shelley and Browning, though so different 'in their writings, their mentality, and their lives', mingled in his thoughts 'almost to the exclusion of other English poets equally, or nearly so, associated with Italy, with whose works he was just as well acquainted'.

Nothing concerning Shelley was too insignificant for Hardy's interest. He told his secretary Miss O'Rourke that he was the poet whom above all others he wished to have met, and many Shelleyan quotations and allusions are to be found in his works. Even before he left Dorset for London in 1862, Hardy had been impressed by Walter Bagehot's essay on Shelley in his *Estimates* of 1858 (afterwards entitled *Literary Studies*). Much later, his romantic interest in the poet was renewed and extended by Edward Dowden's *Life of Shelley* (1886). From Geneva in June 1897 he informed Mrs Henniker that he 'thought of going this afternoon to try to find the cottage in which Shelley and Mary lived, a little way below Byron's "Campagne Diodate" (*vide* Dowden's *Shelley*)'. His own *Life* shows how he loved to think that, when he had his mother travelled in his boyhood to her sister's at Hatfield, they had stayed in the room at the Cross Keys, Clerkenwell, which was occupied by Shelley when he met Mary Godwin there at week-ends. They were married at St Mildred's, Bread Street, to which Hardy took his friend

Sir George Douglas in 1899 to see their signatures in the register; he had been there before, he adds parenthetically. In the story 'An Imaginative Woman' he compares a poet's scribbling on the wallpaper to Shelley's manuscript scraps; in the Apology to *Late Lyrics and Earlier* he refers to his love of sailing paper boats. His visit to the graves of Shelley and Keats in Rome inspired one poem, and the knowledge that Shelley composed 'To a Skylark' at Leghorn led him to write 'Shelley's Skylark' when he was near Leghorn in March 1887.

Hardy's poem is on a more pedestrian level, but it recalls the 'ecstatic heights in thought and rhyme' of Shelley's poem. Believing with St John that 'the truth shall make you free', Hardy recognized in Shelley a fellow-spirit. The implications of 'To a Skylark' had been revealed in *Prometheus Unbound*: the freedom of man would come with enlightenment and love. The bird is

> Like a Poet hidden
> In the light of thought,
> Singing hymns unbidden,
> Till the world is wrought
> To sympathy with hopes and fears it heeded not.

If only the Poet of Liberty, as Hardy called him in *Jude*, had the joy and inspiration of the skylark, the world would listen to his message. Thinking of the 'poet' as a man of vision (writer, artist, or legislator), Shelley wrote:

> The most unfailing herald, companion, and follower of the awakening of a great people to work a beneficial change in opinion or institution, is poetry. . . . Poets are the unacknowledged legislators of the world.

'If you mean to make the world listen to you, you must say now what they will all be thinking and saying five and twenty years hence: and if you do that you must offend your conventional friends', Hardy advised his author-friend Mrs Henniker in 1893.[1]

In London Hardy's Shelleyan fervour helped to kindle his political and revolutionary zeal. In 1865 he listened to a political speech from J. S. Mill, whose treatise *On Liberty* he knew 'almost by heart'. The following year he was intoxicated by the word-magic and passionate revolt of Swinburne's poetry. By the end of 1867 he had completed the first draft of *The Poor Man and the Lady*; it was

> a sweeping dramatic satire of the squirearchy and nobility, London society, the vulgarity of the middle class, modern Christianity, church-restoration, and political and domestic morals in general, the author's views, in fact, being obviously those of a young man with a passion for reforming the world – those of many a young man before

and after him; the tendency of the writing being socialistic, not to say revolutionary.

Yet it was Shelley's (and Swinburne's) fearless attack on the blind or tyrannical Power to whom responsibility was attributed for the cruelty of Nature and the plight of man which made the greatest and most lasting impact on Hardy. In *The Revolt of Islam* winter represents the hardships suffered by man which Shelley believed could be removed or alleviated by revolution and enlightenment. From the euphoric vision of this poem – best summed up in the closing lines of 'Ode to the West Wind':

> Be through my lips to unawakened earth
> The trumpet of a prophecy! O, Wind,
> If Winter comes, can Spring be far behind?

– comes the wintry imagery in Hardy which connotes man's trials, setbacks, and tribulations. 'Crass Casualty' or 'the Frost's decree' can be mitigated by science and enlightenment, by co-operation and 'loving-kindness', but there is much in it which is subject to natural law and seemingly inevitable.

In the face of adversity, Shelley counsels 'Gentleness, Virtue, Wisdom, and Endurance':

> To suffer woes which Hope thinks infinite;
> To forgive wrongs darker than death or night;
>   To defy Power, which seems omnipotent;
> To love, and bear; to hope till Hope creates
> From its own wreck the thing it contemplates;
>   Neither to change, nor falter, nor repent;
> This, like thy glory, Titan, is to be
> Good, great and joyous, beautiful and free;
> This is alone Life, Joy, Empire, and Victory.[2]

For Hardy the essence of this is synonymous with the spirit of Christian 'charity' (which involves long-suffering); he embodies it in Tess, not absolutely but humanly, as far as circumstances and probability allow. More dramatically *Prometheus Unbound* exemplifies the power of love in the salvation of mankind. Influenced also by Comte's stress on altruism to the same end, Hardy says in 'A Plaint to Man' that a brighter future depends

> On the human heart's resource alone,
> In brotherhood bonded close and graced
> With loving-kindness . . .

In this way the will of mankind, by being part of the 'general'[3] or Immanent Will, could, Hardy dared to hope at the end of *The*

Dynasts, do something to make 'the Cause of Things' conscious of suffering in a Darwinian and irrational world.

There can be little doubt that Hardy was influenced by the form as well as the spirit of *Prometheus Unbound.* Its chorus of spirits 'From the depths of the sky and the ends of the earth' suggested the aerial spirits of *The Dynasts,* though Hardy gave them roles more distinct and diversified in accordance with his own modes of thought and feeling. One of Shelley's choruses presents the 'Gentle guides and guardians . . . of heaven-oppressed mortality', and in them Hardy's Spirit of the Pities may be seen. More often they appear as the flower of man's intelligence, like the Chorus at the end of Part First of *The Dynasts.* They come

> from the mind
> Of human kind
> Which was late so dusk, and obscene, and blind,

representing man's highest Thought, Wisdom, Art, and Science. Hardy's Shade of the suffering Earth has its obvious orginal in Shelley's lyrical drama, and the Fore Scene of *The Dynasts* echoes a Shelleyan note when the Chorus of Pities sings to aerial music:

> We would establish those of kindlier build,
> In fair Compassions skilled . . .
> Those, too, who love the true, the excellent,
> And make their daily moves a melody.

In *Prometheus Unbound,* and elsewhere in Shelley, music and musical imagery reflect happiness and the ideal; and it is in accordance with this that Hardy's Spirit of the Pities avers:

> Things mechanized
> By coils and pivots set to foreframed codes
> Would, in a thorough-sphered melodic rule,
> And governance of sweet consistency,
> Be cessed no pain.

The chorus and semi-choruses of *Hellas,* Shelley's second lyrical drama on the subject of human liberation, also affected the form of *The Dynasts.* Perhaps its final expression of uncertain hope weighed with Hardy when he chose to end his epic drama more hopefully than history (or the Spirit of the Years) warranted.

Important though *The Revolt of Islam* and *Prometheus Unbound* are in the development of Hardy's thought, it is doubtful if either affected him quite as much as *Queen Mab* and its extensive notes, completed by Shelley at the age of twenty, and the repository of most of his philosophical and revolutionary thought. Here, like Hardy's 'Cause of Things', Nature is represented as neutral or amoral, loveless and hateless (see the quotation on pp. 94–5). She is referred to as the

'mother', as happens frequently in Hardy's poetry, and more significantly (on the score of influence) in his first published novel, *Desperate
Remedies*. As in *Tess of the d'Urbervilles*, one of the images illustrating
the ruthlessness of Nature in Shelley's poem is the 'ceaseless frost' of
the Polar regions (viii, 58–69).

Among the notes to *Queen Mab* which Hardy must have read with
approval, the following are of special importance:

1. On the plurality of worlds and the immensity of the universe, which
make it inconceivable that the Spirit pervading 'this infinite machine'
(cf. *The Dynasts*) 'begat a son upon the body of a Jewish woman' (cf.
'Panthera'); 'or is angered at the consequences of that necessity'
(natural law throughout the universe), 'which is a synonym of itself'.

2. Necessity as 'an immense and uninterrupted chain of causes and
effects, no one of which could occupy any other place than it does
occupy, or act in any other place than it does act'. 'Motive is to volun-
tary action in the human mind what cause is to effect in the material
universe. The word liberty, as applied to mind, is analogous to the
word chance as applied to matter: they spring from an ignorance of
the certainty of the conjunction of antecedents and consequents.'

Although the general evidence confirms Hardy's belief in a 'modicum of free will',[4] Shelley's statement admirably elucidates what Hardy
implies when he says that we are 'bond-servants to Chance' or subject
to the 'whimsical god ... known as blind Circumstance'. 'Circumstance' includes personal as well as external factors; motivation depends
on character, and character (to some extent) on heredity (cf. Hardy's
poem 'The Pedigree').

3. On marriage. Shelley's views seem more relevant to Hardy than
those of Milton in *The Doctrine and Discipline of Divorce*:

   i. 'Love withers under constraint: its very essence is liberty: it is
   compatible neither with obedience, jealousy, nor fear; it is there
   most pure, perfect, and unlimited, where its votaries live in confidence, equality, and unreserve.' Hardy's familiarity with this
   passage was due primarily to Bagehot's essay on Shelley.[5] Similar
   views may be seen in his poems 'The Ivy-Wife' and 'At a Hasty
   Wedding'. Pre-eminently they are voiced by Sue Bridehead, who is
   afraid that the 'iron contract' of marriage will extinguish tender-
   ness, and abhors the thought of being 'licensed to be loved on the
   premises'. Hardy found its best expression in the words of Thomas
   Campbell:

   > Can you keep the bee from ranging
   > Or the ring-dove's neck from changing?
   > No! nor fetter'd Love from dying
   > In the knot there's no untying.

ii. 'A husband and wife ought to continue so long united as they love each other: any law which should bind them to cohabitation for one moment after the decay of their affection would be a most intolerable tyranny, and the most unworthy of toleration.' This applies to the marriage of Grace Melbury and Fitzpiers, and much more explicitly to that of Phillotson and Sue Bridehead.

iii. 'Has a woman obeyed the impulse of unerring nature; – society declares war against her . . . ; theirs is the right of persecution, hers the duty of endurance.' Hardy's sympathy with this view is clear in 'The Christening'.

His association of the iris or rainbow image with love and hope (see pp. 161–2) was reinforced by Shelley. In *Prometheus Unbound* (i. 708–722) the rainbow arch suggests love and self-sacrifice, after storm and disaster at sea; in *Hellas* (43) Shelley refers to Hope's 'iris of delight'. Two related images in 'Epipsychidion' also find their place in Hardy. The first is proverbial:

> This truth is that deep well, whence sages draw
> The unenvied light of hope.

Phillotson had often drawn from it, but to the boy Jude it appeared 'from his present position' (both literal and allegorical) like 'a long circular perspective ending in a shining disk'. In the next lines (186–9) Shelley describes this world as a 'garden ravaged' or 'wilderness'. It is a favourite image with Hardy, harking back to Eden, and to Hamlet's

> How weary, stale, flat, and unprofitable
> Seem to me all the uses of this world!
> Fie on't! Ah, fie! 'tis an unweeded garden,
> That grows to seed; things rank and gross in nature
> Possess it merely.

It is seen at Talbothays when Tess, her young life blighted, is drawn to Angel. Through the mediation of Swinburne it finds a place in *Desperate Remedies* (see pp. 13–15) and, in association with the onset of winter, following the lead of Shelley in 'The Sensitive Plant', it leaves a trail of significant images in Hardy's novels and poetry (p. 99).

Three of his last four novels suggest that Hardy came to realize the hazards of Shelleyanism in practice. However much one may agree in principle with Shelley on love and marriage, one can never forget the tragic death of the wife Harriet whom he deserted. Imagine a sensualist romantically exalted by the Platonics of 'Epipsychidion', and led on by the Vision or the Idea into philandering and infidelities, and you have someone like Fitzpiers. Basically, but less ideally, he is moulded on the theme of 'Alastor or the Spirit of Solitude'. Like the youth of Shelley's poem, he is 'conversant with speculations of the sublimest and most perfect natures'; and 'the vision in which he embodies his own imaginations unites all of wonderful, or wise, or beautiful, which the poet, the philosopher, or the lover could depicture'.[6] Fitzpiers in his solitude at Hintock reads widely, his mind passing 'in a grand solar sweep through the zodiac of the intellectual heaven' in the course of a year. He is unpractical, a dabbler in science and medicine; and he has no roots in the country. In such circumstances, Hardy writes:

> A young man may dream of an ideal friend . . . but some humour of the blood will probably lead him to think rather of an ideal mistress, and at length the rustle of a woman's dress, the sound of her voice, or the transit of her form across the field of his vision, will enkindle his soul with a flame that blinds his eyes.

The self-centred seclusion of Shelley's idealist brings its 'alastor' or retribution. When he seeks to find the veiled maid of his vision, a companion of similar intelligence to his own, 'a prototype of his conception', he is disappointed and dies an early death. Unlike the youth of 'Alastor', Fitzpiers is a man of corrupted feelings, a dilettante humbug who knows all the virtues of Schleiermacher, tries to flatter Grace by saying that she practises all of them unconsciously, but is incapable of observing any of them himself. In accordance with the idealism of 'Epipsychidion', he pursues the shadow of the idol of his thought (the 'prototype of his conception') from woman to woman, and adopts an irresponsible, Shelleyan attitude towards marriage:

> I never was attached to that great sect,
> Whose doctrine is, that each one should select
> Out of the crowd a mistress or a friend,
> And all the rest, though fair and wise, commend
> To cold oblivion, though it is in the code
> Of modern morals, and the beaten road
> Which those poor slaves with weary footsteps tread,
> By the broad highway of the world, and so
> With one chained friend, perhaps a jealous foe,
> The dreariest and the longest journey go.

In Shelleyan theory 'nothing exists but as it is perceived'.[7] 'Human love is a subjective thing', so that it is very much a matter of chance on whom the 'rainbow iris' is projected, Fitzpiers tells Giles Winterborne, after quoting a verse on his Vision from *The Revolt of Islam* (ii. xxiii): 'She moved upon this earth a shape of brightness . . .'. Grace Melbury first appears to him as a vision, her image being reflected in a mirror as he momentarily wakes. Later he wonders whether he has seen this 'lovely form' in a dream, or whether he could have been awake. 'I fancied in my vision that you stood there', he tells her when she returns; 'I thought, what a lovely creature! The design is for once carried out. Nature has at last recovered her lost union with the Idea!'

Despite his rainbow iris theory, he is 'enchanted enough' to 'fancy' that the Idea or Platonic ideal had found its 'objective substance' in her when he goes to the Hintock wood on Midsummer Eve, ironically to end the night on a haycock with Suke Damson. After his marriage to Grace, the Idea takes this Tannhäuser to Felice Charmond, and he murmurs lines from 'Epipsychidion' as he goes:

> ... towards the lodestar of my one desire,
> I flitted, like a dizzy moth, whose flight
> Is as dead leaf's in the owlet light.

The search for the Idea in one woman after another is presented both tragically and sarcastically in *The Woodlanders*; in the lighter fantasy of *The Well-Beloved* it is viewed for the most part in a comic light. The form the story took owed much to 'the remark of a sculptor that he had often pursued a beautiful ear, nose, chin, etc., about London in omnibuses and on foot'.[8] The sculptor Jocelyn Pierston is neither selfish nor sensual like Fitzpiers. He is a victim of the Vision, the 'migratory, elusive idealization he called his Love' having 'flitted from human shell to human shell an indefinite number of times' before taking up its abode in the first Avice when he is a young man of twenty. 'A young man of forty', and still a 'young man' at sixty, he falls in love with her daughter, and then her grand-daughter. The *reductio ad absurdum* comes when, deciding to confide in the latter, he tells her his past, and she asks whether he had been in love with her great-grandmother. Jocelyn suddenly becomes old; the Vision of the Well-Beloved and his artistic sense abandon him, never to return. After a marriage of convenience, he turns to utilitarian occupations for the benefit of the local community. Hardy described the novel as a tragi-comedy; Edmund Gosse, as 'The Tragedy of a Nympholept'. The title-page quotation 'One shape of many names' comes from *The Revolt of Islam* (I. xxvii), where it refers to 'the Spirit of evil'; and Pierston maintains that he is under a 'curse' or 'doom' as long as he is lured on by the 'Jill-o'-the-wisp' Idea. (For the link with Shelley's 'Alastor', see p. 164.) Nevertheless, Hardy does not seem to have taken the story very seriously in human terms. His most positive statement suggests a rather allegorical significance: 'There is, of course, under-lying the fantasy followed by the visionary artist the truth that all men are pursuing a shadow, the Unattainable, and I venture to hope that this may redeem the tragi-comedy from the charge of frivolity.'[9]

The inadequacy of the Shelleyan lover is presented in Angel Clare. Whether his name alludes to Arnold's description of Shelley as 'a beautiful and ineffectual angel, beating in the void his luminous wings in vain' is doubtful (see p. 127), but his love for Tess is 'imaginative and ethereal' rather than real. 'She was no longer the milkmaid, but a visionary essence.... He called her Artemis, Demeter...'; and he

regards her as the embodiment of 'rustic innocence'. As soon as he
finds the 'vision' of her 'mocked by appearances', he is overcome by
an antipathy which 'warps' his soul. His love had been 'ethereal to a
fault, imaginative to impracticability. With these natures, corporeal
presence is sometimes less appealing than corporeal absence; the latter
creating an ideal presence that conveniently drops the defects of the
real.' Similarly Jocelyn Pierston finds that he loves the first Avice when
she is 'dead and inaccessible as he had never loved her in life'. The
most apposite criticism of Angel Clare from Hardy is implied in his
note of 28 November 1891, when he may well have had the subject of
The Well-Beloved in mind:

> It is the incompleteness that is loved, when love is sterling and true.
> This is what differentiates the real one from the imaginary, the prac-
> ticable from the impossible, the Love who returns the kiss from the
> Vision that melts away. A man sees the Diana or the Venus in his
> Beloved, but what he loves is the difference.

Yet, whatever reservations Hardy formed on some of Shelley's principles and imaginative flights, he never ceased to admire his poetry and
spirit. He had a tendency to think in terms of Shelley's imagery. It is
noticeable in his earliest fiction and in his last (see p. 92 for the
influence of 'When the lamp is shattered'). *'Cold reason'* comes back
to *'mock'* Tess after she has answered some of her friends with
superiority, on her return from The Slopes; when Angel turns against
her, his propensities are as *'dead leaves* upon the tyrannous *wind* of his
imaginative ascendency'. To Pierston, when he is subject to his
'gigantic fantasies', the sight of the new *moon*, 'representing one who,
by her so-called *inconstancy*, acted up to his own idea of a migratory
Well-Beloved, made him feel as if his wraith in a changed sex had
suddenly looked over the horizon at him'.

Nowhere is Hardy's imagining in Shelleyan terms more important
than in *Jude the Obscure*, and the reason is not far to seek. Hardy had
become a victim of the Vision; he had met and fallen, imaginatively
at least, in love with Mrs Henniker. They were, he felt, kindred spirits.
He discovers that they have been reading 'Epipsychidion' at the same
time, and is certain it must have happened by 'mutual influence'. He
then regrets that she 'who is pre-eminently the child of the Shelleyan
tradition' has 'allowed herself to be enfeebled to a belief in ritualistic
ecclesiasticism', and tells her that he must 'trust to imagination only
for an enfranchised woman'. This imaginary woman he depicted in
Sue Bridehead; she is the 'prototype of his conception'. Her ideas on
convention and the First Cause are Hardy's, and she shocks Jude when
he is training to become a curate. Her ideas on marriage are Shelley's,
as has been noted. In the end, disaster gets the better of her reason, and
she becomes a slave to 'ritualistic ecclesiasticism'. When Jude falls in

love with her, he feels it is a cruel chance that 'the one affined soul he had ever met was lost to him, through his marriage'. Sue is 'nearer to him than any other woman he had ever met, and he could scarcely believe that time, creed, or absence would ever divide him from her'. That is how, at first, Hardy, unhappily married, felt towards Mrs Henniker. He thinks of her in terms recalling Shelley's worship of his 'Seraph of Heaven'. When he tells her that she is of that 'ethereal intangible sort which letters cannot convey', the creative influence of 'Epipsychidion' is evident:

> She met me, Stranger, upon life's rough way,
> ... An antelope,
> In the suspended impulse of its lightness,
> Were less aetherially light; the brightness
> Of her divinest presence trembles through
> Her limbs ...

Hardy's imaginative idealization of Florence Henniker[10] is transferred to Jude, and the following passage (III. ix) could be autobiographical in almost every respect:

> Looking at his loved one as she appeared to him now, in his tender thought the sweetest and most disinterested comrade that he had ever had, living largely in vivid imaginings, so ethereal a creature that her spirit could be seen trembling through her limbs, he felt heartily ashamed of his earthliness ... There was something rude and immoral in thrusting these recent facts of his life upon the mind of one who, to him, was so uncarnate as to seem at times impossible as a human wife to any average man.

In comparison, the quoting of 'Epipsychidion' by Sue with reference to herself (IV. v) is factitious; but the conception of her here and elsewhere as an 'aerial being' is typical of Hardy's heightened imagining under the influence of Shelley's poetry, and not inappropriate to Fitzpiers or Pierston.

14 The Iris-Bow and the Well-Beloved

Robert Browning used the iris-bow image once only, very late in his life, in his Prologue to *Asolando* (1889), which begins:

> 'The Poet's age is sad: for why?
>   In youth, the natural world could show
> No common object but his eye
>   At once involved with alien glow –
>   His own soul's iris-bow.
>
> 'And now a flower is just a flower:
>   Man, bird, beast are but beast, bird, man –
> Simply themselves, uncinct with dower
>   Of dyes which, when life's day began,
>   Round each in glory ran.'

In reply, the poet asks whether one prefers 'truth ablaze', 'the naked very thing', or 'falsehood's fancy-haze'. The thought is closely akin to Hardy's rather than to the more familiar theory of the imagination enunciated by Wordsworth and Coleridge. Browning rejoices that a flower is seen distinctly for what it is ('a flower is just a flower'), whereas Wordsworth grieves that the sympathies of Peter Bell had never been awakened, simply because he had no imagination:

> A primrose by a river's brim
> A yellow primrose was to him,
> And it was nothing more.

There must be a Wordsworthian illogicality in the assumption that an imaginative sympathy is identical with the creative imagination, as Coleridge regards it when he laments its loss with the passing years:

> I may not hope from outward forms to win
> The passion and the life, whose fountains are within.
>
> O Lady! we receive but what we give,
> And in our life alone does Nature live:
> Ours is her wedding-garment, ours her shroud!
>   And would we ought behold, of higher worth,

> Than that inanimate cold world allowed
> To the poor, loveless ever-anxious crowd,
> Ah! from the soul itself must issue forth
> A light, a glory, a fair luminous cloud
> Enveloping the Earth.

For Wordsworth and Coleridge the imagination is life; it gives full realization. For Hardy and Browning it is delusive.

The truth seems to be that an imaginative, heightened awareness enhances life only as far as it promotes a realization of the truth, as Wordsworth hinted in *The Prelude* (II. 358–70) when he distinguished the imagination which was 'Subservient strictly to external things/ With which it communed' from that which is 'rebellious' or 'devious', indulging at times in 'vagaries' of fictive fancy such as those he describes in Book VIII of *The Prelude* (365–450).

The inference drawn from Browning's late, solitary use of the iris-bow image is that, consciously or otherwise, he borrowed it from Hardy. In May 1888 the latter sent Browning a copy of *Wessex Tales* as a birthday greeting; and it seems not at all improbable that interest in some of these stories led the aged poet to read Hardy's latest novel, *The Woodlanders*. If this surmise is true (and it seems far from improbable, since the two writers had met frequently), Browning had noticed the remarkable passage in Chapter xvi which runs:

> Human love is a subjective thing – the essence itself of man, as that great thinker Spinoza says – *ipsa hominis essentia* – it is joy accompanied by an idea which we project against any suitable object in the line of our vision, just as the rainbow iris is projected against an oak, ash, or elm tree indifferently. So that if any other young lady had appeared instead of the one who did appear, I should have felt the same interest in her, and have quoted precisely the same lines from Shelley about her, as about this one I saw. Such miserable creatures of circumstance are we all!

This statement fuses the rainbow connotations and a theory of experience or perception in a magic-lantern image which may have derived from Schopenhauer, whose Will operates at varying degrees through the world, finding its 'clearest and fullest objectification' in man. Perceptive functioning is illustrated as follows:

> As the magic-lantern shows many different pictures, which are all made visible by one and the same light, so in all the multifarious phenomena which fill the world together or throng after each other as events, only *one will* manifests itself, of which everything is the visibility, the objectivity, and which remains unmoved in the midst of this change.[1]

Basic to Schopenhauer's reasoning is the Cartesian and Berkeleyan assumption that nothing exists except in a subjective form: 'all that exists for knowledge, and therefore this whole world, is only object in relation to subject, perception of a perceiver, in a word, idea'.[2] It was familiar to Hardy from the time when he noted Shelley's view in Bagehot's *Estimates* that 'nothing exists but as it is preceived'.[3] In 1865 he wrote, 'The poetry of a scene varies with the minds of the perceivers. Indeed, it does not lie in the scene at all.' One suspects that he had read 'The Lover's Journey' in Crabbe's *Tales*, a story written to illustrate views which are summarized in the opening paragraph:

> It is the soul that sees; the outward eyes
> Present the object, but the mind descries;
> And thence delight, disgust, or cool indiff'rence rise:
> When minds are joyful, then we look around,
> And what is seen is all on fairy ground;
> Again they sicken, and on every view
> Cast their own dull and melancholy hue;
> Or, if absorb'd by their peculiar cares,
> The vacant eye on viewless matter glares.
> Our feelings still upon our views attend,
> And their own natures to the objects lend:
> Sorrow and joy are in their influence sure,
> Long as the passion reigns th'effects endure;
> But love in minds his various changes makes,
> And clothes each object with the change he takes;
> His light and shade on every view he throws,
> And on each object, what he feels, bestows.

In 'The King's Experiment' Hardy writes a parallel to Crabbe's tale. It is 'in the comedy of things' that Hodge should find a dull scene 'bright as Paradise' when he goes to see his love, and a bright scene gloomy and accurst after her death. King Doom concludes his answer to Nature's questioning:

> 'And there's the humour, as I said;
> Thy dreary dawn he saw all gleaming gold,
> And in thy glistening green and radiant red
> Funereal gloom and cold.'

This is the principle which Hardy often observes in presenting impressions of scenery in his novels (see pp. 25–30); it can be seen in his poems, as in 'Alike and Unlike', which may have been written long after he and Emma travelled via North Wales to Dublin in 1893.

Hardy carries the subjective theory too far. He states categorically, for example, in *Tess of the d'Urbervilles* (xiii) that 'the world is only a psychological phenomenon' (see p. 132). Sometimes his use of the iris-bow image in his poetry suggests that this point of view has become a reflex one, too rationalistic and mechanical to be validated by experience. Responses are not wholly subjective in the Berkeleyan sense; they result from objective realities. How many would agree with Fitzpiers that 'if any other young lady had appeared', he would have felt just the same about her as he did about Grace Melbury? The second sonnet in the 'She, to Him' series (*Wessex Poems*) and its applied paraphrase in *Desperate Remedies* (xiii. 4) bring us nearer to a true assessment of experience, and to Shelley's view of subjective reality.

Having lost faith in Providence, Hardy took the iris-bow as a sign of illusory hope from the rainbow which was believed to be a token of the covenant between God and his people after the Flood.[4] In *Desperate Remedies* (1.5) he describes sudden hopes as rainbows to the sight which prove to be mists to the touch. In the poem 'To Outer Nature' he looks back wistfully to his youth when he could regard Nature as the handiwork of a God of love:

> O for a moment
> Of that old endowment –
> Light to gaily
> See thy daily
> Iris-hued embowment!

Darwinism had caused this 'glow' to fade, 'Darkness-overtaken'. In these shades can be seen the gloom of Egdon in *The Return of the Native*, a symbolical setting for a philosophy which only a thinker and realist like Clym Yeobright, aware of the 'defects of natural laws', can accept. 'Haggard Egdon appealed to a subtler and scarcer instinct, to a more recently learnt emotion than that which responds to the sort of beauty called charming and fair.' Facing the truth boldly can bring no comfort, Hardy reflects in 'On a Fine Morning', a poem which provides a comment on the conclusion of the song sung on a bright morning in Browning's *Pippa Passes*: 'God's in His heaven – /All's right with the world!' Solace comes, Hardy continues, only from the belief that 'this moment/With its iris-hued embowment' is 'no specious show',

> But as nothing other than
> Part of a benignant plan;
> Proof that earth was made for man.

More often the iris-bow in Hardy refers to love, and this may be due to the influence of Shelley's *Prometheus Unbound* (see p. 153). The most elaborate instance of it occurs in *The Return of the Native*. When Eustacia's 'perfervid imagination' makes her fall 'half in love with a vision' raised by Clym's return from Paris, she has a wonderful dream in which she eventually finds herself dancing with a man in silver armour (II. iii). As he whispers to her, she feels she is in Paradise; then suddenly they dive into one of the pools on the heath and come out 'somewhere beneath an iridescent hollow, arched with rainbows'. He is about to remove his casque and kiss her, when the dream is shattered. Here is the beginning of a 'La Belle Dame sans Merci' motif which ends in the ferny hollow on the heath (III. v), where the scene seems to belong to an age when there was 'nothing but a monotonous extent of leafage, amid which no birds sang'. These scenes are imaginatively related to 'The Hollow amid the Ferns' in *Far from the Madding Crowd*, where Troy's fascination for Bathsheba is dramatized in a dazzling sword-exercise display which makes her see 'a sort of rainbow' one moment, and a succession of gleams which appear by the rapidity of their movement like 'the luminous streams' of an *aurora militaris*.

In the poem 'Her Apotheosis', despite the implications of the title, love hardly seems an illusion. The 'faded woman' who sings this song must have been attractive in her youth. At least that is how she feels as she recalls a time when, though it was not the fashion for 'common maids' to receive 'honours, praises, pleasure' from men, 'an iris' ringed her with 'living light'. She may be indulging a fond fancy, just as the poet of 1890, in stating that he is as subject to 'Love's fitful ecstasies' as he had been in his youth, admits that he is as susceptible to fantasies as he was then ('In a Eweleaze near Weatherbury'; cf. 'I Look Into My Glass').

It is noticeable in 'The Absolute Explains' that the 'irised bow' is restricted to Hardy's 'ever memorable/Glad days of pilgrimage' when he journeyed to meet Emma Gifford in Cornwall. 'Looking at a Picture on an Anniversary' describes his feelings after her death, as he gazes at a portrait of her on the forty-third anniversary of their first meeting. As in other poems recalling their early love and happiness, no astringent note of disillusionment is heard. Hardy's old love is revived, and the 'rainbow-rays' are not so much illusion as idealization.

Elsewhere in Hardy (possibly as a result of his imaginative association of them with the rainbow in Wordsworth's 'Intimations of Immortality') the vision or the irradiation engendered by love is referred to as 'the glory and the dream'. In *A Pair of Blue Eyes*, before passing away with Knight's growing suspicions of Elfride, they had assumed an 'iridescence (see p. 23). As soon as Eustacia heard that Wildeve was 'no longer coveted by her rival', he lost 'the glory and the dream' with which she had invested him. And one suspects that this is the implication of the cryptic note (*Life*, 124) on Hardy's married life at Tooting, when he and Emma 'seemed to begin to feel that "there had past away a glory from the earth"' after their Sturminster Newton 'idyll'. 'To be conscious that the end of the dream is approaching, and yet has not absolutely come, is one of the most wearisome as well as the most curious stages along the course between the beginning of a passion and its end', Hardy observed at Sturminster Newton in *The Return of the Native* (I. xi).

In 'He Abjures Love', like Browning in *Asolando* but for more depressing reasons, Hardy rejects 'falsehood's fancy-haze':

> No more will now rate I
> The common rare,
> The midnight drizzle dew,
> The gray hour golden,
> The wind a yearning cry,
> The faulty fair,
> Things dreamt, of comelier hue
> Than things beholden!

In 'At Waking', a poem written in 1869 before he met Emma Gifford, he imagines the effect of the sudden death of love on the lover when the beloved loses 'her old endowment/Of charm that capped all nigh':

> O vision appalling
> When the one believed-in thing
> Is seen falling, falling,
> With all to which hope can cling.

Far more convincing, almost searingly traumatic, is it when Angel Clare, his 'vision' of Tess 'mocked by appearances', finds his love ('less fire than radiance') die within him; and Hardy introduces a verse from Swinburne's *Atalanta in Calydon* to express Tess's tragic perception that 'he saw her without irradiation – in all her bareness; that Time was chanting his satiric psalm at her then –

> Behold, when thy face is made bare, he that loved thee shall hate;
> Thy face shall be no more fair at the fall of thy fate.
> For thy life shall fall as the leaf and be shed as the rain;
> And the veil of thine head shall be grief, and the crown shall be pain.'

A disinterested disillusioning analysis of the subjective view of love is presented in the poem 'The Well-Beloved', where the lover's idealisation –

> O faultless is her dainty form,
> And luminous her mind;
> She is the God-created norm
> Of perfect womankind!

– is psychotherapeutically dissipated when he meets it in a Shape who tells him that she is what he dreams his love is, and what every lover thinks his bride to be. The shape is the 'ideal beloved one', the Platonic Idea. Man may pursue such a Well-Beloved, but she marries no mortal.

She is an illusion and, as the lover discovers, bears no resemblance to reality:

> – When I arrived and met my bride
> Her look was pinched and thin,
> As if her soul had shrunk and died,
> And left a waste within.

An extension of this idea runs through both versions of *The Well-Beloved*, where the artist's pursuit of the Unattainable has its parallel in 'Alastor'. Shelley's poem, however, is almost wholly allegorical: 'The intellectual faculties, the imagination, the functions of sense, have their respective requisitions on the sympathy of corresponding powers in other human beings.' The poet dreams of a veiled maid whose voice is 'like the voice of his own soul',

> Heard in the calm of thought; its music long,
> Like woven sounds of streams and breezes, held
> His inmost sense suspended in its web
> Of many-coloured woof and shifting hues.

When she is irrecoverably lost, the poet asks –

> Does the dark gate of death
> Conduct to thy mysterious paradise,
> O Sleep? Does the bright arch of rainbow clouds,
> And pendent mountains seen in thy calm lake,
> Lead only to a black and watery depth . . .?

For Shelley the idealistic reformer, Alastor or the avenging spirit is the doom of a 'self-centred' poet; the sub-title of the poem is 'The Spirit of Solitude'. The poet 'seeks in vain for a prototype of his conception. Blasted by his disappointment, he descends to an untimely grave.' Hardy's hero Pierston is continually disappointed, but in retrospect it is his illusive temperament which he regards as his doom or curse. The 1892 serial version of the novel is much gloomier than the final form; its ending becomes leaden with despair and attempted suicide. It conforms to the belief Hardy penned on 9 July 1889, 'Love lives on propinquity, but dies of contact', and anticipates *Jude* in a number of ways, particularly on the question of marriage. Pierston's first marriage hastens the departure of 'the Well-Beloved' from the shell it inhabited, and he declares, when he finds his second wife loves someone else, that 'healthy natural instinct is true law, and not an Act of Parliament'. There can be little doubt that Hardy was expressing principles which he accepted in theory but never thought fit to practise. The light fantastic skiff of this story is almost sunk beneath a heavy weight of contrivance engineered rather hastily to launch an attack on 'licensed' marriage, and the serial ends on a note of ghastly mockery.

In *The Well-Beloved*, serial and novel, both idealization and marriage for love lead to unhappiness. Hardy believed that 'a sympathetic interdependence, wherein mutual weaknesses are made the grounds of a defensive alliance' was required for 'an enduring and staunch affection'.[5] There may be a parallel between the unromantic ending of *Far from the Madding Crowd* and the marriage of convenience which concludes the revised version of *The Well-Beloved*, but the latter holds less promise. Oak and Bathsheba have learned much from mistakes of another kind, but they share many interests and have good prospects; for Pierston and Marcia little remains – they are already shrivelled by time. Furthermore, unlike the poet in Browning's Prologue to *Asolando* who finds it an advantage to shed romantic illusion, the artist is dead. Fortunately Hardy made his Shelleyan lover predominantly the subject of a metaphysical comedy. He knew from experience the danger of the Vision, and could contemplate it at times with amused detachment. He had stated the distinction between true love and imaginary on 28 November 1891 with reference to either Angel Clare or his conception of *The Well-Beloved* (see p. 156).

There is much in Hardy's writings to confirm the impression that in this novel he was adapting his own experience. His first sketch of it had been made when he was 'comparatively a young man, and interested in the Platonic Idea'. From youth to old age he was apt to fall in love not so much with people as with his own dream-creations of them. He seems to be writing autobiographically on this subject as early as *Desperate Remedies* (x. 4), where, with reference to Springrove, he says that his impressionable heart had for six or seven years been yearning in vain for an 'indefinable helpmate to the remoter sides of himself' until 'he developed a plan of satisfying his dreams by wandering away to the heroines of poetical imagination'. Then 'Cytherea appeared in the sky: his heart started up and spoke:

> 'Tis She, and here
> Lo! I unclothe and clear
> My wishes' cloudy character.'

This verse from Richard Crashaw's 'Wishes' has its counterpart from the same poem in the epigraph to Part First of *The Well-Beloved*:

> Now if Time knows
> That Her, whose radiant brows
> Weave them a garland of my vows,
>
> Her that dares be
> What these lines wish to see:
> I seek no further – it is She.

Yet the theme of the later novel, though partly foreshadowed in

Springrove's pursuit of his Well-Beloved, is not the same. For him the Idea is attained; for Pierston it is ever elusive. The earlier Springrove is to some extent a precursor of Angel Clare, as his opposite, Manston, is of Alec d'Urberville. And it is in *Desperate Remedies* (I. 2) that Hardy asserts a general truth which appears to be the key to much in his life and poetry: 'with some natures utter elusion is the one special event which will make a passing love permanent for ever'. 'With these natures,' Hardy wrote of Angel Clare, 'corporeal presence is sometimes less appealing than corporeal absence; the latter creating an ideal presence that conveniently drops the defects of the real' (xxxvi); and of Jocelyn Pierston, when he hears of the death of the first Avice (II. iii):

> The soul of Avice – the only woman he had *never* loved of those who had loved him – surrounded him like a firmament. . . . He loved the woman dead and inaccessible as he had never loved her in life. . . . She had been another man's wife almost the whole time since he was estranged from her, and now she was a corpse. Yet the absurdity did not make his grief the less: and consciousness of the intrinsic, almost radiant, purity of this new-sprung affection for a flown spirit forbade him to check it. The flesh was absent altogether; it was love rarefied and refined to the highest attar. He had felt nothing like it before.

In March 1890, not long before Hardy began to plan *The Well-Beloved*, his married cousin Tryphena had died; and immediately she became his 'lost prize', as the poem 'Thoughts of Phena' shows. This is the supreme truth, it appears, of Hardy's love of Tryphena. Of their personal relationship before he met Emma Gifford in March 1870 little is known beyond the evidence of 'In a Eweleaze near Weatherbury' that they danced together at a kind of 'picnic' or 'gipsying' (possibly like that described in *The Return of the Native*, IV. iii), and that she was one who 'kindled gaily/Love's fitful ecstasies'. The poem (which was written in 1890) continues with what became a leading motif in *The Well-Beloved*, 'Yet I note the little chisel/Of never-napping Time', and confirms that Hardy's novel took its final origin from a critical appraisal of imaginative experience activated by fond recollections of a woman he had for long almost forgotten. Similarly his love for Emma revived after her death and became more 'rarefied and refined' than it had ever been in her presence. 'He loved the woman dead and inaccessible as he had never loved her in life.' Hardy's love flourished most in his imagination; for him it was absence or loss which gave the iris-bow, the Idea, or 'the Well-Beloved' its greatest radiance.[6]

15 Intimations of Immortality

Hardy probably became first acquainted with Wordsworth's 'Intimations of Immortality' in the copy of *The Golden Treasury* which Horace Moule gave him in January 1862. It was a volume he prized all his life, and he knew most of its poems intimately. Concealed or disclosed quotations from 'Intimations' occur in at least six of his novels. In *A Pair of Blue Eyes* he twice uses 'the glory and the dream' with reference to Knight's love of Elfride. Wordsworth's romantic view of childhood is the target of an accusatory Positivist when, on their last night in the old home at Marlott, the youngest of the Durbeyfield family are presented singing a hymn to Tess (li):

> If she could only believe what the children were singing; if she were only sure, how different all would now be; how confidently she would leave them to Providence and their future kingdom! But, in default of that, it behoved her to do something; to be their Providence; for to Tess, as to not a few millions of others, there was ghastly satire in the poet's lines –
>
> Not in utter nakedness
But trailing clouds of glory do we come.
>
> To her and her like, birth itself was an ordeal of degrading personal compulsion, whose gratuitousness nothing in the result seemed to justify, and at best could only palliate.

In *Jude* it is the depressing contrast between the reality and childhood dreams which makes the Wordsworthian reference irresistible. A touching faith in Vilbert's promise to bring him Greek and Latin 'grammars' causes the boy Jude to smile 'with that singularly beautiful irradiation which is seen to spread on young faces at the inception of some glorious idea, as if a supernatural lamp were held inside their transparent natures, giving rise to the flattering fancy that heaven lies about them' (I. iv). How little hope Christminster holds out for him, how much enlightenment can be expected from his 'city of light', may be gauged from the darkness in which he finds the colleges and from 'the outmost lamps of the town' (II. i):

> – some of those lamps which had sent into the sky the gleam and glory that caught his strained gaze in his days of dreaming, so many

years ago. They winked their yellow eyes at him dubiously, and as if, though they had been awaiting him all these years in disappointment at his tarrying, they did not much want him now.

In 'Midnight on the Great Western' Hardy wonders what occupies the mind of an apparently listless boy; whether, in fact, immortality 'broods' over him as it does over the child in Wordsworth's poem – 'trailing clouds of glory' or 'Haunted for ever by the eternal mind'. The 'journey' is life, and the unknowns ('What past can be yours, O journeying boy/Towards a world unknown ...?') extend beyond it. Thinking of the Platonic theory of pre-existence which Wordsworth had in mind, and 'Heaven lies about us in our infancy', the poet asks:

> Knows your soul a sphere, O journeying boy,
>   Our rude realms far above,
> Whence with spacious vision you mark and mete
> This region of sin that you find you in,
>   But are not of?

Hardy's attitude here is less Positivist on the question of pre-existence than in *Tess*, and (as will be seen) on the question of immortality in *Wessex Poems* (1898) and *Poems of the Past and the Present* (1901). In conjunction with the evidence which follows, this might be considered an indication that 'Midnight on the Great Western' was written several years after *Jude the Obscure*.[1]

'The Impercipient' gives us Hardy's sceptical response to Wordsworth's belief that, though the 'vision splendid' of youth fades into 'the light of common day' as we grow up, nothing can destroy its memory, and that,

> Though inland far we be,
> Our souls have sight of that immortal sea
> Which brought us hither,
> Can in a moment travel thither,
> And see the children sport upon the shore,
> And hear the mighty waters rolling evermore.

After saying that his comrades' faiths are fantasies to him, and 'mirage-mists their Shining Land', Hardy comments:

> I am like a gazer who should mark
>   An inland company
> Standing upfingered, with, 'Hark! Hark!
>   The glorious distant sea!'
> And feel, 'Alas, 'tis but yon dark
>   And wind-swept pine to me!'

Long before this was written, Hardy in *Far from the Madding*

Crowd had very quietly shown his interest in, if not his allegiance to, a theory of immortality that discounted the world beyond. Puzzled at finding the authorship of that novel ascribed to George Eliot, he concluded that the attribution was due to his recent reading of Comte's *Positive Philosophy* 'and writings of that school', and to the existence of some of its expressions in his own novel as well as in George Eliot's works. Leslie Stephen was much nearer the mark when he wrote reassuringly to Hardy: 'As for the supposed affinity to George Eliot, it consists, I think, simply in this that you have both treated rustics of the farming class in a humorous manner . . .'.

Hardy's admiration for George Eliot as a thinker rather than a 'storyteller' was no doubt conditioned by his own Positivism, and it is interesting to find that the note he preserved relative to her death is on this 'new religion' (J. S. Mill's 'Religion of Humanity') and what it needed to make it more acceptable (*Life*, 98, 146). Based on the assumption that nothing about God or existence beyond life on earth is knowable, its tenor was that the business of man is to do everything possible for the welfare and progress of the human race. Intrinsically Hardy never gave up this general belief.

The Positivist view of life after death was expressed in George Eliot's lines:

> O may I join the choir invisible
> Of those immortal dead who live again
> In minds made better by their presence: live
> In pulses stirred to generosity,
> In deeds of daring rectitude, in scorn
> For miserable aims that end with self,
> In thoughts sublime that pierce the night like stars,
> And with their mild persistence urge man's search
> To vaster issues.

Hardy's reference in *Far from the Madding Crowd* to this theory of 'heaven' or 'the life to come' occurs in a such trivial context (l) and is so tentative that no reader could make a serious issue of it: 'If, as some thinkers hold, immortality consists in being enshrined in others' memories, then did Black Bess become immortal that day if she never had done so before.' Leslie Stephen, editor of *The Cornhill Magazine*, edgy and professionally prudish though he was in his anxiety not to offend readers, could hardly object to such a non-commital reference, and probably relished it privately, for only a year later he requested Hardy to witness his renunciation of Holy Orders. Whether Hardy gave this avant-garde theory much thought seems doubtful (for in 1888, fourteen years after making reference to it in *Far from the Madding Crowd*, he copied in his notebook the following passage from Pater's *Marius the Epicurean*: 'that secondary sort of life which we can give to the dead, in our intensely realised memory of them – the "subjective immortality", to use a modern phrase ...'. This may have given Hardy the assurance he needed, for, though a little thought shows that the rationalist's 'immortality' is a short-lived one for most people, he boldly adopted this rationalization in his first two volumes of poetry.

'Her Immortality' could refer to his cousin Tryphena, who died in 1890. It expresses sentiments rather than feelings. Though it was probably occasioned by thoughts of her death, it is very much an invention. The narrator imagines that he is joined by the spirit of his 'dead Love' in a pasture where he last saw her 'living smile'. She is drawn to him, she says, because she has discovered since her death that he prizes her above all others:

> Seven years have circled since I died:
>   Few now remember me;
> My husband clasps another bride:
>   My children's love has she.
>
> My brethren, sisters, and my friends
>   Care not to meet my sprite:
> Who prized me most I did not know
>   Till I passed down from sight.

He heroically offers to join her by committing suicide, but she insists that such action would be abortive:

> 'That cannot be, O friend', she cried;
>   Think, I am but a Shade!
>
> 'A Shade but in its mindful ones
>   Has immortality;
> By living, me you keep alive,
>   By dying you slay me.
>
> 'In you resides my single power
>   Of sweet continuance here;
> On your fidelity I count
>   Through many a coming year.'

The central character of this poem is not the poet Hardy, who could never have believed that he would join a 'dead Love' by taking his own life. The poem is a dramatized fantasy, yet it firmly suggests that living intensely in the memory was not a secondary sort of 'immortality' but the only one in which Hardy the rationalist believed at this time.

Two poems in his second volume of poetry, *Poems of the Past and the Present*, show that Hardy had realized that the new 'immortality' was a misnomer. They were both written in February 1899. 'His Immortality' begins:

> I saw a dead man's finer part
> Shining within each faithful heart
> Of those bereft. Then said I: 'This must be
> His immortality.'

As time passed, the lustre of the 'finer part' diminished; in those of the next generation who remembered him, he had shrunk to 'a thin and spectral manikin'; finally all that remained of him was 'a feeble spark/Dying amid the dark' in the mind of the aged recorder. Its companion poem 'The To-Be Forgotten' presents the dead mourning not at being buried but at the certainty that their 'second death' is near, 'When, with the living, memory of us numbs,/And blank oblivion comes!' They have realized that few can live long in human memory after death:

> For which of us could hope
> To show in life that world-awakening scope
> Granted the few whose memory none lets die,
> But all men magnify?

That the dead who live only in others' minds are imagined as persons expressing Hardy's views should create neither surprise nor misprision. In dramatizing his thoughts (as in 'God-Forgotten' or 'A Philosophical Fantasy') the poet ignores the illogicality of the method, and makes the Prime Cause or Immanent Will address him, though he regards it as unconscious of humanity and in general no more than a blind 'propension' or 'unconscious propensity' (*Life*, 168).

A rational 'immortality' is easy to follow, but it was a concept Hardy outgrew. Felt experience disclosed a reasoning of the heart which refused to follow that of the abstract intellect. In 'A Sign-Seeker' he admits that he would like to believe in a future life, and find evidence for it:

> In graveyard green, where his pale dust lies pent
> To glimpse a phantom parent, friend,
> Wearing his smile, and 'Not the end!'
> Outbreathing softly: that were blest enlightenment.

He insists that there is no such evidence, and that death is the end. He has 'Called many a gone and goodly one to shape a sign',

> And panted for response. But none replies;
> No warnings loom, nor whisperings
> To open out my limitings,
> And Nescience mutely muses: When a man falls he lies.

The thought here has a finality akin to that shown in February 1881, when Hardy wrote, 'Carlyle died last Saturday. Both he and George

Eliot have vanished into nescience while I have been lying here'; or, again, to the assurance of a note in 1890: 'I have been looking for God 50 years, and I think that if he had existed I should have discovered him.' He then added, 'As an external personality, of course – the only true meaning of the word',[2] the implication being that God has no existence outside people's minds.

Yet in 'Wessex Heights', a poem written not long after his complex crisis of 1896, we find that the calm and solace of solitude on the hills persuade him that he could have existed there before birth, and may find his spiritual home there after death. This 'seeming' is confirmed by 'The Schreckhorn', the subject of which occurred to Hardy in 1897. He associates the mountain-peak with his friend Leslie Stephen: its aloof, spare, desolate figure appears less 'A looming Alp-height than a guise of him/Who scaled its horn with ventured life and limb'. Then he asks whether 'the eternal essence' of Stephen's mind will enter 'this silent adamantine shape' at his death,

> And his low voicing haunt its slipping snows
> When dawn that calls the climber dyes them rose.

The last two lines are a poetic sentiment of the kind found in Shelley's *Adonais*, on the death of Keats:

> He is made one with Nature: there is heard
> His voice in all her music . . .

The main question, nevertheless, is a serious one, paralleling the possibility Hardy considers of haunting Wessex heights posthumously himself.

In 1901 he wrote:

> My own interest lies largely in non-rationalistic subjects, since non-rationality seems, so far as one can perceive, to be the principle of the Universe. By which I do not mean foolishness, but rather a principle for which there is no exact name, lying at the indifference point between rationality and irrationality.[3]

The passage is hardly explicit, but it is clear that Hardy shows greater humility and wisdom in his attitude to the unknown than had been characteristic of him during a long period of Positivist conviction. It is significant that one of his greatest friends, Edward Clodd of Aldeburgh, who in 1906 became Chairman of the Rationalist Press, had reservations about Hardy in his later years, simply because the latter would not commit himself to a rationalist philosophy.

'You must not think me a hard-headed rationalist for all this', Hardy wrote in 1915:

> Half my time – particularly when writing verse – I 'believe' (in the modern sense of the word) not only in the things Bergson believes in,

but in spectres, mysterious voices, intuitions, omens, dreams, haunted places, etc., etc. But I do not believe in them in the old sense of the word any more for that. . . .[4]

As an example of what Hardy meant here one could point to the spectres which haunt his poems, especially those in memory of his first wife. We see and hear spectres in the 'immortality' poems, the whole import of which is that they exist only in the minds of people. All are recollections or fantasies; their existence is nothing but psychological.

The conclusion I am reaching has its amusing side. 'A Sign-Seeker' expresses Hardy's wish that the old belief in ghosts could be proved true in his experience. At the end of 1919 Florence Hardy informed his friend Sydney Cockerell that, after placing a sprig of holly on his grandfather's grave, Hardy had seen the ghost of a man in Stinsford churchyard. It wore eighteenth-century dress, and said 'A green Christmas'. He followed it into the church, and found it had disappeared. Did he entertain the belief that he had been granted a sign, for which he had long been seeking, of immortality in the old non-rational sense of the word? Two poems suggest that he took the experience seriously. The first is 'Paradox', recalling Mary Hardy, who died in 1915:

> Though out of sight now, and as 'twere not the least to us;
> Comes she in sorrows, as one bringing peace to us?
> Lost to each meadow, each hill-top, each tree around,
> Yet the whole truth may her largened sight see around?
> > Always away from us
> > She may not stray from us!
> Can she, then, know how men's fatings befall?
> Yea indeed, may know well; even know thereof all.

The other poem is 'He Prefers Her Earthly', which was undoubtedly written with the spirit of his dead wife in mind. The last verse tells us little more than the title. Here are the other two:

> This after-sunset is a sight for seeing,
> Cliff-heads of craggy cloud surrounding it.
> –And dwell you in that glory-show?
> You may; for there are strange strange things in being,
> > Stranger than I know.
>
> Yet if that chasm of splendour claim your presence
> Which glows between the ash cloud and the dun,
> > How changed must be your mortal mould!
> Changed to a firmament-riding earthless essence
> > From what you were of old.

There is a fanciful recollection of Emma Gifford's horse-riding here, which has its counterpart in 'A Woman Driving':

> Where drives she now? It may be where
> No mortal horses are,
> But in a chariot of the air
> Towards some radiant star.

The poem 'When Dead', with its reference to a life 'in the Vast' which is resumed after death, may have been written with Emma Hardy in mind. If so, the almost parodic 'Doubt not I shall infallibly/ Be waiting you' alludes to her unwavering belief in immortality. Nothing in Hardy's later years suggests that he ever attained such absolute certainty of faith, but there can be no mistaking the import of 'for there are strange strange things in being,/ Stranger than I know.' The 'Scheme of Things' had indeed become incomprehensible;[5] his dogmatism had been reduced to fragmentary 'seemings', and there could be no return to the confident Positivism of his earlier years.

*   *   *

The conjectural life after death of such poems as 'He Prefers Her Earthly' should not be confused with the remarkable extra-terrestrial world imagined by J. Hillis Miller,[6] where all who have lived will continue to exist, no longer individualized but part of a universal consciousness which is eternal, still aware of their sufferings in an inexorable repetition of the drama of their mortal lives. Characters such as Tess, Jude, and Henchard are assumed to share this existence, though they have never lived on earth except in their author's imagination and in the imagination of countless readers. If one attempts to follow this belief to its logical conclusion, thinking of all the characters of all the writers of imaginative literature throughout the ages, and of all the sufferings from which they can never escape, the magnitude of this amazing theory can be glimpsed. Hillis Miller may well ask if Hardy's writing is the sign of 'a sadistic streak in him', and the same question, based on the same assumptions, could be asked of numerous writers. The theory is based on two poems which Hardy wrote – perhaps not too seriously, and almost certainly with no assurance of their scientific accuracy – after reading Einstein. They are 'The Absolute Explains' and 'So, Time'. Whether Hardy ever shared the contemporary belief in Einstein is not known, but his scepticism is very apparent in the theme of 'Drinking Song', which recognises that all attempts at measuring the infinite are doomed to be outmoded; 'after what [Einstein] says the universe seems to be getting too comic for words', he wrote to Dr J. Ellis McTaggart on 31 December 1919. 'The Absolute Explains' was completed on New Year's Eve, 1922; 'So, Time' is 'The same thought resumed'.

Supplement

Supplement

i. *The Return of the Native* in the Making

It has always seemed puzzling that Hardy, who had finished his previous novel in January 1876, should not, after settling in his first home
(at Sturminster Newton) early in July 1876, have begun his next novel
for another year.[1] He depended on writing for a living, and that meant
novel-writing. There is no evidence that he wrote any short stories
while he was at Sturminster; he may have written some poems (by
1877 he had planned some tragic poems in which he tried, unsuccess-
fully, to engage Leslie Stephen's editorial interest); he certainly thought
about the possibilities of 'a grand drama, based on the wars with
Napoleon, or some one campaign. . . . It might be called "Napoleon",
or "Josephine".' Hardy and his wife enjoyed many outings; in retrospect, their two years at Sturminster were the 'happiest time' they
spent together. It seems inconceivable that Hardy could have been
happy for long, however, had he not been actively engaged in creative
writing; and he tells us in his *Life* that *The Return of the Native* was
his main occupation at Riverside Villa. It took longer, and gave him
more trouble, than is generally known.

The evidence that Hardy wrote a large portion of the novel long
before August 1877 is in Edinburgh, and it is by kind permission of
William Blackwood and Sons Ltd and the National Library of Scotland
that I am able to refer to it publicly.

On 22 February 1877 John Blackwood (George Eliot's publisher)
replied to Hardy, stating that he was glad to make his acquaintance,
that he did not know when he would have room in his magazine for the
serial proposed, and that he hoped Hardy would write again when his
work was further advanced.

It is evident that Hardy had set to work in earnest on *The Return
of the Native* at the beginning of 1877, and equally probable that he
had planned it in some detail before then. It is interesting to note that
he and his wife spent the Christmas of 1876 with his father and
mother at Higher Bockhampton. 'Egdon Heath' extended to the back
of the house, and the highest visible point, half a mile away, was
Rainbarrow. Perhaps at this time Hardy made his ground-plan sketch
of 'Mr C's house' near the well at Higher Bockhampton for reference
when describing Avice's (Eustacia's) home at Mistover Knap. It seems
inevitable that he spent time renewing his impressions of the heath,
and especially at dusk for the opening scenes of the novel.

On 12 April 1877 he sent the first fifteen chapters of his story to John Blackwood. In these he had reached, I estimate, a point in the narrative (whatever the subsequent changes) corresponding to the end of Book II of the final version of the novel. Hardy expressed the wish that the book should be issued 'complete' (in volume form) by the beginning of May 1878. John Blackwood took time to read the manuscript from beginning to end, even though he could not accept it for serialization in 1877. He described the novel as 'excessively clever'; nothing could be 'more graphic than the description of that awful Egdon Heath'; the natives and their conversation showed a 'wonderfully real life', but (he asked) were they not 'more curious than interesting'? He doubted whether Hardy should have spent so long on the opening scenes 'without a thread of light to throw an interest round the rugged figures' he had so vividly painted; there was 'hardly anything like what is called Novel interest until the connection between the villainous Toogood [Wildeve] and that she-devil Avice appears and they are run to ground by the indefatigable reddleman'. It is possible that John Blackwood had other reservations, and even more probable that Hardy suspected he had, for in June 1879 he wished to submit another novel for the publisher's consideration, one nearer to his 'standard of taste'. Though he gave no title, Hardy was obviously thinking of *The Trumpet-Major* (which he describes as 'a cheerful story, without views or opinions, and ... intended to wind up happily') in comparison with *The Return of the Native*.

For financial reasons, one suspects, Hardy was anxious that the publication of *The Return of the Native* should be delayed as little as possible. His former serial editor Leslie Stephen had been disappointed in his last novel, *The Hand of Ethelberta*; nevertheless, Hardy, perhaps hoping that the success of *Far from the Madding Crowd* might weigh in his favour, lost little time in inviting Stephen to consider his new novel. Stephen's reply is dated 28 May 1877, and it shows that Hardy hoped for a 'speedy decision'. Cautious as usual, the editor of *The Cornhill* said he thought he could decide in two or three weeks but would prefer more time. He wished to have 'full details' of the 'intended development' of the story when the manuscript was sent.

The sequel was told by Hardy, and is to be found in F. W. Maitland, *The Life and Letters of Leslie Stephen* (London, 1906). Unlike John Blackwood, Stephen was impressed by the opening scenes, but as the editor of 'a family magazine', with his weather-eye open for the appearance of Grundyan clouds over the horizon, he feared that the relations between Avice (Eustacia), Toogood (Wildeve), and Thomasin (originally Clym's sister) might develop into something 'dangerous'. The 'villainous Toogood' has misled Thomasin into thinking that they were legally married; they had been away a week after the ceremony; and the 'marriage' was threatened by 'that she-devil Avice'. Stephen refused to have anything to do with the story unless he could see the whole of it. This was impossible, and Hardy needed a contract for serialization as soon as possible. Not much time was lost, for on 16 June he invited the editor of the magazine *Temple Bar* to accept his story.[2] Eventually he was glad to accept terms for its publication in *Belgravia* ('of all places', he adds disparagingly in his *Life*). There is evidence at Princeton University Library which suggests that he received £20 for each monthly instalment; and this would have meant security until the end of 1878 at least.

It must have been obvious to the Hardys that for serial publication the story had to be altered without delay. Many of the manuscript pages of the first two books are in unusually fair hand, showing that much was completely rewritten; deletions, alterations, and additions on some of the other pages give some idea of the extent of the textual changes which made rewriting a necessity. Hardy read Matthew Arnold's essay 'Pagan and Medieval Sentiment' not later than the middle of June 1877, and that may have imparted a new or greater thematic emphasis to the contrasting outlooks of Clym and Eustacia. By 28 August 1877 seven chapters were ready; modification of the remainder of the first two books, which Hardy had hoped were ready for publication the previous April, was not completed until the beginning of November. Changes in the text of *The Return of the Native* have been the subject of extensive research,[3] but the full extent of the differences between the text of the present novel and its original design can never be known. This must have been planned before Hardy and his wife spent their 1876 Christmas at Higher Bockhampton, and there can be little doubt that the writing of the novel was under way soon after their return to Sturminster Newton, probably more than six months earlier than has been generally assumed.

ii. Hardy and Pater

Hardy seems to have met Walter Pater for the first time at one of Mrs Jeune's receptions in Wimpole Street in the summer of 1886. He noted his manner, that of 'carrying weighty ideas without spilling them' (*Life*, 180). Two years later the Hardys were lodging in Kensington, and Pater 'sometimes called on them from over the way'. On 14 July 1888 they dined at the London home of this Oxford scholar, and there they met 'Miss —, an Amazon, more, an Atalanta, most, a Faustine. Smokes: handsome girl: cruel small mouth: she's of the class of interesting women one would be afraid to marry' (*Life*, 212). Hardy had discovered that there was a social side to the writer whose intellectual profundity and subtlety he no doubt admired.

Whether he had read 'Winckelmann' soon after its appearance in

The Westminster Review for January 1867 is doubtful. It was included with later essays in *Studies in the History of the Renaissance* (1873), and Hardy's interest may have owed something to his growing friendship with Edmund Gosse (who became acquainted with Pater in 1874) when *The Return of the Native* was being planned or replanned. It was the conflict, first between Hellenism and Christianity, and secondly between the desire for enjoyment and repose, on the one hand, and, on the other, intellectual integrity in a world where the new scientific outlook was destructive of old basic assumptions, which drew Hardy to the concluding essays in Pater's Renaissance studies. The merging of the second aspect of this conflict with the story of *The Return of the Native* is a manifest consequence of this interest.

Besides defining this dilemma, the essay on Winckelmann affirmed other things which Hardy felt. For example, the statement that 'a universal pagan sentiment' survives in all religions, and is 'the anodyne ... to the law which makes life sombre for the vast majority of mankind' has a special relevance to the dwellers on Egdon Heath:

> Moreover to light a fire is the instinctive and resistant act of man when, at the winter ingress, the curfew is sounded throughout Nature. It indicates a spontaneous, Promethean rebelliousness against the fiat that this recurrent season shall bring foul times, cold darkness, misery and death. Black chaos comes, and the fettered gods of the earth say, Let there be light.

It is echoed in the passage on 'the determination to enjoy' (quoted on p. 88) which Hardy wrote on 16 July 1888, two days after meeting Pater; and in *Tess of the d'Urbervilles* (xxx): 'The "appetite for joy" which pervades all creation, that tremendous force which sways humanity to its purpose, as the tide sways the helpless weed...'. Pater's setting of this pagan sentiment against 'irresistible natural powers, for the most part ranged against man' is at the very heart of Hardy's imaginative scheme for *The Return of the Native*. It is significant that the paragraph in the essay on Winckelmann which contains these words refers to pagan forms of belief such as 'charms and talismans', 'the kindling of fire', and 'dances', all of which supplied hints to Hardy for some of the imaginative Wessex scenes and actions which are related to the main theme of his novel.

The concept of the 'great web' to which Hardy gives particular expression in *The Woodlanders* seems to have originated from his reading almost coincidentally John Addington Symonds (see p. 43) and the essay on Winckelmann, where Pater states that 'the chief factor in the thoughts of the modern mind concerning itself is the intricacy, the universality of natural law, even in the moral order'. Necessity, he continues, is 'a magic web woven through and through us ... penetrating us with a network, subtler than our subtlest nerves, yet bearing in it the central forces of the world'. These natural forces 'we shall never modify, embarrass us as they may', he adds, asserting that 'this network of law' creates the tragic situation in romances by Goethe and Victor Hugo, and 'some excellent work done *after* them'. In this respect, no doubt, Hardy hoped that he would belong to their school.

The subject of universal scientific laws is continued in the 'Conclusion' to Pater's Renaissance studies. Thinking of our physical life and all the outer forces which have come to work within it, he writes:

> Far out on every side of us those elements are broadcast, driven in many currents; and birth and gesture and death and the springing of violets from the grave are but a few out of ten thousand resultant combinations. That clear, perpetual outline of face and limb is but an image of ours, under which we group them – a design in a web, the actual threads of which pass out beyond it. This at least of flame-like our life has, that it is but the concurrence, renewed from moment to moment, of forces parting sooner or later on their ways.

The intellectual vision of such a passage must have made a deep impression on Hardy, possibly playing a part in creating the idea for poems such as 'Voices from Things Growing in a Graveyard', 'Heredity', and 'In a Museum', though they were written many years later.

Pater's 'Conclusion' subsequently stresses the isolation of the individual, 'each mind keeping as a solitary prisoner its own dream of a world'. The thought was not new to Hardy (it occurs in the second 'She, to Him' sonnet, written in 1866), but I doubt if he ever found it more beautifully and analytically expressed. He may have been jolted by a reference to Comte's 'facile orthodoxy', but the poet in him must have been reinvigorated by Pater's insistence on the primary value of 'a quickened, multiple, consciousness', and of the pre-eminence of vital experience over philosophy and abstract theory. Hardy's interest in scientific philosophy was too strong for him ever to be as intensely exclusive as Pater. It moulded the thought of both, and carried Hardy into a world of speculation productive of inconsistent and unpopular points of view which he attempted to justify as 'seemings' that were never intended to be part of a coherent philosophy.

An entry on 'subjective immortality' in Hardy's notebook shows that he read Pater's *Marius the Epicurean* (1885) in 1888. The transcribed passage confirmed a Positivist idea which he had met years earlier, and which encouraged him to express unequivocal views on the subject in three poems, though his confidence in such rationalism waned in his later years (see pp. 169–74). Most of the conclusions reached by Marius as he developed were those formed by both Pater and Hardy, but one seems to have been overlooked by the Hardy who describes the world as 'only a psychological phenomenon' in *Tess*, and persisted in his disillusioned theory of the iris-bow. It relates to the Heraclitean philosophy of flux as opposed to the conventional view which attributes 'permanence or fixity' to the 'phenomena of experience'. Unfortunately, Pater adds:

> Heracliteanism had grown to be almost identical with the famous doctrine of the sophist Protagoras, that the momentary, sensible apprehension of the individual was the only standard of what is or is not, and each one the measure of all things to himself. The impressive name of Heraclitus has become but an authority for a philosophy of the despair of knowledge.

In one of his closing chapters, 'Sunt Lacrimae Rerum', Pater's thought coincides remarkably with Hardy's on the defects of nature, the development of man's awareness of sorrow and desolation, and the need for compassion or altruism 'as an elementary ingredient of our social atmosphere, if we are to live in it at all'. The implications of the first two views bear a close resemblance to those which led Hardy to formulate his theory of the Unfulfilled Intention (*Life*, 149). The last had been an article of faith with him for a long period; his hope for the human race depended on it, though it was sorely tried in his last years. Pater becomes more eloquent as he expresses his thought, and ends with the suggestion of a hope the influence of which may have persisted with Hardy when he concluded *The Dynasts*:

> A protest comes, out of the very depths of man's radically hopeless condition in the world, with the energy of one of those suffering yet prevailing deities, of which old poetry tells. Dared one hope that there is a heart, even as ours, in that divine 'Assistant' of one's thoughts – a heart even as mine, behind the vain show of things!

The reference appears to be not so much to the Holy Spirit or Paraclete ('advocate, one summoned to aid') of the Christian Church as to the Stoic conception of an intelligence in man, which is an 'efflux of the Deity', his guardian and guide, indicative of His will. There is an obvious difference between this conception and that of Hardy's 'Cause of Things', but the ultimate similarity of the hopes (that 'the Deity' or 'the Immanent Will' will respond sympathetically to suffering on earth)[1] makes it seem very probable that one seed at least for the conclusion of *The Dynasts* was sown in 1888, though Hardy had no conscious recollection of it twenty years later, when he stated his belief that 'the idea of the Unconscious Will becoming conscious with flux of time' was his own (*Life*, 454).

iii. *Les Misérables*

Lennart Björk's research on some of Hardy's later jottings in his '1867' notebook[1] has disclosed that Hardy read Charles E. Wilbour's translation of Victor Hugo's *Les Misérables* soon after its appearance in 1887 and again in 1889. Most of the notes Hardy made from his literary readings show little more than his interest as a writer in subject, expression, facts, and points of view. Entries from *Les Misérables* do not suggest that he was influenced significantly by that novel.

Hardy honoured Hugo. He read his poetry as well as his prose, sent a card for a wreath at his funeral, and wrote, at the invitation of a continental newspaper, the following tribute for the centenary of his birth:

His memory must endure. His works are the cathedrals of literary architecture, his imagination adding greatness to the colossal and charm to the small.

Hardy's reference to this tribute[2] is remarkable for his emphasis on Hugo's 'genius as a poet', and no doubt he found poetry as much in his prose as in his verse. The characteristics of the imagination which Hardy's cathedral metaphor conveys are particularly true of *Les Misérables*.

To enhance the epic grandeur of his masterpiece, Hugo cunningly linked many minor structures (sometimes of unusual solidity for a novel) to his main narrative edifice. Hardy's interest in one of them, the battle of Waterloo, was undoubtedly great. Yet from the first he must have been held by the excitement of the story. The impression made by certain scenes was so vividly cogent that features entered *The Mayor of Casterbridge*. As is well known, it is in that novel that the word *misérables* occurs, and there can be little doubt that Hardy first read Hugo's story in French.

The following notes are based almost entirely on the narrative sections of *Les Misérables*. The first relate to resemblances between Hugo's novel and *The Mayor of Casterbridge*. They show that Hardy was influenced particularly by the final scenes in the life of Hugo's hero Jean Valjean. (The references at the beginnings of items in this section are to *Les Misérables;* those at the end, to *The Mayor of Casterbridge*.)

i. (Fantine) The hero of each story is successful in business, and becomes a mayor, after committing a crime.

ii. (Jean Valjean, iv. i) When Javert, the police inspector, contemplates suicide he goes to one of two bridges, very close together over the Seine, and leans over the parapet in deliberation. The scene could have suggested the two bridges for the *misérables* of different classes at Casterbridge (xxxii).

iii. (ibid.) His prospects are unendurable, and the darkness is complete as Javert leans over the whirlpool. In Hardy's novel there are two scenes with these features: the first (xxxii) draws attention to the deep pool called Blackwater, and reveals a landscape which grows blacker until it is like a picture blotted with ink; in the second (xli) Henchard's prospects are unendurable, and the land ahead is as darkness itself as he proceeds to Ten Hatches, intent on drowning himself.

iv. The ex-mayor lives for Cosette. She is not his daughter, but all his fortune is hers when she marries Marius. Henchard is ruined, but all he has in life is the girl he once thought his daughter, Elizabeth-Jane.

v. (ibid., vi. ii) Jean Valjean is not missed at the wedding-banquet, so happy are the young lovers (xliv).

vi. (ibid., vi. iv) Can Valjean's past remain a secret? If it is revealed, he will be disowned and have nothing to live for. Rather than lose Elizabeth-Jane, Henchard lies (xli).

vii. (ibid., vii) After Valjean's confession, Marius, who had always been suspicious and afraid of him, turns against him, and regards him as an 'outcast'. Valjean pleads to see Cosette, and would willingly enter by the back-door. He visits her in the basement, but his reception gets colder and colder in every way with each succeeding visit. Cosette's married happiness makes her forget him when his visits cease (xlv, Elizabeth-Jane begs her husband Farfrae to help her find Henchard, and make his life 'less that of an outcast'; xliii, 'He proceeded to draw a picture of the alternative . . .'; xliv).

viii. (ibid., vii. ii) He is a 'remorseful Cain' (xliii).

ix. (ibid., ix. ii) As he lies dying in his poor tenement, he has only the portress, 'this good woman', to attend him. The doctor says he is dying from the loss of a dear friend. With this one can compare the loyal service of Whittle, Henchard's death in an abandoned heath cottage, and the effect of his rejection by Elizabeth-Jane (xlv).

x. (ibid., ix. iv, v) After Marius has discovered the true story of Valjean, he and Cosette hire a fiacre to bring him back. Hugo's ending is a happy one, though Valjean dies. Unlike Hardy, both believe in Providence (xlv).

xi. (ibid., ix. v) Cosette, looking forward to Valjean's return, tells him how pretty her garden is and of her sorrow that a nesting redbreast has been killed. It would be charming to live together and hear the birds in the trees, he replies. Then he announces his imminent death, and immediately refers to the redbreast. The symbolism is simpler than that of the caged goldfinch which Henchard brings hopefully as a peace-offering and wedding-present (xliv), but it could have suggested it via Lear's short-lived hopes of happiness with Cordelia: 'We two alone will sing like birds i' th' cage.'

Similarities between *Les Misérables* and *Tess of the d'Urbervilles* may be too slight to denote influence. The main one relates to the courtship of Marius and Cosette. The contrast between 'the lusty and vigorous vegetation' which 'trembled full of sap and intoxication' in the overgrown garden on May evenings and the innocence of the young lovers who met there (St Denis, VIII. i) is comparable to that between 'the ooozing fatness and warm ferments of the Froom Vale' and the ethereal, idealizing, Shelleyan love of Angel Clare for Tess (xxiv); unlike Cosette's, the garden in which Tess's love for Angel grows, is blighted (xix). Marius is 'pure and seraphic', and Cosette is the embodiment of 'artlessness, ingenuousness, transparency, whiteness, candour, radiance' (essential attributes in Hardy's conception of Tess); she is 'a condensation of Auroral light in womanly form'. Like Angel, Marius becomes indurated by principle: he rejects Jean Valjean, whose reformed life is one of saintly compassion and forgiveness, just as Angel hardens his heart against Tess, who is the essence of Christian charity.

One passage relative to Cosette's garden (St Denis, III. iii) shows a philosophical awareness of universal interdependence which would appeal to the imaginatively scientific mind of Hardy (cf. 'In a Museum', 'A Kiss'). Hugo writes antithetically on 'decompositions of forces resulting in unity. All works for all': 'the radiance of the star benefits the rose; no thinker would dare to say that the perfume of the hawthorn is useless to the constellations. ... Every bird which flies has the thread of the infinite in its claw ... the universal life ... entangling, from the highest to the lowest, all activities in the obscurity of a dizzying mechanism. ... Enormous gearing, whose first motor is the gnat, and whose last wheel is the zodiac.'

Hugo's vivid presentation of the battle of Waterloo, and his pronounced views on the subject, seem not to have had the least influence on its pictorial and dramatic re-creation in *The Dynasts*.

Bishop Bienvenu and his life of compassion (Fantine, I–III) must have been held in high veneration by Hardy, who believed more and more firmly with the years that only brotherhood and loving-kindness stood between man and disaster. The bishop's pity for all God's creatures, including the spider and the ant, is reminiscent of 'An August Midnight'.

Hugo's preface to *Les Misérables* must have made a strong impact on Hardy. 'So long as there shall exist, by reason of law and custom, a social condemnation, which, in the face of civilization, artificially creates hells on earth ... so long as ignorance and misery remain on earth, books like this cannot be useless.' This apologia would commend itself as a charter to Hardy when he was contemplating *Tess of the d'Urbervilles* and *Jude the Obscure*, and there is an echo of it in 'Why Do I?', the last poem of *Human Shows*.

iv. During Wind and Rain

Throughout the poem of this title Hardy presents a duality of youth and decay, or of time remembered and time present. The bright scenes of the past are blotted out one by one until, with the slow-down of the inexorably erosive rain on the inscriptions, the poem closes with the thought of oblivion:

> Ah, no; the years, the years;
> Down their carved names the rain-drop ploughs.

Preceding images of sick reeling leaves, white storm-birds winging, and the rotten rose ripped from the wall, are all manifestations of the late autumnal wind and rain which form a threnodic accompaniment until time past and time present meet with finality on the tombstones.

Wind and rain as an image of trials and tribulation came to Hardy from the clown's song at the end of Shakespeare's *Twelfth Night*:

> With hey, ho, the wind and the rain,
> For the rain it raineth every day.

He seems to have had the last line in mind in 'An Autumn Rain-Scene', where the rain as a setback is associated with people of varying outlooks, from those who accept to those who endure, the final thought being that peace is found only in the grave.

Whereas the rain which brings death to Giles Winterborne is no more than natural, there are tragic scenes in Hardy when wind and rain have a poetic or symbolic import. In *The Return of the Native*, Clym's anxieties when he decides to leave home and marry Eustacia are reflected in wet boisterous weather and the damage it inflicts on the beeches in a young plantation:

> at every onset of the gale convulsive sounds came from the branches, as if pain were felt. In a neighbouring brake a finch was trying to sing; but the wind blew under his feathers till they stood on end, twisted round his little tail, and made him give up his song.

On the open heath, however, the storm gnashed ineffectively; 'gusts which tore the trees merely waved the furze and heather in a light caress'. The 'defects of nature' are felt more as human nature has evolved and knowledge has grown.[1]

On a much grander scale, wind and rain combine with funereal darkness to intensify the tragedy of Eustacia as she stumbles to her death across the heath. More incidentally, but just as impressively by reason of their recurrence, Hardy uses the same effects to express the final dual tragedy of *Jude the Obscure*. When Jude leaves his sickroom at Christminster, he seeks Sue and death, encountering cold driving rain on the way, and struggling over the down by the Brown House 'in the teeth of the north-east wind and rain' on his return. As Sue prepares for her last sacrifice, Mrs Edlin observes, 'What a wind and rain it is to night!' Again, at the end of the scene, 'How it do blow and rain!' This fourfold conjunction in consecutive chapters on the catastrophes of two allied lives seems to confirm Hardy's symbolical intention.

v. Oxford and *Jude*

At a London party in 1896 Lord Rosebery asked Hardy why he had called Oxford 'Christminster'. 'Hardy assured him that he had not done anything of the sort, "Christminster" being a city of learning that was certainly suggested by Oxford, but in its entirety existed nowhere else in the world but between the covers of the novel under discussion.'[1] Up to a point he was right: 'Christminster' exists only in a book or (more precisely) in the minds of readers. As he maintained, he did not slavishly copy the 'architecture and scenery' of Oxford. He was to speak similarly and with equal validity of 'Casterbridge' in 1910, pouring scorn on photographic writing.[2]

Irrespective of whether Hardy answered Lord Rosebery's question, his reply was partial and evasive. However far Oxford is represented in *Jude the Obscure*, there can be no doubt that it was Hardy's model for 'Christminster'. The distant view of it from 'the Brown House' on the ridgeway which is identified as 'the Icknield Street and original Roman road through the district' makes it clear from the outset that no other university city was intended. In fact, Hardy supplied a key to most of the colleges in his novel (see the plate in Clive Holland, *Thomas Hardy*, London, 1933), and some are easily recognisable. He knew Oxford well enough to ensure that his 'Sarcophagus College' could not be identified.

In recent years it has been stated emphatically that Hardy knew little of Oxford, and did not visit it before June 1893. The truth is that nobody knows how often he visited the city, or when he first stayed there. His *Life* shows that, in preparation for *Jude*, he visited Fawley, Berkshire, in October 1892, and Oxford the following June. Thinking possibly of his hero's role, and anxious no doubt not to let it be known that he was planning a novel about Oxford, he deliberately went 'as a stranger', observing such proceedings as 'Christ Church and other college balls, garden-parties, and suchlike bright functions'. Even though a friend received an honorary degree, he 'viewed the Commemoration proceedings from the undergraduates' gallery of the Sheldonian'.[3]

The result of these observations is clear in the final section of *Jude*;

but Hardy does not appear to have spent much time in Oxford in 1893, and it seems impossible that he gained all his impressions of 'Christminster' from a day visit, or from that and an hour or two two days later.[4] He had been to Oxford previously.

According to Clive Holland (who had the benefit of a number of discussions with Hardy in his later years), he was sent to Oxford while he was employed by the architect Arthur Blomfield, in connection with the building of the chapel at the Radcliffe Infirmary. Although this statement has not been confirmed, it cannot be ignored.

More important for Hardy was the opening in 1869 of St Barnabas Church in the 'Jericho' district of Oxford. Arthur Blomfield was its architect, and Hardy may have seen, or heard of, plans for it before he left Blomfield's office in 1867. It is the church of St Silas in *Jude the Obscure*, and Hardy's accomplished programme does not suggest that he had time to visit it in June 1893.

He was in Oxford in 1875. With *Far from the Madding Crowd* he had gained recognition as an important new novelist. The result, as may be seen in the library of Princeton University, was an invitation from the editors of *The Shotover Papers* to attend a dinner and accept a place for viewing the 'Eights'. The second annual dinner of the student Shotover Society was held on 11 May, and the toast to Literature on that occasion was responded to by Austin Dobson and Thomas Hardy.[5] The latter probably said little, but no doubt he enjoyed the privilege of watching the 'Eights' from a barge or boat, and recalled some of the spectacle in the closing chapter of *Jude*. He may have found time on this occasion, if not earlier, to visit St Barnabas and examine its impressive interior.

Whenever he visited it, the memory of this church undoubtedly played an important part in directing the course of the tragedy in *Jude*. Sue's *volte-face*, her surrender to 'Sacerdotalism', is dramatized in 'the Church of Ceremonies – St Silas', for which the Anglican church of St Barnabas is a fitting original; (Jude found work in the neighbourhood, and could not afford to live in a more expensive part of the city):

> High overhead, above the chancel steps, Jude could discern a huge, solidly constructed Latin cross – as large, probably, as the original it was designed to commemorate. It seemed to be suspended in the air by invisible wires; it was set with large jewels, which faintly glimmered in some weak ray caught from outside, as the cross swayed to and fro in a silent and scarcely perceptible motion. Underneath, upon the floor, lay what appeared to be a heap of black clothes, and from this was repeated the sobbing he had heard before. It was his Sue's form, prostrate on the paving.

This scene could not have occurred to Hardy when he visited Oxford in June 1893. It arose from discovering that he could not persuade his new, idealized friend Mrs Henniker to abandon her High Church beliefs for his progressive Positivist views. Expressing his disappointment, he told her in July 1893 that he would have to 'trust to imagination only for an enfranchised woman'; and the result was the transference of his 'new religion' to Sue Bridehead. Jude's impassioned criticism of her conversion was a dramatic heightening of Hardy's protest that Mrs Henniker 'should have allowed herself to be enfeebled to a belief in ritualistic ecclesiasticism' for the satisfaction of some emotional need.[6] From this it was but a short step to the conviction that even an 'enfranchised woman' would break down under the stresses of a terrible personal calamity.

'Strange difference of sex,' Jude concludes, 'that time and circumstance, which enlarge the views of most men, narrow the views of women almost invariably'; and that Sue, whose intellect once 'played like lambent lightning over conventions and formalities' had now become a slave to 'forms'. There can be little doubt that the character of the heroine and the ending of *Jude the Obscure* changed significantly in the second half of 1893, and that the Anglican church of St Barnabas offered the ideal setting for the symbolical dramatization of her final crucifixion and 'enslavement'.

vi.   One Rare Fair Woman

In my introduction to *One Rare Fair Woman*[1] I endeavoured to show that the love which Hardy felt for Mrs Henniker (the extent of which she did not know, he wrote in 'Wessex Heights'), at a time when his relations with Mrs Hardy were often strained or warped, entered phases of the story of *Jude the Obscure*, helping to give imaginative life and poignancy to some of its dramatic scenes. Expressions in some of his letters are a key to the plot, and demonstrate that important changes in his plan for the novel took place in the latter half of 1893, if not in the early part of 1894, when the novel got under way with some difficulty. The evidence confirms the truth of Florence Hardy's statement that Sue Bridehead was drawn to some extent from Mrs Henniker.[2]

Hardy's imaginative susceptibility to beautiful women was part of his artistic temperament, and the main reason for his interest in the Platonic theory of the Idea or 'the Well-Beloved'. It remained with him to the end; in his eighties, his wife Florence discovered a poem on an imaginary elopement with a captivating woman he had recently met, and promptly burnt it. The two items which follow relate to poems sent by Mrs Henniker to Hardy, and they are provided as further evidence in support of the view that, more truly than anywhere else, Hardy disclosed his feelings towards her in the words which he

wrote of Jude and Sue: 'the sweetest and most disinterested comrade
that he had ever had, *living largely in vivid imaginings*' (my italics).[3]

*   *   *

After meeting Mrs Henniker for the first time at the end of May 1893,
the Hardys continued their 'season' in London. At this time (before he
wrote *Jude*) his fame made him 'welcome anywhere'. He met Mrs
Henniker in town, and kept in correspondence with her. At the end of
June she sent him some of her translations, which he acknowledged as
follows:

> What beautiful translations those are! I like the two verses from the
> Spanish best. You are a real woman of letters: and must be invited to
> the next Mansion House dinner to literature. It was lively there
> last night: but many ladies did not come, I am told, because their
> husbands were not invited. So much for their independence.[4]

Three of Florence Henniker's translations were inserted in Hardy's
second literary notebook, where they are dated 'June 30. 93' in his
writing. The first consists of two stanzas 'From the Spanish of G.
Bécquer'; the second, of four stanzas, headed 'An Autumn Lyric' (after
Drèves).[5] The third, entitled 'Affinity' is a free translation of Théophile
Gautier's 'Affinités Secrètes' in *Emaux et Camées*. This poem is based
on four images: two blocks of stone in an ancient Athenian temple, two
pearls that whispered secrets in a sea-shell, two roses in a rare Spanish
garden, and two doves on a golden dome in Venice. All have passed
away, but each is born again and renewed, until the marble is found in
'limbs that are white and warm', the pearls in 'mouths of velvet', the
roses in 'red lips that kiss', and the doves 'in hearts of lovers'. How
otherwise can one explain

> the strange and sweet affinity
> That warms two souls in this desert of earth,
> They must claim each other, where'er they be?

They recall 'the dreams of their mystic long ago'

> Till my heart, that within me burns and glows,
> Would read *your* heart, and ask you whether
> You were pearl, or marble, or dove, or rose
> In that fairer world, when we were together?

Mrs Henniker's choice of translations was probably prompted by little
beyond a degree of pride, but Hardy was impressionable (rather like
Boldwood on the receipt of Bathsheba's valentine), and the thought
'that the one affined soul he had ever met was lost to him' through
marriage smote him 'with cruel persistency'.[6] In August 1895, reflect-

ing on ill-chance in marriage, including his own, he wrote the verse on
'ill-affin'd' hearts which appears on the title-page of *The Woodlanders*.[7]

* * *

On 29 July 1894 Florence Henniker sent, or presented to, Hardy a
copy of *Selections from the Poetical Works of Robert Browning*. There
can be little doubt that Hardy's interest in this volume accounts for the
inclusion of most of the Browning quotations in *Jude the Obscure*, and
that many of the poems meant much to him. The passages he marked[8]
may be divided into four categories: incidental felicities of expression,
sensory observation, and graphic portrayals giving situations at a
glance; thoughts and sentiments of which he approved or disapproved;
passages which reflected his private position; and passages illustrating
admirable poetic skills, especially in dramatic lyricism.

The selection which is given below seems to reflect a position which
Hardy knew too well. Most of the excerpts present it from his point of
view; one or two, from his wife's:

1. —So is my spirit, as flesh with sin,
   Filled full, eaten out and in
   With the face of her, the eyes of her,
   The lips, the little chin, the stir
   Of shadow round her mouth.   ('Time's Revenges')

2. What I seem to myself, do you ask of me?
   No hero, I confess.   ('A Light Woman')

3. She turned on her side and slept. Just so!
   So we resolve on a thing and sleep.
   So did the lady, ages ago.

   Where is the use of the lip's red charm,
   The heaven of hair, the pride of the brow,

   Unless we turn, as the soul knows how,
   The earthly gift to an end divine?
                         ('The Statue and the Bust')

4. Stanza iii and the last five lines of stanza v   ('Cristina')

5. And find her soul as when friends confer,
   Friends – lovers that might have been.
   . . .
   If you join two lives, there is oft a scar,
   They are one and one, with a shadowy third;
   One near one is too far.

   When a soul declares itself – to wit,
   By its fruit – the thing it does!   ('By the Fire-side')

6. Since mine thou wast, mine art, and mine shalt be,
    Faithful or faithless, sealing up the sum
    Or lavish of my treasure, thou must come
    Back to the heart's place here I keep for thee!

    ('Any Wife to Any Husband')

7. Stanzas i, viii, and x   ('In a Year').

The art richly displayed in the volume which Hardy received from
Mrs Henniker could have had some influence on his decision to abandon the writing of novels earlier than he had intended, and turn to
poetry, a form he had always rated more highly than prose fiction and
in which it had been his ambition to excel from the outset of his writing
career. The situations in many of Browning's short poems, and their
admirable lyrical and dramatic qualities brought home to Hardy, at a
time when his marital relations made it extremely difficult, if not
impossible, to meet the sustained demands he set himself in his major
novels, how much more sensible it would be to do at last what he could
now afford to do: write poems whenever he wanted and on whatever
subject he pleased, knowing that thereby his 'instinctive' urge would
be satisfied, and that he ran far less risk of annoying the public in verse
than in prose fiction.[9]

vii. Abdication of a Novelist

It is becoming fashionably axiomatic among critics to assume that
Hardy could have taken the novel no further than he did in *Jude the
Obscure*, and that he was irresistibly driven to the writing of poetry
when he ceased to write novels. Behind this belief (already set to
become one of the clichés bedevilling Hardy criticism and biography)
there seems to be a vague thaumaturgic insistence which is rather like
a resurrection of the Platonic idea of divine inspiration. A study of
Wessex Poems (1898) could lead to different conclusions. The only
compulsion that produced most of this verse was Hardy's long thwarted
desire to succeed as a poet. It would not be difficult to find passages of
greater poetic appeal and intensity in Hardy's fiction than are to be
found in almost the whole of this volume. Most of the poems bear
inescapable evidence of labour rather than inspiration. Hardy's decision
to turn to poetry was to be vindicated later, but the evidence of his
early volumes does not suggest an inner compulsion to switch suddenly
from prose to verse in order to express himself. His frustrations in 1894–
1895 came from other, more mundane, more compelling sources.

With *The Woodlanders* and *Tess of the d'Urbervilles* Hardy had
reached a higher sustained level of achievement than ever before. Not
long after the completion of *Tess*, his relationship with Mrs Hardy took

a serious turn, and the result was such recurrent discord and unsettlement that Hardy regarded the last twenty years of his life with her as 'division' and 'death'. 'The Dead Man Walking' (1896) is one of several poems on this subject. As Florence Hardy recorded, he had to bear 'bitter denunciations' and 'long evenings spent in his study, insult and abuse his only enlivenment'. He was wounded, and at times in despair. Some of the earlier shadows of this unhappiness increase the gloom of *Jude* and the bitterness of its attacks on marriage. It was difficult for Hardy to attain the regular and sustained detachment for a work of such length and complexity. Such was his harassment that no settled period was predictable.

The novel had already been on his mind too long. 'The scheme was jotted down in 1890, from notes made in 1887 and onwards.' He wrote an outline in 1892 and in the spring of 1893, but it is clear that, although he modified his plans after meeting Mrs Henniker, he was neither happy with the design nor making headway by the end of the year. On 1 December he informed Mrs Henniker that he was not 'so keen about the, alas, unwritten, long story' as he ought to have been. 'However,' he adds, 'as it is one I planned a couple of years ago I shall, I think, go on with it and probably shall warm up.' By 15 January 1894 he was 'creeping on a little' and 'beginning to get interested' in the heroine.[1] He did not finish until March 1895. At the revision stage the following August he found that his interest in 'the Sue story' was greater than in any other he had written.

One cannot say that *Jude* shows a pent-up poetic urge; its greatest intensity lies in those dramatic scenes into which Hardy could project vivid and passionate imaginings prompted by his idealization of Mrs Henniker. One reason for his initial lack of enthusiasm was that he had failed to recapture the original freshness of much of his plan; the professional skill with which he worked is great, but it is more deliberate than inspired.

At times his difficulties were aggravated by the restrictive demands of serialization: how could he satisfy his own imaginative and moral integrity without upsetting Victorian readers?[2] He knew what was involved from falsifying and emasculating the narrative of *Tess*; he had done it with cynical amusement, and in normal circumstances he could have repeated the process, but in April 1894 he tried to cancel his serial engagement with *Harper's Magazine* (*Life*, 263). Relief from this burden would have helped, for in August the following year he found that 'the labour of altering *Jude the Obscure* to suit the magazine, and then having to alter it back' had exhausted him, and he was unable to revise the novel as he had intended (*Life*, 269). Sir George Douglas, who was with Hardy at Max Gate on the day of publication, noted that he was not 'lifted up by a sense of work well done'. There is genuine regret (and something by way of excuse) in Hardy's letter to Gosse (*Life*, 271), where he says that his correspondent can hardly conceive 'how poor and feeble the book seems . . . as executed' compared with his own 'idea of it . . . in prospect'. But for his troubles *Jude* would have been as intensely revised as *Tess* had been, and Hardy would have continued to write prose fiction, as he had planned. The theory that with *Jude* he had completed his course as a novelist is an ideal one which ignores the evidence.

Towards the end of 1893, in an interview at Max Gate with Frederick Dolman of *The Young Man*,[3] Hardy indicated that he had much fiction in mind, and gave the impression that he could continue writing it for the rest of his life if he wished:

> '. . . I have far more material now than I shall ever be able to make use of.'
> 'In note-books?'
> 'Yes, and in my head. I don't believe in that idea of a man's imaginative powers becoming naturally exhausted; I believe that if he liked, a man could go on writing till his physical strength gave out. Most men exhaust themselves prematurely . . . Scott and Dickens, for example.'

As writers who wrote as well as ever to the end, he instanced Hugo and Carlyle. Earlier he had stated that he liked writing a short story occasionally, 'if only as a relief to the tension of writing three-volume novels. In the midst of a book one is chained to one's task, so to speak; even if you are not under contract to finish it by a certain time, the "fever of composition" is upon you, and nothing can be enjoyed till the last chapter is written.'

In his *Life* (291) Hardy characteristically ignores his personal difficulties at the time he gave up novel-wriitng, and stresses the 'misrepresentations' which arose after the publication of *Jude* among the public 'who had not read him'. Mrs Hardy, according to the testimony of Alfred Sutro,[4] maintained that 'the book had made a difference to them in the County'. It may seem odd that Hardy was influenced by this kind of unpopularity, but 'Wessex Heights' confirms that he was. 'The onslaught upon *Jude* started by the vituperative section of the press – unequalled in violence since the publication of Swinburne's *Poems and Ballads* thirty years before – was taken up by the anonymous writers of libellous letters and post-cards, and other such gentry.' Sustained abuse of this kind 'wellnigh compelled him, in his own judgment at any rate, if he wished to retain any shadow of self-respect, to abandon *at once* a form of literary art he had long intended to abandon *at some indefinite* time, and resume openly that form of it . . . which he had just been able to keep alive from his early years, half in secrecy, under the pressure of magazine writing'.[5] One must conclude from this that Hardy had not expected to give up novel-writing as soon as he did, and it is possible that some of the stories he wished most to write were serious enough in their issues to make him think that they could damage his reputation still further. 'The wider public which reads novels was not yet ripe for his gospel, and he bowed to its decision', Sir George Douglas wrote after his death.

The notes in Hardy's *Life* for 14 January, 9 March, 28 March, and 8 July 1888 show how readily he responded to experience with creative ideas for fiction. He had already written (*Life*, 177):

> Novel-writing as an art cannot go backward. Having reached the analytic stage it must transcend it by going still further in the same direction. Why not by rendering as visible essences, spectres, etc., the abstract thoughts of the analytic school?

The observations and thoughts in these recordings suggest what an original and exciting novel he may have planned on 'psychical' lines. One thing is certain: he had several stories in mind (more than those he subsequently wrote in fulfilment of contracts) when he finished *Jude the Obscure*. He told his friend Edward Clodd that the public reaction to *Tess* and *Jude* made him give up novel-writing when he had scores of plots in his head.[6] Hardy may be accused of hyperbole, but nobody can dispute that his plans were upset. No doubt he confided in his friend Sir George Douglas, who stated that it was 'a literary tragedy if ever there was one' that Hardy should have been diverted from his natural development as a result of finding or imagining himself a pariah.[7] It took time to show that this setback was a blessing in disguise; it was only 'ultimately' that the 'misrepresentations' which made Hardy turn to poetry proved 'to be the best thing that could have happened' (*Life*, 291).

Whatever the gains or losses, one consequence was unfortunate. In the writing of serials and short stories, Hardy had often chosen to sacrifice art to expediency. As, after the crisis of 1895–6, he lost interest in his fiction and learned to enjoy the amenities which he could now afford of writing for himself, he took the view that his prose had been mere journey-work. To some extent this was the defensive reaction of an injured spirit; he could never forget public disapproval. How remote the judgement of his later years could be from the creative reality of some of his greatest writing may be seen in the statement that, when he was writing *The Woodlanders* (and presumably *Tess of the d'Urbervilles*), he had 'quite resigned himself to novel-writing as a trade' and 'went about the business mechanically' (*Life*, 182–3). This attitude led on the whole to rather perfunctory revisions of his fiction for new editions; had he been keenly interested, most of the more superficial weaknesses could easily have been removed.

viii.   Wessex Topography

The zeal for Wessex identifications among Hardy topographers sometimes leads to 'discoveries' which strain the reader's credulity, and
would, one suspects, have brought amazement (and some amusement)
to Hardy himself. It is true that he commonly sets his stories in and
around places which he knew from direct experience or from books;
but he was an imaginative writer, and more interested in general impressions than in detail. Speaking of the artistic liberties he had taken
with Dorchester in the creation of 'Casterbridge' (when he received
the freedom of the town in 1910), he dismissed photographic representation as an 'inartistic species of literary produce' (*Life*, 351).

So little detail from the original is added to the general description
of High-Place Hall (Lucetta's house in *The Mayor of Casterbridge*)
that it would be hard to identify but for the archway with the keystone
mask in the high wall which once stood beside it. In the novel the court
to which it gave access was moved in relation to the house, and both
were transferred to a corner of the market-place. Again, only a few
architectural details such as period, pilasters, chimneys, and gable
finials indicate what resemblance there is between Bathsheba's homestead and Waterston House near Puddletown. Hardy leaves so much to
the imagination that, regardless of the fact that the accepted 'original'
is a mile further from 'Weatherbury' than Bathsheba's dwelling, one
must ultimately doubt whether he had more than a few features of this
large manor house in mind for the heroine's farmhouse in *Far from the
Madding Crowd*, even though in the preface which he wrote more than
twenty years later he refers to this 'fine old Jacobean house' as the
original.

Hardy's distances are unreliable, and occasionally inconsistent. Trantridge is given locations which are miles apart in two stories. Over-
combe in *The Trumpet-Major* is composed of features from different
places, and its situation below Bincombe Down does not seem to
coincide with any particular hamlet or village. It is generally assumed
that Welland House in *Two on a Tower* is Charborough Park, a house
which Hardy never saw at close quarters until he visited it a few
months before his death (*Life*, 441). From the novel it is impossible to
discover anything with certitude about its position, except that it is five
miles from 'Warborne'. The prototype of Rings-Hill Speer is at least
seven miles to the west. In the novel the house and tower are but
walking-distance apart, and on opposite sides of the road. Careful
investigation shows that Hardy makes it impossible to deduce on which
side of the road either is, just as he ensures that the railway-station
where Louis Glanville caught Lady Constantine's cheek with his whip-
lash is also beyond identification.

Such topographical divergences are to be expected in an imaginative writer who created stories around actual places, and two more examples of wider application must suffice. In his General Preface to the Wessex Edition of 1912 Hardy wrote, 'the portraiture of fictitiously named towns and villages was only suggested by real places, and wantonly wanders from inventorial descriptions of them'. He made deliberate changes in *A Pair of Blue Eyes* 'to avoid drawing attention to ... St. Juliot while his friends were living there' (*Life*, 92), though his making the Cliff without a Name a 'composite' one had other, more exciting and essential reasons. Most, if not all, of his knowledge for the Wessex settings in *A Laodicean* came from books and his imagination. 'Looking over the novel at the present much later date,' Hardy wrote in 1912, 'I hazard the conjecture that its sites, mileages, and architectural details can hardly seem satisfactory to the investigating topographist, so appreciable a proportion of these features being but the baseless fabrics of a vision.' His map of Wessex may indicate that Dunster Castle was the original of 'Stancy Castle', but it ought not to be forgotten that the latter was burnt down and left in ruins.[1]

The above reservations are in most respects familiar and generally accepted. There is another, which appears to have been overlooked and can have more widespread effects: Hardy sometimes shifted the settings of his stories from one district to another, or from one Wessex region to another, without any significant change in their description. In other words, a Hardy topographer intent on thorough research, needs to study manuscripts, serial versions, and even different volume editions, before he can be certain just what part of Wessex Hardy is describing. The place-names will suggest one area, while in fact he may have had another in mind.

Perhaps the most striking of these changes relates to 'The Romantic Adventures of a Milkmaid'. The contrast between this story and the adventures of Tess Durbeyfield is such that Hardy very sensibly decided to transfer it from the Frome valley (the Valley of the Great Dairies in *Tess*) to the Exe valley (in Devon or 'Lower Wessex') when he revised the story for inclusion in *A Changed Man* (1913). In the Summer Number of *The Graphic*, 1883, the Frome is the 'Swenn', and Margery Tucker lives at 'Stickleford Dairy-house'. In the final version of the story, this becomes 'Silverthorn Dairy-house', 'Casterbridge' becomes 'Exonbury', and so on. Occasionally very slight alterations in the text can be found, but no changes whatever in the scenic background. The most important changes are in the place-names; some, such as 'Chillington Wood' and 'Rook's Gate' were allowed to remain, since they are not used in other Wessex stories. It would be a wild goose chase to search for any of the background in or near the Exe valley. Some of the original topography is interesting. The yacht which carries the Baron away to sea had waited in a cove which must be Lulworth, from 'the miniature Pillars of Hercules' which form its mouth.² Jim's chase of the Baron and Margery began at the review which was held on a hill outside Casterbridge. This must be Poundbury or 'Pummery' (outside Dorchester). When he came to Winford (Stinsford) Hill, he was misdirected along the London road, and did not stop until his horse became weary. On the return journey he was forced to rest his horse at the hamlet of Letscombe Cross. Wessex topographers may have little difficulty in ascertaining whether Jim, in this somewhat supernatural story, had reached the crossroads at Winterborne Whitchurch near Lower Whatcombe and Whatcombe House, or at what other intersection 'rose the remains of the old medieval cross which shared its name with the hamlet'.

Similar changes occurred in 'What the Shepherd Saw' when Hardy revised it for inclusion in *A Changed Man*. They prompt the question when and how did Hardy discover the trilithon west of Marlborough which became the focal point of the story. In the Christmas Number of *The Illustrated London News*, 1881, the 'Druidical trilithon' is situated in 'a sheltered portion of that wide expanse of rough pasture-ground known as Verncombe Down, which you cross in its lower levels when following the turnpike-road from Casterbridge eastward, before you come to Melchester' (Salisbury). This seems to be a part of Wessex which had a special interest for Hardy. Vernditch Chase is north of Pentridge, the 'Trantridge' of *Tess of the d'Urbervilles*, and Woodyates Inn, where (according to *The Trumpet-Major*) George III's coach-horses were scheduled to be changed on his way to Weymouth. Once again the description of the setting remains wholly unaltered. Among the few changes there is one which reflects Hardy's characteristic manner of taking the surname of a principal character from a village in the locality which provides the setting. As a result, 'Fred Pentridge' has become 'Fred Ogbourne'.

There are minor changes in 'The Withered Arm' which can upset calculations. The first published version, in *Blackwood's Edinburgh Magazine*, January 1888, shows that Farmer Lodge and his young wife were parishioners, not of Holmstoke but of Stickleford (Tincleton), at least six miles nearer Casterbridge than the villages which suggested Holmstoke. It can be seen that anyone unfamiliar with the magazine topography and in search of where Rhoda Brook or Conjuror Trendle were imagined to have lived needs to start afresh. In both versions of the story Trendle lives five miles from Rhoda Brook's cottage. When Gertrude Lodge sets out on the journey which will take her across the heath to Casterbridge, her 'cunning course' is exactly the same in the magazine as in *Wessex Tales*; the earlier version runs, 'went from her husband's homestead in a course directly the opposite of that towards Casterbridge', without any reference to 'the direct route thither through Stickleford'. The first part of her ride was therefore imagined several miles further west than might be surmised from *Wessex Tales*.

The manuscript of 'The Winters and the Palmleys' throws new light on the topography of the saddest story in 'A Few Crusted Characters', a minor collection which contains some of Hardy's most entertaining tales. They were published serially as 'Wessex Folk', and later included in *Life's Little Ironies*. It can be seen that the story belonged originally to the region of King's Hintock (Melbury Osmond, where Hardy's mother was born), and that the setting was changed to one twelve miles south-east in order to fit in with a narrative framework which demanded stories relating to people in the neighbourhood of Longpuddle. In all probability the story is based on incidents Hardy heard his mother relate in his boyhood, combined with details told by his father of the hanging of a youth for alleged complicity in arson as described in 'The Withered Arm'.

Further research may reveal other 'transfers', but the number made by Hardy can never be known, for too many of his manuscripts have been lost. We have seen that he did not think it his duty in the cause of imaginative fiction to present places, routes, and scenes with exactitude of detail or siting; he selected features or generalized 'with an eye to being more truthful than truth', claiming that such selectivity (for significance and vividness) was the 'just aim of Art'.[3] There were circumstances, too, which required him to transfer some of his stories to other parts of Wessex. He made such changes with due care that nothing essential was lost, but always with the slightest descriptive changes, if any. The best illustration of this is afforded by the shift in the whole setting of *The Woodlanders*.

I described this at some length in the 1971 number of *The Thomas Hardy Year Book*.[4] The main topographical points are that Rubdon (Bubb Down) was the original 'axis of so many critical movements' in the lives of Marty South, Grace Melbury, and Fitzpiers (xlv), and that from the 1895 edition onwards this became High Stoy (four miles to the east). Similarly Great Hintock and Little Hintock (Melbury Osmond and an imaginary hamlet on its eastern side) were transferred about six miles east from one woodland area to another near the Sherton Abbas–Abbot's Cernel (Sherborne–Cerne Abbas) road. There were several collateral changes. Giles Winterborne, for example, met Fitzpiers at Calfhay Cross (east of Melbury Bubb) in the first edition, and near Reveller's Inn (Revels Inn Farm, two miles east of High Stoy) in the later version (xxviii); on his return from Middleton Abbey, Fitzpiers allowed his horse to stop and drink at Holy Spring, where he heard the church clock at Owlscombe (Batcombe) strike midnight; the corresponding places in the new setting (xxix) are Lydden Spring and Newland Buckton (Buckland Newton). There are no significant changes in the description of the setting, yet we are led to believe that most of the main action took place several miles to the east of where it was imagined and delineated. One result is that, while no 'Hintock' church can be found on a hillside in the woodland area north of High Stoy, there can be no doubt that the description at the end of the novel, with reference to Marty South, the churchyard, the hill, and 'Little Hintock', is appropriate to Melbury Osmond.

When, on 5 April 1887, Hardy told Edmund Gosse that Great Hintock was Melbury Osmund (so it was spelt then), he told the truth. In 1926 the truth was less simple, and in answer to an inquiry whether Little Hintock was Minterne (south of High Stoy) he wrote to say that he did not know where it was, and that it contained features of places north of High Stoy and near, and also of Melbury Bubb (*Life*, 432). He had to throw a wide net; there was always the chance that some inquisitive reader might remember or meet the Wessex names in the 1887 editions.

The only explanation, I believe, for the sweeping ostensible changes in the topography of *The Woodlanders* is that Hardy, knowing that he was likely to incur disfavour with the Ilchester family when 'The First Countess of Wessex' was published (a risk he was prepared to take because he believed that his story was substantially verified by records as well as local tradition), realized how foolish it was to create annoyance quite gratuitously by fictionally associating Mrs Charmond with Melbury House, south of Melbury Osmond. He had disguised 'Great Hintock House' by placing it in a hollow; he decided that a better plan would be to transfer it (and the hollow) to a woodland region where no prototype could be found.

ix.   Shockerwick House

Writers on Hardy's use of history in *The Dynasts* seem to have ignored the question why the scene in which the Younger Pitt hears the news of the shattering of his European alliance against Napoleon at Austerlitz was set in Shockerwick House near Bath. According to Earl Stanhope's *Life of the Right Honourable William Pitt* (new edition, London, 1879), Pitt proceeded to Bath on 7 December 1805, and stayed there 'upwards of a month' to alleviate 'flying gout'. Reports from 'domestics' in immediate attendance on him indicate that, after receiving the Austerlitz despatches, 'he desired a map to be brought to him and to be left alone' (vol. III, p. 337). This detail will be found in *The Dynasts* (Part First, VI. vi), and it seems certain that Hardy knew Earl Stanhope's biography of Pitt.

When Pitt left Bath on 9 January 1806 he was so weak that the journey to his home at Putney took three days. 'It is said that on leaving his carriage, and as he passed along the passage leading to his bedroom, he observed a map of Europe which had been drawn down from the wall; upon which he turned to his niece and mournfully said, "Roll up that map; it will not be wanted these ten years." ' (Stanhope, III, p. 382). It can be seen that Hardy's conflation of two scenes is a daring poetic licence, but one which is artistically justifiable in a three-volume epic dramatizing ten years of European conflict in more than one hundred and thirty scenes.

In his biography of Pitt, Lord Rosebery refers to a tradition that Pitt 'was looking at a picture gallery' when the news of the disaster reached him at Bath. Hardy studied histories and local records of the Napoleonic era for many years, and it has always seemed probable that he found evidence in one of the byways of history for locating the scene at Shockerwick House.

In a letter which he wrote to Sir George Douglas on 2 December 1902 we approach the subject without solving the mystery: 'About a month ago we were staying in Bath. I stayed close to where Pitt was living when he received the news of Austerlitz which is said to have killed him.' Hardy's *Life* (p. 317) shows that his visit to Bath took place during a period of research for Part First of *The Dynasts*.

Most probably it was at this time that he became interested in R. E. Peach's *Historic Houses of Bath*. On page 13 of the Second Series (published in London in 1884) there is a footnote in small print with this preliminary acknowledgement.

> The author is indebted to the Rev. E. W. L. Davies for the following note, relating to W. PITT, in 1805, when he visited the Earl of Harrowby, who was living at the time in the Duke of Northumberland's mansion, 11, Laura Place.

The probability that this was the source of Hardy's knowledge of where Pitt stayed in Bath is strikingly confirmed by the Rev. E. W. L. Davies' story:

> In the summer of 1860, a great treat was in store for me: I had been promised a view of no less than seven of Gainsborough's grand pictures, two of them perhaps the finest he ever painted; namely, 'The Return from the Harvest Field', and 'The Bradford Parish Clerk'. They were at Shockerwick, where Mr. John Wiltshire, the owner of these treasures, kindly acted as showman on the occasion. We were standing together, looking at the famous portrait of Quin, the comedian, when Mr. Wiltshire turned to me and said, 'A remarkable incident occurred to me once when, as a boy and in the absence of my father, I was showing that picture to a gentleman; who, as I soon discovered, was no less a man than Mr. Pitt, the distinguished statesman, and at that time Prime Minister of England. He was looking intently at the picture through the hollow of his two hands;

when suddenly a sound caught his ear – it was that of a horse gallop-
ing furiously up the gravel road leading to the house. "That must be
a courier", he said eagerly, "with news for me!" and almost immediately a man, booted and spurred, and splashed from head to foot,
entered the room and handed his despatches to the Minister, still
standing before the picture. Tearing them open, he became intensely
agitated, and exclaimed, "Heavy news, indeed! do get me some
brandy"; on which (said Mr. Wiltshire) I rushed out, and brought
in the brandy myself; and can at this moment well remember the
little water he added to the spirit, as he tossed off a tumbler-full at
a gulp; he then took another, and I believe if he had not done so, he
would have fainted on the spot. The Battle of Austerlitz had been
fought and won by Buonoparte. The Emperors of Russia and Austria
had commanded at it, and the coalition had been mainly due to a
brilliant effort of Pitt's genius, by which he hoped to crush the hydra-
headed power of Napoleon. The disappointment overwhelmed him;
it was more than he could bear, and in less than two months from
that date he sank under the weight of it. Austerlitz was fought on
the 2nd of December, 1805, and the great statesman died on the
23rd January, 1806.'

Comparison with the scene in *The Dynasts* soon reveals that Hardy
has followed this account in almost every detail, notably in the concentration on Gainsborough's picture of Quin, the gallop of the approaching horse, the arrival of a courier splashed with mud, the 'heavy news
indeed' uttered by Pitt on reading the despatch, and his request for
brandy to sustain the shock.

One important difference will be noted. In *The Dynasts* it is Mr
Wiltshire, the owner of Shockerwick House, who is Pitt's guide and
support; in the source it is the boy John Wiltshire who plays the host,
in the absence of his father. Could Hardy have overlooked this when
working from his notes? Or is this another poetic licence? And, if so, is
it justified?

Credit for the discovery of this note is due to Mr Norman Atkins,
who very generously sent me the information in February 1969, after
visiting Shockerwick House and finding that nothing was known there
of Pitt's visit. The detail of the story gives it a high degree of probability, though it does not constitute proof of its authenticity. The only
claim for it is that it was almost certainly the source of the evidence
which Hardy used for setting a highly historic and dramatic scene
in Shockerwick House.

Notes

1. An Early Influence
1. Kenneth Robinson, *Wilkie Collins* (London, 1951), pp. 330–31.
2. 'Thomas Hardy, Some Recollections and Reflections', *The Hibbert Journal* (Apr. 1928).
3. See Charles Morgan, *The House of Macmillan, 1843–1943* (London, 1944), pp. 93–4.
4. Compare Walter Bagehot, *Literary Studies* (London, 1920), vol. i, p. 260, on Shelley's father: 'Lord Chesterfield himself was not easier on matters of morality. He used to tell his son that he would provide for natural children *ad infinitum*, but would never forgive his making a *mésalliance*.'
5. John Ashton, *Chap-books of the Eighteenth Century* (London, 1882), p. 41. When Hardy first read this story is not known; there is a reference to it in *The Woodlanders* (1887), ii.
6. It is sometimes assumed that Emma Gifford's experience as a child may have given Hardy a hint for the scene; see *Life*, 66.
7. See 'Fellow-Townsmen', viii (*Wessex Tales*) and 'Hap' (*Wessex Poems*).
8. See 'Ditty' (*Wessex Poems*), 'The Young Churchwarden' (*Moments of Vision*), and Purdy, 220.
9. *Life*, 114, 120.
10. 'After a Romantic Day' (*Late Lyrics and Earlier*) and 'The Change' (*Moments of Vision*).
11. *Life*, 239, 252, 150, 176.
12. See examples on pp. 50 and 55.

2. Poetical Extravagance in Fiction
1. The chapters in the respective novels are: (1) xliv, (2) v. vii, (3) xlii.
2. With this in mind Hardy wrote the date 'December 15, 1870' against Hamlet's 'But thou wouldst not think how ill all's here about my heart; but it is no matter' (*Life*, 83).

3. Pictorial Art
1. *Life*, 216.
2. 'Pictorial Imagery in the Novels of Thomas Hardy', *The Review of English Studies* (1961).
3. *Life*, 177.
4. See *After Strange Gods* (London, 1934), pp. 54–8. In *To Criticize the Critic* (London, 1965) Eliot's retraction is implicit in his wonder 'whether it might not have been better never to have written' about an author as antipathetic to him as Hardy.

5. The 'great tradition' is not confined to one genre of literature. One line of influence runs from Fielding via Scott to Hardy; another (possibly more important) may be traced via the poet Wordsworth and George Eliot.

6. Hardy's note and sketch of the picture are in the Dorset County Museum.

7. A recollection from Hardy's own experience; cf. *Life*, 96 and *Desperate Remedies*, viii, 3: 'The shovel shone like silver from the action of the juice, and ever and anon, in its motion to and fro, caught the rays of the declining sun and reflected them in bristling stars of light.'

8. Compare Hardy's note for the end of November 1877, at Sturminster Newton (*Life*, 118).

4. Chance, Choice, and Charity

1. *The Revolt of Islam*, VIII. v.
2. *ORFW*. 17.
3. 'Goethe's Helena', quoted with reference to Faust and Bellerophon in *The Mayor of Casterbridge*, xvii.
4. From 'Ditty' (1870) in *Wessex Poems*.
5. *Desperate Remedies*, vi. 4.
6. Ibid., ix. 3.
7. *A Pair of Blue Eyes*, xxx and xxxii.
8. *Life*, 149.
9. Basil Willey, *Nineteenth Century Studies* (London, 1955), p. 278.
10. *Culture and Anarchy*, i.

5. The Wild Duck

1. *Life*, 104; cf. ibid., 53, 87.
2. The Bank of England.
3. *ORFW*. 26.
4. See Robert Gittings, *The Young Hardy* (London, 1975), pp. 113, 119, 207; and his edition of *The Hand of Ethelberta* (paperback ed., London, 1975), p. 27 (or hardback, 1976), p. 26.

6. Mephistopheles, Satan, and Cigars

1. Whether the book was given by Moule to Hardy or inherited after Moule's death is uncertain. It was published in 1865, and has two autographs on the title-page, 'H. M. Moule' and 'Thomas Hardy' (Lennart A. Björk, Notes on *The Literary Notes of Thomas Hardy*, Göteborg, 1974, vol. 1, p. 286).

2. Evelyn Hardy, *Thomas Hardy, A Critical Biography* (London, 1954; New York, 1970), p. 51.

3. See note 3 to Chapter 3 above.

4. A facsimile copy of Hardy's version of the story appeared in the handbook for the Thomas Hardy Festival at Dorchester in July 1968.

5. See note 5 to Chapter 1 above.

6. In *The Mayor of Casterbridge* there are two reminders of *Macbeth*: the 'haggish' furmity-woman with her 'three-legged crock' when Henchard sells his wife, and much later (xxvii) when he wonders whether someone has been 'stirring an unholy brew to confound' him.

7. The passage Hardy quotes from occurs near the end of Matthew Arnold's essay 'Pagan and Medieval Religious Sentiment'. Arnold states that 'the poetry of later paganism lived by the senses and understanding'; that of medieval Christianity, 'by the heart and imagination'. The main element of 'the modern spirit's life' is neither of these; it is 'the imaginative reason'. The modern dilemma, Hardy seems to be saying, is to find a new set of values reconciling head and heart, fusing reason and imagination, or endowing belief in scientific and technological progress with sentiments as reassuring and romantic as those attached to tradi- tional beliefs and institutions of the past. Paula cannot help regretting the decay of old romanticisms, but the more resolute Somerset, a repre- sentative of 'the modern spirit', will be 'glad when enthusiasm is come again'.

7. Hardy's Humour

1. From Hardy's General Preface to the Wessex Edition of 1912.
2. Orel, 30–31.
3. June 1896. See *ORFW*. 52.
4. 'The Profitable Reading of Fiction', Orel, 117.
5. See *The Times Literary Supplement*, 14 March 1935.
6. See *Life*, 48 and Charles Morgan, *The House of Macmillan, 1843–1943*, pp. 87–91.
7. R. G. Cox (ed.), *Thomas Hardy, The Critical Heritage* (London and New York, 1970), pp. 1 and 5.
8. The view (based on a statement by D. H. Lawrence: 'Study of Thomas Hardy', iii) was first developed by J. F. Danby in 'Under the Greenwood Tree', *The Critical Quarterly* (1959). The quotation that follows is from J. Hillis Miller, *Thomas Hardy, Distance and Desire* (Cambridge, Mass., 1970), p. 152.
9. *Desperate Remedies*, xv. 3: 'a wild hill that had no name, beside a down where it never looked like summer'; cf. the poem 'It Never Looks Like Summer'. Hardy's sketch of the scene (with Beeny Cliff in the back- ground) indicates that the remark was made on 22 August 1870.
10. According to a note in her 1889 edition of *Far from the Madding Crowd*, Rebekah Owen thought Hardy told her that Henery Fray and Joseph Poorgrass were founded on Isaac West and John Amey.
11. For example, when Poorgrass groans, 'Cain Ball, you'll come to a bit of bread!' (xxxiii) – a reference to Proverbs, vi, 26: 'For by means of a whorish woman a man is brought to a piece of bread.' A scriptural allu- sion may be suspected in the name 'Poorgrass'; cf. Psalm xcii, 7.
12. See 'The Dorsetshire Labourer' (Orel, 168–91) and *Tess*, xviii, xxii.
13. The vicar's first remark is a Hardy allusion to the burning of Mary Channing less than a mile away in 1705; see *The Mayor of Casterbridge*, xi and 'The Mock Wife' in *Human Shows*.
14. See 'Rake-Hell Muses' in *Late Lyrics and Earlier*.

8. The Frost's Decree

1. *Life*, 213.
2. Ibid., 149. Compare the poem 'The Mother Mourns'.

3. The passage is quoted on p. 29 (from *Tess*, xliii).

4. *ORFW*. 75.

5. Charlotte Brontë, *Jane Eyre*, xxvi.

6. *Life*, 444. See V. Collins, *Talks with Thomas Hardy* (London, 1928), pp. 36–7.

7. *Life*, 23–4.

8. *Desperate Remedies*, vi. i.

9. *ORFW*. 14–15, 17, 26.

10. From 'The Subalterns'.

11. According to a note by Sir James Barrie (based, no doubt, on information from Florence Hardy) in Hardy's copy of *Queen Mab and Other Poems* (Cottage Library), which he acquired in 1866. See Phyllis Bartlett, 'Seraph of Heaven', *PMLA* (1955).

12. The three inset quotations are from *The Revolt of Islam*: VIII. v; IX, xxviii; IX. xxi–xxiv.

13. Hardy may have intended a contrast with the image of the psalm sung by Cytherea, when she was thinking of Edward, who sat in front of her with her rival Adelaide Hinton (xii. i):

> Like some fair tree which, fed by streams,
>   With timely fruit doth bend,
> He still shall flourish, and success
>   All his designs attend.

14. From 'Thoughts at Midnight' (*Winter Words*).

15. From 'We Are Getting to the End' (ibid.).

9. Hardy and Myth

1. See p. 179. Hardy's notebook shows that he read Arnold's essays not later than June 1877.

2. See Romans, xiii. 9–10 and I John, iii. 23.

3. Hardy's Positivism is also seen in Angel Clare; cf. *Tess*, xviii, where, in answer to his father's question on what good his university education has been 'if it is not to be used for the honour and glory of God', Angel replies, 'Why, that it may be used for the honour and glory of man'. See also *Life*, 332, where Hardy says, (until we can find a Lord to magnify) 'let us magnify good works, and develop all means of easing mortals' progress through a world not worthy of them'.

4. *Life*, 330.

5. See the poem 'Why Do I?' at the end of *Human Shows*.

6. See pp. 186–7 ('During Wind and Rain').

7. See the poem 'Yell'ham-Wood's Story'.

8. *Life*, 149.

9. *ORFW*. 15, 18.

10. There is reason to think that the 'Christminster' theme developed from a chance suggestion by Rebekah Owen that the distant towers and spires at Oxford appeared to Hardy, on his visit to Fawley and the Ridge Way in October 1892, 'like the New Jerusalem'. See Carl J. Weber, *Hardy and the Lady from Madison Square* (Waterville, Me., 1952), pp. 77 and 100–101.

11. *The Positive Evolution of Religion* (London, 1913), p. 213. Compare Hardy's use of 'Prime Mover' in the passage quoted on p. 14.

10. *Tess* and *Clarissa*

  1. See the passage on 'the inherent will to enjoy' (p. 88).

11. A Pure Woman

  1. For the gradual ennoblement of Tess's character by Hardy, see J. T. Laird, *The Shaping of 'Tess of the d'Urbervilles'* (Oxford, 1975).

  2. In *Memories* (1953) Desmond MacCarthy reports Hardy's statement that if he had thought *Tess* was going to be such a success he would have made it a 'really good book'.

  3. Cf. Laird (note 1 above), pp. 71–2.

  4. For this information I am indebted to J. M. Grindle.

  5. From the first chapter of *Studies in Classic American Literature*. Lawrence is more explicit in a previous statement: 'Art-speech is the only truth. An artist is usually a damned liar, but his art, if it be art, will tell you the truth of his day.'

12. Bird Imagery

  1. From Hardy's 'General Preface to the Novels and Poems'.

  2. The influence of Hudson was pointed out by Carl Weber in his *Hardy of Wessex* (New York, 1965), p. 234. For the passages and other influences including Keble's, see F. B. Pinion, *A Commentary on the Poems of Thomas Hardy* (London and New York, 1976), pp. 53–4. See also 'What the Thrush Said' ('O thou whose face hath felt the Winter's wind') in Keats's letter of 19 February 1818 to J. H. Reynolds.

  3. *Life*, 220.

  4. See Ruth Firor, *Folkways in Thomas Hardy* (Philadelphia, Pa., 1931; New York, 1962), pp. 2–4.

  5. See the note for 30 May 1877, when Hardy walked from Sturminster Newton to Marnhull (*Life*, 113).

  6. In a letter to Sir George Douglas on 5 January 1896, Hardy described it as one of the best of Scott's novels, 'the best, indeed, in point of style'. His quotation, 'an owre true tale' (Orel, 142) comes from the ending of *The Bride of Lammermoor* (xxxiv), where it is printed in capitals.

  7. Compare the figurative 'Sportsman Time but rears his brood to kill' in the first of the 'She, to Him' sonnets (1866), and a much later poem, 'The Puzzled Game-Birds', first entitled 'The Battue'. For interesting light on Hardy's knowledge of the subject, see J. O. Bailey, *The Poetry of Thomas Hardy* (Chapel Hill, N.C., 1970), p. 164.

13. The Influence of Shelley

  1. *ORFW*. 26.

  2. *Prometheus Unbound*, IV. 562, 570–78.

  3. See the poem 'He Wonders About Himself'.

  4. The question of free will or 'liberty, as applied to mind' seems insoluble. Necessity for Shelley is the scientific principle of cause–effect. He states that if man were omniscient and could see all cause–effects ('the conjunction of antecedents and consequents'), he would not think in terms of chance. Hardy would have agreed with this, and he sometimes uses the terms 'Law', 'Necessity', and 'necessitation' in ways which seem to

approximate Shelley's absolutism. Natural law includes heredity, but man, when not swayed by prejudices and passions, is capable of reflecting and making rational decisions, and it is in this sense that Hardy refers to man's 'modicum of free will'. If he had not believed in its existence, he could not have held out hope of human progress. The Apology to *Late Lyrics and Earlier* (1922) contains his most important passages on this question, and it was written later than his less qualified statements on the rule of Necessity (see *Life*, 337 and Orel, 145–6).

5. See Walter Bagehot, *Literary Studies*, vol. 1 (London, 1902), p. 252.
6. From the preface to 'Alastor'.
7. Hardy had read this more than once in Bagehot's essay on Shelley, op. cit., p. 270.
8. *ORFW*. 66.
9. *Life*, 286.
10. Hardy wanted to name the heroine of *Jude* after Florence Henniker (cf. *ORFW*. 31), and did, rather surreptitiously (III. vii, IV. ii).

14. The Iris-Bow and the Well-Beloved
1. *The World as Will and Idea* by Arthur Schopenhauer, trans. R. R. Haldane and J. Kemp (London, 1883) vol. 1, pp. 199–200. The relevant passage is quoted by W. R. Rutland (*Thomas Hardy, A Study of His Writings and Their Background* (New York, 1962), p. 95), who states that Hardy owned all three volumes of the above translation.
2. Ibid., p. 3.
3. Compare *Hellas*, ll. 776–85, an adaptation of Prospero's speech (*The Tempest*, IV. i. 151–8).
4. See Genesis, ix. 12–17.
5. Quoted from *The Woodlanders*, xxviii; cf. *Tess*, xxv.
6. See Alma Priestley, 'Hardy's *The Well-Beloved*: A Study in Failure', *The Thomas Hardy Society Review 1976*.

15. Intimations of Immortality
1. The description of the journeying boy in *Jude* will be found in Part v, Ch. iii.
2. Notes of 7 February 1881 and 29 January 1890 (*Life*, 148, 224).
3. *Life*, 309.
4. Ibid., 369–70.
5. From Hardy's letter to Alfred Noyes, 19 December 1920 (*Life*, 410).
6. In *Thomas Hardy, Distance and Desire* (Cambridge, Mass., 1970).

SUPPLEMENT

i. *The Return of the Native* in the Making
1. It has been assumed that the first seven chapters were written by 28 August, and the first two books by 8 November, 1877 (Purdy, 27).
2. Michael Millgate, *Thomas Hardy, His Career as a Novelist* (London, 1971), pp. 124, 380.

3. Otis Wheeler, *Nineteenth-Century Fiction*, 1959; and John Paterson, *The Making of 'The Return of the Native'* (Berkeley, Calif. and London, 1960).

ii. Hardy and Pater

1. Hardy's hope, based on his theory of the Unfulfilled Intention, is that the more advanced conscience of humanity will gradually influence the 'general Will'; see 'He Wonders About Himself'.

iii. Les Misérables

1. Lennart A. Björk, *The Literary Notes of Thomas Hardy*, vol. 1, Text and Notes (Göteborg, 1974).
2. *Life*, 311. I suspect that the cathedral metaphor came from the essay on Sir Walter Scott in the first volume of Leslie Stephen's *Hours in a Library*, and that Hardy's views on *Clarissa* (p. 120) and his emphasis on artistic form in *The Bride of Lammermoor* owe something to the essay on Richardson's novels in the same volume.

iv. During Wind and Rain

1. The human parallel to the contrast between the cultivated plantation and natural growth on the heath in the gale may be seen in the first two paragraphs of Book iii, Ch. i.

v. Oxford and Jude

1. *Life*, 278.
2. Ibid., 351.
3. Ibid., 257.
4. *ORFW*. 6.
5. For some further details, see *The Thomas Hardy Society Review 1975*.
6. *ORFW*. 15, 18, 26.

vi. One Rare Fair Woman

1. *ORFW*. xxxii–xxxviii.
2. Purdy, 345.
3. *Jude the Obscure*, iii. ix. See *ORFW*. xxxvi.
4. *ORFW*. 11.
5. For this detail I am indebted to R. N. R. Peers, Curator of the Dorset County Museum. My attention was drawn to the third translation by James Gibson.
6. *Jude the Obscure*, ii. vii.
7. *ORFW*. 44.
8. This copy (published in 1893 by Smith, Elder & Co.) is in the Dorset County Museum, and my attention was drawn to some of the marked passages by Tom Paulin.
9. See *Life*, 284–5, where Hardy stresses possibilities which were realized particularly in *Poems of the Past and the Present* (1901).

vii. Abdication of a Novelist

1. This suggests he had not made much progress, for the opening chapters of the original composition related to Sue's early history. See John Paterson, 'The Genesis of *Jude the Obscure*', *Studies in Philology* (1960), p. 88.
2. Hardy's best statement on the subject occurs in 'Candour in English Fiction' (1890). The novelist should be able to assume 'untrammelled adult opinion on conduct and theology': 'the position of man and woman in nature, and the position of belief in the minds of man and woman – things which everybody is thinking but nobody is saying' (Orel, 133).
3. *The Young Man* (1894), pp. 75–9.
4. In *Celebrations and Simple Souls* (London, 1933), p. 58.
5. *Life*, 270, 291. The italics are mine.
6. Edward Clodd, *Memories* (London, 1916), p. 146.
7. For the Douglas references, see his article on Hardy in *The Hibbert Journal* (Apr. 1928).

viii. Wessex Topography

1. As a result of inquiry through an intermediary, I was misled into stating in *A Hardy Companion* that extracts from the history of the castle (1. xiii) were taken from Collinson's *History of Somerset* with reference to Dunster Castle. As far as I know, they have not been traced, and could have been invented by Hardy.
2. Compare *Far from the Madding Crowd*, xlvii.
3. From 'The Science of Fiction' (Orel, 134).
4. Toucan Press, Mt Durand, St Peter's Port, Guernsey.

Index